Boston Mass-Mediated

Boston
Mass-Mediated

URBAN SPACE AND CULTURE
IN THE DIGITAL AGE

STANLEY CORKIN

University of Massachusetts Press
AMHERST AND BOSTON

Copyright © 2024 by University of Massachusetts Press
All rights reserved
Printed in the United States of America

ISBN 978-1-62534-824-1 (paper); 825-8 (hardcover)

Designed by Sally Nichols
Set in Minion Pro by Westchester Publishing Services
Printed and bound by Books International, Inc.

Cover design by adam b. bohannon
Cover photo by mandritoiu, *Rush hour traffic on Tobin Bridge (a.k.a. Mystic River Bridge) heading towards Zakim Bridge and Boston skyline at sunset*. AdobeStock_122196487.

Library of Congress Cataloging-in-Publication Data
Names: Corkin, Stanley, author.
Title: Boston mass-mediated : urban space and culture in the digital age / Stanley Corkin.
Description: Amherst : University of Massachusetts Press, 2024. | Includes index. | Summary Provided by publisher.
Identifiers: LCCN 2024016827 (print) | LCCN 2024016828 (ebook) | ISBN 9781625348241 (library binding) | ISBN 9781625348258 (hardcover) | ISBN 9781685750954 (ebook) | ISBN 9781685750961 (ebook)
Subjects: LCSH: Boston (Mass—Civilization. | Boston (Mass.)—In mass media. | Boston (Mass—In motion pictures.
Classification: LCC F73.52 .C67 2024 (print) | LCC F73.52 (ebook) | DDC 974.4/610904—dc23/eng/20240618
LC record available at https://lccn.loc.gov/2024016827
LC ebook record available at https://lccn.loc.gov/2024016828

British Library Cataloguing-in-Publication Data
A catalog record for this book is available from the British Library.

For Jana

Contents

Illustrations ix
Acknowledgments xi

INTRODUCTION
Mediated Streets and Digital Images: The Case of Twenty-First-Century Boston
1

SECTION I
Space and the Crisis of the Post-Industrial City
21

CHAPTER 1
Mapping Boston's White Spaces: Busing, Policing, and Privilege
25

CHAPTER 2
Crime, Silence, and Southie: Priestly Abuse and Whitey Bulger
53

SECTION II
Sports and Mass Culture
95

CHAPTER 3
Branding Red Sox Nation and Its Homeland
99

CHAPTER 4
Race and Celtics Pride
127

SECTION III
Boston on Location: Filming the City
163

CHAPTER 5

The *New* Boston and the Grip of Tradition
167

CHAPTER 6

History, Fact, and Nostalgia
195

CONCLUSION

Ray Donovan and the Essence of "Boston"
228

Notes   237
Index   255

Illustrations

FIGURE 1. Greater Boston and Its Neighborhoods   xiii
FIGURE 2. The Prudential Tower in Boston   8
FIGURE 3. The School Buses Bringing Students from Roxbury to South Boston   29
FIGURE 4. Louise Day Hicks Celebrates Her Win in the 1971 Mayoral Primary   35
FIGURE 5. "The Soiling of Old Glory"   38
FIGURE 6. A Characteristic Three-Decker House in Hyde Park   57
FIGURE 7. Defense Attorney Mitchell Garabedian Questions Cardinal Bernard Law   65
FIGURE 8. The Cathedral of the Holy Cross   67
FIGURE 9. The Old Harbor Housing Project   86
FIGURE 10. Fenway Park, October 5, 2018   105
FIGURE 11. Boston Garden and North Station, 1929   138
FIGURE 12. Banners above TD Garden   142
FIGURE 13. Eddie Coyle and Dillon Watch the Bruins   181
FIGURE 14. Will Hunting and Sean Take Their Session to the Boston Public Gardens   191
FIGURE 15. Opening Shot of The Flats in *Mystic River*   197
FIGURE 16. Final Shot of *Mystic River*   207
FIGURE 17. Mickey Donovan on His Way to Kill a Priest   229

Acknowledgments

This book has been a long time in the making. I thank the many who contributed in various ways including my children, Jesse and Roxanne Corkin, who always listen and help, and sometimes join me in Boston. I thank Kirk Boyle, erstwhile scholar, friend, and interlocutor, for reading and commenting on an earlier version of the manuscript, as well as Tom Leclair, who read the Celtics chapter and has made himself available "to discuss" for over three decades. I appreciate the support of my family—Jon Corkin, Michael Corkin, and Susan Kalish in Boston—as well as my many Boston friends, including Frank and Caren Steinberg. I have valued the support and interest of John and Andrea Kornbluh, and Mark and Miriam Raider Roth in Cincinnati. My colleagues and friends in the Society for Cinema and Media Studies Urbanism/Geography/Architecture Scholarly Interest Group provided an intellectual home for the project: Erica Stein, Lawrence Webb, Amy Corbin, and Josh Gleich. I'd also like to single out Mark Shiel for his friendship and astute commentary over the years. I am grateful to Peter Niehoff, Michael Gott, and Todd Herzog who were instrumental in developing the film studies program at the University of Cincinnati, my academic home in my last years of teaching, as well as Buck Niehoff for his generosity and support of the humanities. My appreciation to Adrian Parr, formerly at the Taft Center of the University of Cincinnati and now at the University of Oregon, for her encouragement of my scholarship and this project in particular. Both the Taft and the Niehoff funds at the University of Cincinnati provided vital funding, including travel funding, over a number of years. Thanks to archivist Peter Higgins at WGBH-TV in Boston and to Rosemary Franklin and Sally Moffitt at the University of Cincinnati Libraries for their assistance, and to Stanley Forman for his permission to reproduce his powerful photograph and Spenser Grant for his permission to use his wonderful image of Louise Day Hicks. I also appreciate the efforts of Matthew Lutts at the Associated Press for responding so quickly and efficiently to my queries. Matt Becker at UMass Press offered patience and astute advice as he guided this project toward publication.

But above all, I thank my wife, Jana Braziel, whose love and support are in every page of this book. Her devotion truly made this possible. She enriches all things I do and for that no amount of thanks and love can express my full appreciation.

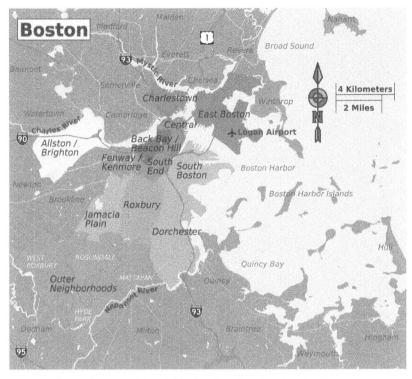

FIGURE 1. Greater Boston and its neighborhoods. —Courtesy Creative Commons.

Boston Mass-Mediated

INTRODUCTION

Mediated Streets and Digital Images

The Case of Twenty-First-Century Boston

As a native Bostonian, I have long been engaged by tropes that people routinely affix to that city; these include, among others, the prominence of its Irish-descended citizens, of Catholicism, of its working-class presence and ethos, and of its immovable racism. The frequency of these definitional terms seem to be eroding as we move well into the 2020s, but their persistence intrigues me. What does it mean to call a city racist? Is Boston more racist than New York, Philadelphia, or Chicago? The association of Boston and a certain ethnic character and an ethos of racial subjugation and exclusion finds its way into any number of narratives, so much so that the very liberal local paper devoted a week of coverage to the phenomenon in late 2017. A *Boston Globe* investigation into the basis for this reputation began: "Google the phrase 'Most racist city,' and Boston pops up more than any other place, time and time again."[1] The piece details the persistence of racial inequities in the city, primarily based in historical racism and demographics: the relatively small size of the city's African American population and its relative lack of wealth both limit its ability to garner political and economic power. But those who invoke the broad contours of the city's civic image tend to insert facts of the past as simple realities of the present. Writes reporter Akilah Johnson in this Spotlight series introduction and overview, "There is no doubt that Boston has made gains in overcoming its history of racism. Gone are the days when Black people crouched in cars, windows rolled up, hats pulled low so as not to be seen driving through the streets of South Boston or Charlestown, fearing racial slurs or real physical violence. . . . Yet this is a city that still stumbles and, in doing so, rekindles seething images of racial discord beamed into televisions during the school desegregation battles of the 1970s."[2]

Johnson's view recognizes the vicissitudes of the recent past and their relative hold on the present. As Johnson points out trenchantly, the Boston of 2017 was not at all the city of the 1950s, 1960s, or early 1970s. That city was indeed very white and insular. The Boston of today is decidedly multiethnic, white collar, and certainly more expansive than it was in those years. Yet, certain identifiers of place persist. This study is an investigation into at least some of their means of persistence, as well as of their historical roots and, even more significantly, means of transmission. As such, this is a study of the intersections of media and history. I begin my study—in chronological terms—in 1973 (with the film *The Friends of Eddie Coyle*) and 1974 (ground zero for the busing crisis as a national story), moments when Boston was both at a kind of nadir economically and demographically, a city shrinking in many ways. I end in 2015 through my discussion of two feature films based in news stories of national prominence, stories that I also discuss in their journalistic expression in part two: *Spotlight* (dir. Tom McCarthy, 2015, about the crisis of sexual abuse by Catholic priests and its coverage by a *Globe* Spotlight team) and *Black Mass* (dir. Scott Cooper, 2015, a film about the South Boston–based criminal Whitey Bulger). I also discuss relatively briefly in my conclusion the Showtime television series *Ray Donovan* (created by Ann Biderman, 2013–20, with a film released in 2022, dir. David Hollander). While in this span of years the city changed markedly, narratives about the city changed more slowly.

One of the definitional aspects of the postmodern, gentrified city is the power and allure of its brand. Arguably, a city's dynamism draws extensively from its resonant meanings and visibility in national and international milieus. These conceptions of place are connected to its materiality but not commensurate with it, and they are conveyed through a variety of associations triggered through electronic means. The twenty-first-century metropolis is the city of aspiration and image, a place that has been commodified and sold to a consuming populace. This conception of the urban is distinct from, but not unrelated to, the role of the city in the age of massive urbanization in the late nineteenth and early twentieth centuries. This earlier demographic shift was substantially a result of the city becoming an economic center that featured industrial production and employment. Although other economic activities clearly grew from this central cause, the city, as we have seen in multiple narratives, also possessed a kind of allure, signifying the adventure of modernity and the creation of a new way of life. Industrial work served as an alternative to the ardor and increasing redundancy of agricultural labor. Municipalities such as Chicago and

Detroit, which had been relatively unimportant in the mid-nineteenth century, became powerhouses of production due largely to fortuitous geographies and growing demand for certain commodities. As a complement to these activities, they became centers for the creation and managing of wealth—banks, brokerages, and exchanges all proliferated. For older U.S. cities, such as New York, Boston, and San Francisco, previously banking and shipping centers, industrialization provided a means to add that dynamic dimension to their already central place in their regional and increasingly interregional and international economies. In the contemporary city, the relative absence of industrial work and the increased presence and role of finance capital has made the city significantly a playground for the rich, and while those of the less fortunate classes continue to find their way to urban spaces, increasingly it is the abutting suburbs and beyond that serve as their spaces of residence, as the gentrified urban core is more and more economically unattainable.

***

In the 1950s, Boston was a city in notable decline. Its population was diminishing, as was its economy. Between 1950 and 1980, the city's population shrank from around 800,000 to 562,000, a trend that only slowly began to reverse in the 1980s. (The city's 2020 population was around 675,000.) Writes Harvard-based urbanist Edward L. Glaeser, "By 1980 Boston was just another of America's formerly great declining cities." He notes its slide into "high poverty and urban decline, on its way to urban irrelevance."[3] In the mid-1950s, civic leaders began to see it primarily as a place where some of those who had—logically—moved to the suburbs would come to work, and then return to their enclaves beyond the city limits.[4] In keeping with such a vision, development focused on roads that would allow easy traverse for suburban commuters but that would do violence to urban neighborhoods. Clearly this was not the formula for a healthy and dynamic urban space.

Boston as a place and space are distinctive and related entities. For example, in political and geographic terms, the spatial contours of Boston are easily defined, covering 48 square miles of land and 89.6 square miles including land and water. It is bound by the Massachusetts Bay to the east and the Charles and Mystic Rivers, as well as by various towns to the west, south, and north—Newton, Brookline, Cambridge, Somerville, Quincy, Dedham, Everett, and Chelsea. Yet, once we move beyond the empirical definition provided above, the *concept* of space and then place become elastic, potentially providing a means of inquiring into the various social processes that define relations, including those of politics, economics, and mass communication, all of which can elaborate distinction and restriction. Space need not be a rigid concept defined by a surveyor but can afford a means of conceiving a discrete body of related and apparently contiguous areas and their limits. These organizing connections at a particular temporal juncture are a matter of historically perceived and contemporarily elaborated meanings, connected both to materiality and its perpetual and ever-changing mediation. Geographer John Agnew reminds us that even in a media-saturated environment in which new technologies seem to define new understandings of geographies, space and place remain mutually constitutive terms that shift not only in relation to one another but also in relation to a perpetually shifting and revised historicity.[5]

The city of Boston has become notable in the last decade of the 1900s and into the 2000s as a capital-rich, post-industrial locale. This has resulted from a number of material factors, including its strategic and site-specific arrangement of capital, finance, and cutting-edge technology, a matter of the infrastructure that arranges around a considerable body of elite educational institutions—for example, Harvard, MIT, Boston University, Boston College, and Tufts. Those who employ Boston as a place are also—implicitly or explicitly—able to attach to that tech-heavy success a residual sense of the historical city, which includes its legacy of prosperity from the late eighteenth to the mid-nineteenth centuries, when merchants based in Boston participated in and further developed trade with China and thus created a place-specific wealth. This capital became the basis for elite Protestant families, such as the Forbes, Perkins, Cabot, and Higginson families, whose investments and philanthropy would significantly define the city for generations.[6] The Perkins family founded the Bank of Boston, and many of these families were involved in the creation of the region's valuable educational infrastructure through their gifts to Harvard and then later to MIT.

The mid- to late nineteenth century was also a period of mass immigration to the city from Ireland. This migration would put its stamp on the city and impact its historical development in cultural and economic ways that both complemented and opposed those largely Protestant institutions and legacies. These new Bostonians primarily came to escape poverty and starvation, initially stemming from the potato blight of 1845. In 1847 alone, 37,000 immigrants settled in the city, which then numbered 115,000. According to one historian, "By 1880, Boston had more than 70,000 Irish-born residents, making up more than half of the city's foreign-born population, which was larger than in any other American urban center."[7] The centrality of the ethnic Irish, Catholic population and the ongoing immigration from Ireland has been a defining part of the city's history since that initial surge. Irish Americans have dominated local politics and civic life almost since the election of the city's first Irish mayor, Hugh O'Brien, in 1884. It was only in the 1990s that the city elected its first Italian American mayor, Tom Menino, and not until the recent election of Michelle Wu in 2021 has there been a nonwhite person or a woman elected to City Hall, though Kim Janey, an African American woman who was elected to the city council, was appointed mayor in 2021 when Mayor Marty Walsh became Joe Biden's secretary of labor. Yet, despite the prominence of this Irish-Catholic population, it has historically been at odds with the economically dominant Protestant oligarchs of the city, a situation that has seen some amelioration over time but which remains embedded in the city's social fabric.

With the solidifying of the terms of the post-industrial economy after 1980, high-tech and financial services industries became the basis for a wider economic and then demographic dynamism. But the fact of *that* city—cosmopolitan, highly educated, ensconced in the global information economy—would be eclipsed by a very different Boston, as represented in mass culture. In *Boston Mass-Mediated*, I argue that our comprehension of cities is always mediated by our prior knowledge and expectations of those places and that our contemporary sense of place is substantially gained through devices of mass communication. In the case of cities with a significant media presence, the role of such mediation can grow exponentially until it is, for most observers, indistinguishable from the thing itself, or it may result in such mediated impressions becoming the thing itself.

In this book, I argue that "place" in the postmodern and digital world often becomes a virtual concept that builds on prior narratives of locale—narratives that include elements of history, contemporary social life, and more narrowly topical amalgams of both. This virtual process creates its own *mythos* of place by accentuating certain elements that simultaneously reduce its nuance and complexity. For example, the idea that New York City as a place is commensurate with Wall Street and the financial services industry is shorthand that ignores the textured economic and ethnic diversity of place, especially as it exists outside of a certain region of Manhattan. Indeed, the same shorthand that finds Los Angeles as a small swath of West LA also ignores most of its scattered and extensive urban geography and diversity. In the case of Boston, I trace how, as the city increasingly prospered and gentrified into the 2000s, its ethnic neighborhoods; Catholicism; working-class culture; and attendant, but not monolithic, racism nevertheless remain central to its "brand," even as other aspects of its reality are proportionately diminished. In looking at various types of powerful and resonant public media—journalism, professional sports branding, and feature films—I define an ever-intensifying feedback loop that distills elements of place with a prior media and historical existence and refines those elements so that they become increasingly recurrent, synecdochal, and thus definitional. During the historical time period considered in this book, we move from the beginnings of satellite communication (cable television) to the emergence and actualization of global communication in the digital age with all its immediacy and seeming spacelessness and timelessness. This shift in available and dominant media becomes, among other things, a means by which place is branded and then rebranded in connected ways. Thus, national sports coverage disseminated by satellites projects digital images of Boston often featured in local and national news outlets, and feature films traffic in connected images and tropes.

Since this book is organized by topic and discipline, it queries discrete histories of media events writ large and shows how the post-industrial moment of the early 1970s segued into the media-saturated environment of the 2000s, where certain images and narratives of space became calcified and redolent of meanings that constituted an important dimension of a city's image, its brand. Mikhail M. Bakhtin's concept of the *chronotope* provides a means of conceptualizing such recurrent images and representations that memorialize a moment and continue to project it into the future. This analytic concept that Bakhtin—a literary theorist—applied to the novel, in this urban geographical case helps us to see narratives of place as centrally employing apparent unities of time and space, or as references to a kind of static historical formation, thereby "materialising time in space."[8] Through this framing, one may descry the chronotopes that recur among apparently disparate areas of expression, creating a more and more distinctive—yet reduced—definition of place. These later expressions take—as important elements of their constitution—events and narratives that occurred in the early moments of the post-industrial age, an age that would become media saturated, and employed them in apparently affirming continuities of social life.

* * *

Boston is not an iconic world city. It is not Rome, Paris, Shanghai, or London. Nor, in U.S. terms, is it New York, Los Angeles, or even Chicago. It is a locale that was a center of trade and culture in the nineteenth century eclipsed by New York City, its regional rival some two hundred miles to the southwest, by the time of the Civil War. By the mid-twentieth century, Boston was in decline, but it has, as a matter of its tech-heavy commerce and educational infrastructure, burgeoned in the twenty first century, becoming the city of massive redevelopment in Boston, Cambridge, and the Route 128 corridor, and significantly has become a site of rocketing real-estate values and gentrification.

Physically, the "new" Boston began to emerge through the devices of a few major redevelopment projects in the late 1950s and early 1960s, including the Prudential Center (an urban development that includes as its centerpiece the Prudential Tower), which was preceded by the West End Redevelopment Project (Charles River Park) and the razing of Scollay Square, a place of burlesque theaters and bars frequented by visiting sailors that was sanitized to become Government Center.[9] These projects combined what was in the parlance of the day known as "slum clearance" with a vision of benign and efficient residential and office spaces, offering an altered and decidedly modern landscape and the image of a city that was changing appropriately with the times.[10] Perhaps the most forward looking of these projects was the Prudential Center and its central skyscraper, the Prudential Tower, which not only transformed a sector of the city that was remote from the central business district and home to a largely moribund railyard; the Prudential Tower's majesty affirmed an image of a city, a chronotope that remains resonant in the early twenty-first century, a visual fact appearing in all kinds of media as the digital era emerged and became definitional in the late 1900s and early 2000s, bridging the incubus of a "new" Boston with an emergent gentrified city with a working-class gestalt.

But in the post-1973 era, a time of gradual reinvestment in the city by both public and private entities, the emphasis of development had already changed from redevelopment to gentrification, as large-scale projects that included extensive new construction gave way to the reimagining of extant

FIGURE 2. The Prudential Tower in Boston. —Photograph by author.

buildings and neighborhoods, including the South End, the Back Bay, and parts of Charlestown.

This was in contrast to the 1950s, when the use of federal highway funds had gradually routed both businesses and population out of the city. In that era, it was the construction of the inner-belt highway of Route 128, largely completed as a limited access road by 1951, which dispersed urban populations to inner-line suburbs and which created the tech campuses that lined that highway's central section in towns such as Waltham, Newton, Lexington, and Burlington. By 1957, there were 140 companies located on that road; by 1973, the number was over 1,200. And the existence of Route 128 inevitably led to the further construction of major contiguous highways—the I-90 extension, I-495—which ultimately had a related impact on work and residential locales by the early 1970s, moving people and jobs beyond the city's limits.[11]

In his excellent study of Boston's rise from the ashes, Elihu Rubin traces both the specific matters that led to the building of the city's Prudential Tower and the symbolic significance of that construction.[12] The Prudential Tower opened in 1965, symbolizing not only investment and significance but also the city's role as a player in the capital-intensive environment that emerged in the post–Bretton Woods world, a world dominated by the fluidity of trade and production in a system of global exchange. As blue-collar work and population declined, the city's financial, insurance, and real-estate sectors (FIRE), the hallmarks of the urban neoliberal economy of the 1980s to the 2010s, were relatively slow to emerge. Prudential's investment in the city was not only symbolically significant but also introduced the insurance sector as a pillar of the "new" Boston. That John Hancock Insurance built a new and bigger tower not far away—completed in 1976—was a further statement of the city's rebirth and its prominence in the FIRE-dominated economy of the later century.

While the city received significant national attention as part of the nation's bicentennial coverage in 1975 and 1976, its present was visibly fraught. More nationally resonant than the bicentennial celebration was the negative publicity attached to the city of Boston for the ongoing racial antipathies displayed in response to a court-ordered desegregation order of the city's schools in 1974, a response that resulted from a continuing refusal of the city's school committee to implement a desegregation order issued some nine years before. The resistance of working-class whites to school integration, particularly in Charlestown and South Boston, suggested a place stuck in time and mired in antipathies that dated back to the mid-nineteenth century. They revealed the deep roots of the city's ethnic and class divisions: the city where abolitionism had coalesced around the efforts of William Lloyd Garrison and where liberal politicians, including its current senators—Democrat Ted Kennedy and Republican (and African American) Edward Brooke—had long supported civil rights, also included a significant constituency that resisted such causes. While abolitionism had important roots in the city during the period immediately prior to the Civil War, Boston also included a recalcitrant population that resisted the draft for that war and denounced the intended emancipation of slaves. In the 1960s and 1970s, it was a place where ethnic whites attended rallies for George Wallace, and whose population included the founder of the "Wake Up America" campaign of 1969, Arthur Stivaletta, a self-described superpatriot whose cause was a northeastern version of the John Birch Society. Again, these facts do not make the city distinct from, say, New York or Philadelphia. But they enlarge the busing story and provide further power to an extant and powerful narrative.

My study begins with that 1974 Boston busing crisis, focusing on it not only as a social event but also as a media event. I argue its occurring as a national news story on all three television networks and featured in various national newspapers, magazines, and later a bestselling book (*Common Ground*, J. Anthony Lukas, 1986) was replete with images of place that seemed to define and fix the idea of South Boston and Charlestown as Boston itself; a certain segment of an element of its working-class, largely Irish American population as indicative of the whole; and that racism was a monolithic community value. These images became predictive and recursive in many narratives that came to be definitional over time, seemingly fixing the city in a conceptual bracket, even as the city's fortunes and materiality changed significantly. Such factors played into its becoming a place with certain definitional parameters in the twenty-first century. It became a placeholder for a particular idea of authenticity and tradition, notions tied to conceptions of whiteness and celebrating the immigrant groups from the late nineteenth and early twentieth centuries. Such definitions are not only evident in the mass culture fictions that feature Boston during the twenty-first century but also derive from the ways in which it was situated on the periphery of the national imaginary in the decades before.

Arguably, Boston emerged and grew as a virtual, mediated "place" in the wake of a changing economic environment and in relation to a related media environment. Both of these things have significant implications for urbanism and notions of the urban. The images and social activity circulating around the busing crisis attest that Boston's neighborhoods, though decaying and eroding, were at that time still relatively intact. The resistance to busing speaks both to the relative social stasis of places like South Boston and Charlestown in the early 1970s as well as to the precarity of those places as social environments. The resonance of the busing moment as a marker of time and place certainly spoke to an overt and embedded cultural racism in Boston and beyond. It also highlighted a broader crisis in authenticity that had as its result the elevation of urban locales that seemed to capture an earlier epoch of housing and neighborhood. At a moment when a macro-shift in the mode of production, from industrial to service and financial, became undeniable throughout the United States, it enhanced an extant crisis of authenticity. Boston emerged as a site of working-class and racist resistance within this crisis, and thus was valorized and mythologized for that recalcitrance. And that identification and elevation of place through these qualities remained and deepened over the next forty years.

Sharon Zukin insightfully defines this "crisis of authenticity" as occurring in response to post-industrialization and the related phenomenon of gentrification, contrasting the "corporate city" and the "urban village" as development models that defined competing schools of urbanism in the late 1950s and 1960s. The quest for authenticity, then, became a response to a sense of "placelessness" or the proliferation of "no places." The aesthetics and sociability of the urban village, the idealization of the self-contained ethnic urban neighborhood of the 1920s to the 1950s, became a virtual anchor and "place," just as it was being supplanted by urban renewal and the decline of unionized labor in the late 1950s. Explains Zukin of development pressures that would transform the US city, "Elected officials in different cities marched to the same drum. Though they did not admit it, they were chiefly motivated, suggests the urban sociologist Herbert Gans (1962), who studied the demise of Boston's Italian North End in the 1950s, by the desire to attract affluent residents who would pay higher rents and spend more money in downtown stores."[13] Zukin recognizes the role of an imagined past in elevating the urban in the late twentieth century. Gentrification relies on such a valorization of the idealized past, and as Zukin notes, by definition can only take place in locales where older housing stock is being rehabbed and remarketed. Otherwise, the process is a more architecturally comprehensive and transforming redevelopment, one that is commensurate with the large projects that defined urban renewal in the 1950s and earlier 1960s.

The role of historical touchstones in the physical sense and then the significance of referencing and building virtually on an extant and corporeal history is part of the allure of late twentieth- and twenty-first-century Boston. The city became a placeholder for a nostalgic vision of urban life that valorized the bonds of community found in an idealized past, no matter how toxic or criminal. I look at the expressive presence of Boston in the post-industrial and digital age, employing that city as a means to a broader inquiry into the meaning of place—and urban places, more generally—as I explore the synergies that create a discursive and recursive process of city branding, one that is both place-specific and materially based. As such, Boston is not simply being offered as a distinct example; rather, it is being provided as a case study in how concepts of cities, and not simply images of cities, are developed and ultimately formed in a world of virtuality and digital media.

My study has three sections, each of which moves farther from texts with a clear anchor in time and space. I begin with a section that analyzes highly visible Boston stories from journalism as they address certain temporal moments. I look at their embedded conceptions and images of place while unpacking their narratives. Such stories are indeed the first draft of history with their connection to the available *here* and *now* and their fairly straightforward narrative structure. Section 1 draws on the national coverage of events though the major networks of the era: NBC, CBS, and ABC, as well as national print media (*New York Times*, *Washington Post*) and the national news magazines, including *Time* and *Newsweek*. I also look at local media: newspapers and local broadcasting, including radio. In the first chapter of section 1, I focus on the Boston school busing saga (1974–75) as both a historical and media event, and then segue into consideration of a related racial/spatial media event, the Charles Stuart murder case (1989–90). It is remarkable how the news stories of this part became historical points of reference in section 3, which is concerned with feature films. Busing seems to be the signature story of place, complete with its images of South Boston and its residents. And South Boston—as a place that defines or becomes a synecdoche for the whole—is involved in all chapters except those in section 2, though its shadow looms over those chapters as well. The Charles Stuart case did not take place in South Boston nor was its principal character an Irish American. But Stuart's working-class Catholic roots and Italian American ethnicity map easily onto our existing narrative of place. Similarly, the narratives around this episode are also those of racial exclusion with a distinctly spatial dimension.

The coverage of these stories builds on extant narratives lodged in the known and accepted history of place. The city was largely off the national radar in the 1950s save for the emergence of John F. Kennedy as a national politician. Perhaps not coincidentally, as a man of Irish extraction and the grandson of one of Boston's first Irish mayors, Kennedy (to some degree) fits the contours of the regional stereotype. The city also received intermittent mention as a matter of its famous rogue mayor James Michael Curley, as well as his fictional counterpart in the Edwin O'Connor novel *The Last Hurrah* (1955), which was adapted to the screen in 1958, directed by John Ford and starring Spencer Tracy as Frank Skeffington, O'Connor's stand-in for Curley. True to its origins as a studio production of the era, the film was shot entirely on sound stages in Burbank, eschewing the cost of location shooting. Curley, originally of South Boston and then of the tonier environs of Jamaica Plain, served multiple terms as mayor and as a congressional representative, as well as a term in federal prison for accepting a bribe. And while the very polished Senator Kennedy was a Harvard graduate and an heir to great wealth, his personal story at least touched on that of the stereotypical rogue politician.

The city's connection to a kind of working-class culture and political populism predated the busing crisis but informed its reception. The core of those elements took on definition and drama through the media environment of the 1970s. But the Stuart case was of a different media world, one in which satellite-generated cable television had emerged and the internet was just appearing. It built on notions of place generated and accelerated by the busing story, with its images and narratives of racism and insularity. What became remarkable to me was the way in which the busing story of racial resistance and geographic insularity developed a presence in narratives of place that stretched well into the twenty-first century. We see busing recur in any number of Boston film noirs of the early twenty-first century—in *Mystic River* (dir. Clint Eastwood, 2003), in *The Departed* (dir. Martin Scorsese, 2006), in the television series *Ray Donovan* (2013–20), and in *Black Mass* (dir. Scott Cooper, 2015), leaving the fall of 1974 as a signature moment in the definition of the city.

This book takes into account how ideas of place are beholden to prior narratives and images. In such a reckoning, we may reevaluate the significance of certain past events. The further and intensified power of the analog images of busing resulted from their repeated digital placement in popular feature films from three and four decades later, and informed, at least indirectly, all manner of narratives of place. These stories elaborated an entrenched racism among their principal actors, and the way in which that racism was not only accepted but became definitional for social inclusion in the discrete white space of focus.

In the second chapter of section 1, I look at the media phenomena of the sex abuse scandal in the Catholic church, a story that goes back to the 1970s but which broke in the early 2000s, and the saga of Whitey Bulger, a South Boston–based thug who became locally known in the late 1970s and who disappeared in 1995, only to be apprehended in 2010 after several years on the FBI's most wanted list. Both of these stories are creatures of the digital news era, though each had its roots in a previous period. They proliferated through cable news, websites, and social media platforms. These tales are strongly visual and took on a cultural resonance related to the Stuart case and the busing story, but in these cases the shift in widely available media served as an accelerant. While other stories, such as the Big Dig and the Boston Marathon Bombing, are considered, I refer to them only in passing. This is both a matter of limiting sprawl in my study but also of noting that their coverage seems more event-specific than site-specific. Certainly, the Big Dig transformed the material city significantly, but its coverage tends only to focus primarily on its scale and overruns. The marathon bombing fits better, with its many human-interest stories and its elevation of front-line workers, not to mention the apprehension of the bomber in the working-class suburb of Watertown. The bombing also led to a feature film starring Mark Wahlberg, one that contains many of the tropes that define place in other films I discuss.

The priest abuse story speaks to the defining powers of Catholicism in the working-class communities of the city, apparently creating a kind of social glue that fed into narratives of place and authenticity. The media coverage of the scandal touched on definitions of religious community and ethnic whiteness that had also defined the busing crisis. Rather than focusing primarily on the church and its miscreants, the coverage of the tale exploded into a treatment of place with the same markers of authenticity that formed the busing story—working-class housing, families in crisis, Boston accents, insular neighborhoods. Similarly, Whitey Bulger, through the powers of digital media and larger-than-life definitions of place, became the signature rogue criminal of the city. His backstory as the brother of a prominent South Boston politician is intriguing, but it was also his connections with a romance of place that advanced both his persona and the attendant narrative of South Boston and "Boston" in the national and international imaginary. Not coincidentally, Bulger and his brother William were prominently involved with the anti-busing movement, with Whitey taking it as his mission to organize some of the protests and violence against the bused African American students attempting to enter South Boston High, while William rode his resistance to busing into a position of power in the state legislature. As Whitey's story burgeoned, the narrative returns to South Boston for visions of streetscapes and for interviews on local news stations and national news shows with working-class residents of the neighborhood who knew him, knew of him, or participated in his legend. Again, the visuals of these stories could be largely moved from one tale to another without any major disruption. These later stories had the power to refine and accelerate predigital notions of place, as well as reference those stories in a more powerful platform.

All of these stories, through their vision of the ethnic city and its working-class spaces, have the quality of addressing the crisis in authenticity that marks post-industrial urbanism and employs a dimension and definition of Boston as a key term. Moreover, as we look at the rough chronology of these stories, we can see the recurrence of their visual images, providing a vital thread of connection. Indeed, they constitute vital anchors for our narrative of place and a through-line in defining "Boston."

In section 2, I explore two prominent Boston-based sports teams, the Red Sox professional baseball team and the Celtics professional basketball team, for their connections to prevailing articulations of place and their role in representing concepts of place, as sports branding increasingly became connected to place branding in the 2000s. As in the previous section I look at the extensive national coverage of these two teams in a variety of media, both print and electronic. I also consult the fairly extensive book-length studies concerned both with sport and these teams. This section connects to that of the journalistic narratives of section 1 in that sports journalism is a specific type of genre that became more and more ubiquitous as digital technology burgeoned. Such technology was largely responsible for the boom in sports revenues and cultural prominence in the 1990s and 2000s. (That sports were played before empty arenas during the COVID pandemic attests to their reliance on mass transmission.)

But more than discrete stories of teams, I am interested in the aggregated narratives that became definitional for teams and for teams as related to place. I look at the received histories of these franchises to consider what vision of history is operative and how that history connects to notions of place. I did not choose either the Bruins or the Patriots as foci in this section for various reasons: hockey as a sport in the United States has a narrow fan base and presence, though that is certainly not true in Boston, and the Patriots are a creature of the outer suburbs, without even a Boston designation, a regional team and not a city team. In ways, these Boston sports teams are the most visible of all place-related markers and the most effective means of furthering the power of a brand. And in the media coverage of such teams in the digital age, place, as a limited concept, is reinforced. Both teams involve their brand with notions of authenticity that include elements of actual authenticity. Particularly in the case of the Red Sox, notions of authenticity derive from their shrine-like Fenway Park and its location in an older neighborhood of the city. Similarly, the Celtics have lore around place, the old Boston Garden, though it was demolished in 1998. I find the pairing of these teams intriguing for their overlapping of narrative, though there actually should be almost no overlap. The existence of this confluence suggests the power of place and its increasing role in branding.

In section 3, I consider the presence of the city in feature films from 1973 to 2015. By moving into the world of fiction, albeit cinematic fiction, I distend the line from journalism in order to approach these realist narratives as directly commenting on the materiality and *mythos* of place. But as works of fiction, they have far more latitude to craft the contours of their stories, thus delving into furthers aspects of local culture that can inform the myth of place. They take many elements and images found in the first two sections, which are more explicitly tethered to a palpable reality, and employ them in the service of complex narratives that self-consciously feature place and do the cultural work of affirming certain conceptions of Boston while also furthering them. In chapter 5, I consider three films from the immediate post-industrial era, and then *Good Will Hunting* from 1997 (dir. Gus Van Sant), which signaled a transition in the way Boston is featured. They tap into a broad sense of the city but lack the specificity and more refined sense of place that would mark the later 1990s and 2000s productions. These first of these films, *The Friends of Eddie Coyle* (dir. Peter Yates, 1973), preceded the busing crisis by a year yet contains some of the same regional markers that we find in that coverage. Similarly, the other two films of this chapter, *The Brinks Job* (dir. William Friedkin, 1975) and *The Verdict* (dir. Sidney Lumet, 1982), are broadly evocative of place but lack the celebration and branding savvy elements that would mark most post-1997 films (those produced and released after *Good Will Hunting*). In this chapter, I employ *Good Will Hunting* as a point of contrast and transition into the more place-branded and media savvy films of Boston in the 2000s.

Moving into the twenty-first century, chapter 6 focuses on *Mystic River* (dir. Clint Eastwood, 2003), *The Departed* (dir. Martin Scorsese, 2006), *Gone Baby Gone* (dir. Ben Affleck, 2007), *Spotlight* (dir. Tom McCarthy, 2015), and *Black Mass* (dir. Scott Cooper, 2015). This list of films, while representative, is by no means comprehensive. These Boston-filmed productions present a vision of place that is intertextually coherent and strongly wedded—both in terms of narrative and images—to past conceptions, one that is increasingly articulate and static. These films are both the cause and effect of Boston's emergence as a second-tier world city, even as it retains the cultural function of serving as a placeholder for notions of urban authenticity. The proliferation of films that work within roughly the same geography and cultural terrain is both astounding and indicative of the resonance of definitions of place over some forty-five years.

Chapter 7, the book's conclusion, focuses substantially on Showtime's *Ray Donovan*, a series that makes place an element of its central focus on the Donovan family of South Boston. Yet, the film is largely filmed in Los Angeles, making its Boston elements a distillation of the media hooks that have crystallized around place. It includes the accent, the religion, intertextual references to all of the journalism stories, and many references to the Red Sox, and some to the Celtics. That seven seasons of a series can develop on the basis of a conceit about a place that barely appears in the series suggests the power of the narrative of authenticity connected to "Boston."

SECTION I
Space and the Crisis of the Post-Industrial City

SECTION 1 looks at four major Boston-based news stories. These stories became important in recurring definitions of place over the next four decades. They are replete with references to race and space, as well as connections to ethnic group and religion. Within the two chapters that comprise this section, I traverse the shifts that occurred in media and their implications for definitions of time, space, and place. The narratives changed from analog media to digital modes of representation and access. Analog and cable television in chapter 1 gave way to various digital devices employing increasingly powerful and ubiquitous wired and wireless technologies in chapter 2.

I explore how certain chronotopes that became definitional for "Boston" are elaborated in the busing story and then became place identifiers as they recurred in these more available stories of the 2000s. The distinctions between this earlier era of communication and the later digital period are significant for what they project, how they project it, and to whom. The highly interactive dimension of the digital environment creates a virtual space that is far more enveloping and dynamic than that implied by one-way systems of mass communication, such as radio and television. Interactive mass media in 1974 and in 1989 was limited to telephones and their projection in talk radio, which was emerging as a right-wing force during the busing crisis, and particularly so in Boston, where local conservatives like Jerry Williams and Avi Nelson were fanning the flames of white resentment.[1] This same aspect of the local media, now including the incendiary Howie Carr, would also be active in fanning the flames of rage at the death of Carol Stuart.[2] But it is important to keep in mind the relatively lesser impact of this medium when compared with the proliferation of internet chat sites and all manner of social media in the twenty-first century. These earlier stories were limited by the absence of a digital feedback loop that implicates millions in a personal or quasi-personal way. Talk radio in the 1970s and 1980s certainly had its adherents. But such forces would not become truly powerful until the digital age, when the Rush Limbaughs of the world made media presences with a regional scope and a fixed timeslot look slight. By the 2000s, the key chronology of chapter 3, media had become digital and therefore exploded in access and power, making those events all but ubiquitous and powerful in defining Boston.

As we look at the crises of space that defined the conflicts over busing in the 1970s and the Stuart murder in the late 1980s and early 1990s, the scale and issues of the battles are quite different than they would be in the cases that became widely known after 2000. In both of the stories of chapter 2, at issue would be the ability of white populations to control access to their defined spaces at a moment when economic decline made those populations feel vulnerable to displacement. The narratives of this chapter emerge from the historical circumstances of a place that at the end of the industrial era was one that produced economic, social, and psychological dislocation for its workers and their families—both white and Black. But the circumstances of the earlier part of the sixteen-year period from 1974 to 1990 are distinct in their degree of economic decline and disinvestment, with the number of industrial jobs in Boston decreasing from 55,792 to 31,459, and manufacturing in all of the inner-belt suburbs declining even more steeply.[3] Such dislocation contributed to the sense of disorientation and the embrace of increasingly intransigent and spatial definitions of race and ethnicity during the beginning of the latter part of the twentieth century.

This first chapter of section 1 looks at two news stories in detail, both of which originated in Boston and are replete with racism. These stories gained significant national attention throughout the United States. Each in some ways orients around a crisis of scale brought on by the era of globalization. These stories—that of court-ordered busing, largely in 1974 and 1975, and the related story of the Charles Stuart, who killed his wife in late 1989, blamed a Black man for the murder, and then committed suicide in January 1990—show us a city in crisis, riven by entrenched racialized conceptions of space, a city where boundaries of white space loomed as both absolute and sufficiently at risk to warrant reassertion and enforcement.

The second chapter of section 1 looks at the scandal in the Catholic church over multiple cases of priests' sexually abusing children among their parishioners. This public scandal emerged largely in 2002–4, after a series investigating these incidents broke in the *Boston Globe*, but the incidents referred to went back more than two decades. This narrative of clerical criminality exemplifies the tensions between the past and present, the shifting states and definitions of communities and their institutional glue, as well as the relative power of those institutions and the narratives that deflate and/or enhance that power. These incidents allow us to see the disenchantment of an older, Balkanized city of ethnic enclaves and intergenerational residency. It shows us a city that was in the process of maintaining its identity in a conceptual way, even as it morphed into something somewhat different materially.

In this chapter, I also discuss the related saga of Whitey Bulger, a South Boston–based gangster strongly identified with his home turf. Bulger became the object of a massive national manhunt after he vanished in 1994, but even more so after 2002, as the internet became widely available and used by more than 50 percent of those in the United States, a shift abetted by the advent of smartphones and a 3G network in 2001. Bulger's whereabouts and story were extensively tracked though digital means until his capture in 2011. In each case, the scale of the story and its spatial footprint varied dramatically over time and space. As part of my inquiry into reputation and associations, I am interested in the ways in which the coverage of these stories positioned the city—both verbally and visually—and became part of its contemporary presence, even as they referenced the historical city. The stories of chapter 2 are distinct from those of chapter 1 in their emphasis on religion and its relationship to a kind of social insularity, as opposed to the related discourse of race and racism.

In the period between the two major stories that anchor each chapter—from 1974 to 2002—Boston experienced remarkable economic growth thanks to its situation in an increasingly digital mode of international commerce and communication. Yet, motifs recur in the coverage and even some images were repeated. These stories resonated due to their power to address the cultural weight of broader social changes and reorientations.

CHAPTER ONE

Mapping Boston's White Spaces

Busing, Policing, and Privilege

Boston—as a city with a particular national image—was not only a place where the busing crisis occurred: it was the place where a certain narrative affixed to that crisis could be facilely produced and reproduced. It is no accident that predominantly Irish South Boston was ground zero for national coverage, since the association between that group and the city as a whole had long since been established, dating back to the mass migration of the mid-nineteenth century and the emergence of an Irish American political class around the turn of the twentieth century. My focus is less on the *issue* of busing than on how the coverage of that issue came to inform a mass characterization of space and place, including the visual and conceptual definition of the city that emerged in these stories. Such definitions assert embedded historical tropes of place and therefore help to produce a kind of social stasis.

Ronald Formisano in his study of busing in Boston accurately refers to a post-1970 "suburban noose consisting of over a million and a half persons, more than 98 percent white," while also noting that "jobs as well as population flowed out to the suburbs."[1] The impact of such spatial strictures on employment left those caught within the noose increasingly concerned about protecting their turf, however defined, whether economic, social, or geographic. This anxiety, derived from economic decline, was further exacerbated by looming gentrification: by 1974, the city was just beginning to morph into the "new" Boston of the 1990s and 2000s, with certain neighborhoods beginning to gentrify and some large-scale commercial renewal initiatives, such as the Faneuil Hall (begun in early 1975) and Quincy Market (completed in 1976) projects and the waterfront renovations, coming to fruition or looming in the near future.[2] But even with a change in the city's circumstances emerging, the news coverage, and particularly national news coverage, was defined by embedded definitions of place, tied to certain historical associations and given further resonance through mass media.

The spatial segregation of the post-industrial period exacerbated an already extant tendency toward ethnically and racially distinct neighborhoods. Such ethnic exclusion shows the busing crisis—and the Charles Stuart murder case—as taking place in a social cauldron experiencing a rapid rise in heat as a result of the twin impacts of decline in employment opportunities and a slowly escalating process of gentrification. Into this historical and sociological morass, I interject Henri Lefebvre's idea of the production of space, a concept that explains how discrete spaces are created by social forces. That production takes place not necessarily materially as it did in the nineteenth century, as Boston's Back Bay was formed by a massive project of landfill, the literal creation of new lands; or in the case of the Big Dig, a project that took place between 1992 and 2004 and which, among other accomplishments, added three hundred acres of parks and open spaces to the city.[3] Rather, this late twentieth-century creation was a matter of a mediated environment defined by the proliferation of electronic means of communication, a system of information dispersal with an exponential social impact. Writes Lefebvre, "Social space is not a thing among other things, nor a product among other products. . . . Social space is produced and reproduced in connection with the forces of production (and with the relations of production)."[4] As economic dislocation and the threat of geographic dislodging struck those in areas that were historically both insular and powerfully restricted by class and sometimes race, journalists reporting on issues of interest to those vulnerable populations often trafficked in terms that exacerbated such fears. The unstated assumptions that recurred in print, audio, and visual coverage of the busing crisis treated the racial makeup of discrete regions of the city as sacrosanct, as virtual islands of ethnic whiteness within a city that was "changing." Space was created as distinctly racialized and relatively closed to outsiders. The story that was told in the media of busing and of the Charles Stuart murder case was that some space is definitionally white and will—and should (according to insiders)—tend to remain perpetually so.

But such spatial systems of organization are not inherent; they are a matter of specific acts of law and other, less formal agreements. As they are treated as natural and inevitable, they may come to be perceived as such. Coverage of these events in all manner of mass media reaffirms the character of segregated spaces and defines the broader city in static terms. It employs definitions of race, particularly ethnic whiteness, which has the effect of "reproducing" the white enclaves of South Boston and Charlestown—a neighborhood immediately to the north of downtown that was overwhelmingly white. Because of its geography and historical housing, Charlestown was already gentrifying in the mid-1970s. But it was also the site of a considerable poor and working-class white population ensconced in substandard housing, much of it high-density public housing. This mix of classes made it a particularly volatile locale. Other schools also were the sites of integration and protest, but those received far less attention nationally than the marked Irish Catholic, working-class enclave of South Boston, and then later Charlestown.

Conversely, those spaces were defined in opposition to the Black and Brown spaces of places like Roxbury and Mattapan, which were noted but far less frequently pictured. News coverage, including its supporting images, largely failed to open up the common analytical frame organized around simple definitions of race and space to discuss the contextual factors that exacerbated white resentment. It also failed to reconsider visual strategies that restricted spatial understanding of the larger domain of the city and its relational aspects. This unconsidered treatment of race and space had the effect of recreating a fortress mentality that situated whites and people of color on different sides of an apparently solid and fixed line. Such transmissions reinforced the broad racial narrative that inflamed participants in these events and the viewers who sought information about them.

The busing story in Boston had its roots in the *Brown vs. Board of Education* U.S. Supreme Court case of 1954, and then the civil rights struggles of the 1960s. It took on a clearer urgency with the passage of a state law in 1965 outlawing segregation in Massachusetts's urban schools. From this point on, this northern incarnation of segregation, referred to as de facto, was under duress. The city's schoolboard resisted the law and offered no plan to address the condition it targeted. This crisis accelerated in 1974 when a federal court order mandated that white and African American students be sent to high schools beyond their neighborhoods to achieve racial integration.

In the later decades of the twentieth century, working-class Bostonians of all races experienced social insecurity. This precarity among Bostonians was not unique to that place, but its specific terms provide a window into a broader, multi-geographic condition. While ultimately some jobs would return to the city and inner-belt suburbs, those would substantially require skills and education not readily available to people who had been mired in declining inner-city neighborhoods and schools for the previous decades. This sense of having been left behind by a world that was becoming increasingly complex and subject to innovations in technology which changed the nature of work fueled a determination by many to hold onto residual and simple social definitions and orientations. The logic of such resistance becomes even more apparent when one considers that the Boston plan for school busing had the effect of moving poor Black students to underperforming white schools within the city limits or poor white students to underperforming Black schools, likewise within the city.

More substantial opportunities for access to better education in the form of a countywide or regional system of public education—a system that might include the high-performing schools just outside the city limits in, say, Newton and Brookline—a system that would not make poorly funded and poorly resourced inner-city education a matter of apparent destiny, was initially rejected by Judge W. Arthur Garrity, the federal judge presiding over the case. Soon after, the Supreme Court ruled against regional solutions to school segregation in the *Milliken v Bradley* case, eradicating the prospect of a more fully interclass and interracial system of education, leaving parents and students in economically disadvantaged regions to fight over which failing schools their children would attend.

These historical circumstances found their visual and verbal expression in the journalism of the day, both national and local, but particularly national. Journalists tend to use and reuse particular ethnic identifiers as definitional for certain urban neighborhoods, reifying their demographics as well as the spaces associated with them. One example of this is the way that network news broadcasters in the fall of 1974, as the crisis over busing in Boston exploded, constantly referred to "white students" as opposed to "Blacks," apparently making a case for the primacy of non-minorities in the schools. Similarly, the preponderance of network newscasts showed African American students entering previously all-white schools. The images of those white neighborhoods tended to locate them as virtual fortresses, places with restricted access and escape, thus creating narratives of intrusion that conflicted with embedded stories of belonging.[5]

Photographers and videographers working for network newscasts and national magazines and newspapers generally shot the anti-busing

FIGURE 3. School buses bringing students from Roxbury to South Boston, escorted by police, roll toward South Boston High School. —AP Images.

demonstrators across narrow streets or in the midst of crowds, images that became totalizing, or with barriers of some type defining the extent of a viewer's field of vision. Such recurring tropes both can seem to match and to define the facts of the moment and make them apparently inevitable. One iconic shot was up the hill on G Street in South Boston as the buses rolled down to the school. In many of these television shots we can see and hear an angry crowd and more police in the foreground. The use of such tight shots creates claustrophobic images that support reportage emphasizing insularity. In figure 3, perhaps the most iconic and reproduced image of the crisis, we see an apparent intrusion into discrete and narrow spaces, as African American students are transported to white schools in white neighborhoods, in this case South Boston, escorted by a phalanx of white centurions. The streetscape emphasizes the very working-class, three-decker housing that would become a place identifier in subsequent treatments of the city.

Such emphases create and recreate the narrative of space and place that aligns with a broad cultural and historical understanding of Boston and which would become even more powerful over time. The predominant coverage of the busing crisis reduced space, so that the entire city became identified with this recurring image of a particular locale and then locales like it. As a corollary, historically complex notions of place collapse into a more restricted one, as defined by the temporal resonance of the space and people pictured. Although as Matthew Delmont points out, network newscasts at times employed maps, these schematics tended to emphasize distance rather than minimize it, asserting the relative geographic isolation of both South Boston and Charlestown, or even the distance between white Hyde Park and African American Roxbury.[6] Such spatial representations, with their assertion of "objective space," tended to affirm both division and the core definitional chronotopes of white space that would mediate perceptions of Boston for the next decades.

As economic insecurity burgeoned among working-class whites, geographic mobility for those with little capital all but dried up—until gentrification came of age in the 1990s–2000s and forced residents to inner-line and decaying suburbs. We can see the results of those trends in the shifting demographics of discrete regions of the city. South Boston increased from 97 percent white in 1970 to 98.5 percent white in 1980 before falling dramatically to 84.4 percent white in 2000 and just over 80 percent in 2015. Spatial segregation, which was already a fact, became even more entrenched as the economy shifted from industrial production to a more knowledge- and information-based mode of employment, and white working-class neighborhoods became even more so during the busing era. But then as gentrification took hold, districts like South Boston became both wealthier and less white.

Conversely, the historically African American region of the city, Roxbury, which had been substantially Jewish until the 1940s, was around 82 percent African American and Hispanic in 1970 and 89 percent by 2000, suggesting the lines that formed around both race and class in providing housing opportunities for people of color. The abutting neighborhood of Mattapan was 86 percent Black and Hispanic in 2000, while it was 21 percent in 1970. Roxbury in 1970 was 8.1 percent foreign-born and Mattapan 13.8 percent. In 2000, Roxbury was over 20 percent foreign-born and Mattapan over 31 percent. Such numbers suggest not only the persistence of racialized patterns of housing but also the ways in which the city's institutions accepted that spatial order. Such demographics show how legacies of segregation are re-elaborated with new populations, as immigrants of color succeed native-born populations of color.[7]

Reproducing Assumptions of "White Space" in a "White" City

Images of a self-evidently white city proliferated as a means of denaturalizing that concept for framing the spatial dimension of both the busing and the Charles Stuart sagas. Evidence of this may be found in Elijah Anderson's definition of white space, which shows how such regions are made and enforced. Writes Anderson, "The Civil Rights Movement is long past, yet segregation persists. The wider society is still replete with overwhelmingly white neighborhoods, restaurants, schools, universities, workplaces, churches and other associations, courthouses, and cemeteries, a situation that reinforces a normative sensibility in settings in which Black people are typically absent, not expected, or marginalized when present. In turn, blacks often refer to such settings colloquially as 'the white space'—a perceptual category—and they typically approach that space with care."[8]

Indeed, both incidents are testimonies to the prevalence of "white space," and it is in the visual representation of that space, including terms that define it as white, that we are provided a window into the contours of "Boston." Although the city was around 20 percent Black and Brown in 1970, 30 percent in 1980, and 40 percent in 1990, it was largely still represented as a city populated by mainline Protestants of an earlier vintage and white ethnics, particularly Catholics of Irish and, to a lesser degree, Italian extraction. The predominant images of the busing story are of African Americans being compelled to enter decidedly white spaces, and that upon entering those spaces treated with the precise behaviors that Anderson defines as marking the racial dominance of the white group, even though the schools were, as of the 1974–77 academic year, 61 percent white and 31 percent African American, so far from monolithically white.[9] Anderson explains, "For the white space is where many social rewards originate, including an elegant night on the town, or cultural capital itself—education, employment, privilege, prestige, money, and the promise of acceptance. To obtain these rewards, blacks must venture into the white space and explore its possibilities, engaging it to the extent that they can while hoping to benefit as much as possible."[10] Certainly, these factors are assumed as definitional for school busing, at least as presented to a mass public. Nightly newscasts on all three networks showed African American adolescents under police protection, leaving yellow school buses and traversing angry white mobs in order to enter a guarded edifice—that is, a public high school built in the earlier century, so far from "elegant" but still assumptively better than the alternative. We repeatedly saw images of African American students complying with the court order and entering the zones defined by white-only schools, only to be harassed and physically assaulted.[11]

The rationale for busing was based in the need to redress segregated residential spaces. When Arthur Garrity wrote his order for mandatory school busing in June 1974, it threatened those who had derived comfort from the city's very clear spatial organization, a regime that resulted in people of Irish ancestry residing in certain areas, Italians in others, Jews in others, and African Americans in a very few and highly circumscribed districts. In the post–World War II era, this social practice was enforced at a variety of tiers. Realtors were unlikely to show a property in Irish South Boston to those of Italian descent, while Jews were, after 1950 or so, unlikely to be shown a house in Roxbury. This practice of segregation by both race and ethnicity resulted from a combination of both ground-level market choices by consumers and macro-policy as a matter of custom and fiat (Federal Housing Authority practices; agreed-upon lending policies by banks; and quasi-official acts by realtors, neighborhood associations, and civic groups of various kinds). Indeed, in a very revealing episode, the Boston Banks and Urban Renewal Group (BBURG) made a judgment in 1968 that the formerly Jewish area of Mattapan would be opened to African Americans, who would eventually become the prevalent population of that neighborhood, along with recent migrants of color, including a significant Haitian American population and those who had come to Boston from Cape Verde. This initiative did in fact come to pass and is revealing for the ways in which it defined that neighborhood as racially monolithic and subject to pressures by institutions within the city.[12]

It was this spatial segregation that court-ordered school busing attempted to redress in 1974. By reading the data and concluding that African Americans were underserved by the racially segregated school system, the federal court instituted a plan to shift the city from neighborhood schools to schools that were populated by students of different races who resided in different sectors of the city.[13] Since school populations were defined by attendance boundaries that were contiguous to schools, segregated housing resulted in segregated schools, and the resources available for predominantly African American schools were always less than those for white schools. The result was all manner of resistance and social violence by a subset of working-class whites who protested the order and physically obstructed entry to African American school children bused to their neighborhoods. The most famous images of this activity were of groups surrounding buses as they entered the environs of South Boston High School, displayed in any number of news reports, both in print and in television newscasts.[14]

The story of busing is, on the surface and in its depth, one fundamentally about race in the city as a whole and in distinct regions as well. And this emphasis was well defined in both local and national coverage, although in the national coverage, it was more a given and less a matter for explicit exploration. In other words, local coverage tended to go more deeply into the spatial and racial issues that underlay the various groups' positions, perhaps because viewers were assumed to have more basic knowledge of the surface elements of the situation. As Delmont shows in his excellent analysis, the mass-media treatment of the issue of busing as a means of school integration and its specific Boston case left much to be desired. He points out that the usual framing of the national rancor over court-ordered busing largely failed to address the central issues of racism and white privilege. Rather, it fell into a far more localized narrative about white resistance to the act of "busing," which was, for the most part, accepted—as a matter of the reportage—as an intrusion into everyday life. Such on-the-ground reporting failed to address the systemic, deep structures of racial segregation and subjugation.[15]

Delmont further illustrates his point by detailing the journalistic emphases: stories focused on "clashes between white protesters and police but said little about the students or schools that were ostensibly at the center of the story."[16] The national version of the Boston story almost immediately became one about events and localized conflicts, one that lent itself to a kind of reduction that allowed undue credibility to affix to the case of the protesters, even as the particular actions associated with them were clearly reprehensible. But that judgment was so self-evident that it was beyond comment. In a signature event from the beginning of the crisis, protesters jeered Senator Edward Kennedy off of a stage on the Boston Common just as school began in 1974. Coverage of the event was far more concerned with the conflict than the issue, noting of one man in the crowd, like many of the demonstrators, he saw the integration plan "as being forced on the city's working class neighborhoods by wealthy suburbanites and outside liberals who do not have to bear its burdens, and he feels deeply threatened and resentful."[17]

Boston's Irish and the Terms of White Resentment

Boston had a certain limited national visibility for its resistance after 1965 to integrating its schools. By the mid-1970s, the city, both its image and its actuality, had started to change through a number of devices—sports, politics, the 1976 bicentennial, increased economic development—but the terms of the busing crisis and the media coverage of its major players—schoolboard chair Louise Day Hicks, Mayor Kevin White, and Judge Garrity, among others—well played into an embedded national definition of place: its insularity and its resistance to change. That is, the mediated Boston was a place defined by a very traditional narrative of the urban, one closely related to the image of the first Irish Catholic presidential candidate, New York Democratic governor Al Smith, who in 1928 ran for president unsuccessfully as a symbol of urban America, particularly of the Northeast.

It is indeed interesting that the Irish American angle of the story is a far more prominent part of the busing crisis' national coverage than its local. Local coverage tended to focus on matters of race—antipathies between Black and white people—and logistics—where the buses went, how they got there, impediments to their safe arrival—while national stories focused far more on particularized ethnic tensions between people of Irish descent, not simply "white" and "Black" African Americans, as well as on South Boston in particular, a locale that reinforced the emphasis on Irish-ness. The local stories told daily in the *Boston Herald*, *Boston Globe*, and the network television stations—WBZ, WCVB, WNAC, and public television's WGBH—tended to provide relatively greater context than the networks. This may be of course inevitable, as a matter of broadcast time devoted to the story and a matter of their consumers being more versed in the embedded details of the events covered. But those national outlets were far more powerful as framers of the story and disseminators of a certain narrative.[18]

The national face of the anti-busing movement was local politician Louise Day Hicks. Hicks was a classic Boston politician, a woman from South Boston, an heir to a powerful family. Her father, William J. Day, was a municipal court judge who became wealthy through his law practice and real-estate holdings. She was first elected to the schoolboard in 1961 and served as its president when the initial order to address racial imbalance in Boston Public Schools came from the state in 1965. Hicks was a galvanizing figure but one who readily took on, and was granted in the press, both local and national, the crown of a champion for the beleaguered white working-class. Although she was far from working class, Hicks dressed and spoke the part, with a heavy Boston accent and decidedly frumpy clothing, including hats. Her motto, "You know where I stand," affirmed her predilection toward segregation and the sanctity of Boston's ethnically homogeneous neighborhoods. It also connected her with a public that shared her spatial and racial politics. In television news, Hicks was the face of white recalcitrance and fidelity to her own tribe. Beyond appearing on the cover of *Newsweek* magazine on November 6, 1967, she was a noted presence in an anti-busing march on Washington covered by CBS news in April 1972 and frequently appeared in newspapers such as the *New York Times* and *Washington Post*.[19] She served in Congress from 1971 to 1973, when she replaced the former Speaker John W. McCormack, and lost two hotly contested mayoral elections to Kevin White in 1967 and 1971. Figure 4 shows her celebrating her win in the 1971 primary.

FIGURE 4. Louise Day Hicks celebrates her win in the 1971 mayoral primary. Spencer Grant, "Louise Day Hicks Wins Mayoral Primary, Boston," photograph, 1971. —Courtesy Digital Commonwealth, https://ark.digitalcommonwealth.org.

In a 2017 fifty-year retrospective in the *Boston Globe*, reporter Andrew Ryan wrote of the 1967 mayoral election as a turning point in Boston's history, citing Hicks's appeal to the ethnic loyalties and antipathies as a decided look to the past. He quoted her invocations of a "Boston for Bostonians," positioning herself as an advocate for the "forgotten man." Ryan wrote, "She caught fire as a populist phenomenon, a symbol of white backlash against a changing world."[20] But this fifty-year retrospective is too schematic, too embedded in the relative political dynamics of the city and the time. While eventual mayor Kevin White was relatively more progressive and a supporter of busing, he was not outside of the historical political machine, either personally or politically. The son of a prominent Irish political family that had made its way from South Boston to the more genteel Jamaica Plain, he was not anti-busing; he also failed to stand in the forefront of the movement for school integration. Further, White easily fit the mold of place and its dominant political class, and thus reinforced extant narratives. As he continued to serve from 1968 to 1984, his reformer image gave way to his big-city-machine-mayor persona before he finally left politics under a cloud of investigation.

For the sake of contrast and elaborating the relative emphasis on Hicks and the Irish angle to the story, there was the situation, far less visually available in print and electronic media, of East Boston, where integration was largely exempted from the busing order "for geographic reasons."[21] That region included its own galvanizing, race-baiting advocate, Elvira "Pixie" Palladino, a leader of the East Boston chapter of ROAR (Restore Our Alienated Rights), which was founded by Hicks in 1974. And though Palladino would be elected to the city schoolboard in 1975, the face of the anti-busing insurgency in the national press perpetually belonged to Hicks, a condition that followed the almost daily focus on South Boston High School.

In looking at the images of the busing crisis, there are a few that are distinctly iconic. These include the aforementioned Ted Kennedy debacle at the anti-busing rally on September 9, 1974. It shows the still young and vital senator, at the time just over forty years old and the last surviving brother of that notable family. The newscasts were shot with an intimacy that puts viewers in the bodily space of the senator. The crowd that surrounds him is monolithically white and angry. As we watch the clips, we see Kennedy denied the speaker's platform.

Such visual images only buttress existing impressions of a place that was defined by its whiteness and resistance to change. The scene that day, as documented by all three television networks and the national print press, as well as all three local newscasts and the two major daily papers, was distinctly urban—crowded streets, concrete buildings, few trees, and little grass. As that scene took place on the mall of the new city hall, a place characterized by its coldness and brutalist architecture, the city is anything but inviting.[22] The setting and scene seamlessly provide an alienating sense of place. Ultimately, we see security guards move Kennedy inside in order to get him out of the angry throng, and we hear a man say, "The people do not care to hear you," and a voice yell out, "Bus *your* kids, Teddy." As Kennedy retreated to the building, the crowd continued to surge forward, eventually breaking one of the large plate glass windows that begin at ground level. Those last images were shot from inside the building through the space where the glass had been. Such a view further emphasizes the viewer's space outside of the crowd and its mob-like quality. Not coincidentally, this mall became something of a symbol of the city during this era, and had been a focal location in the Boston-based film *The Friends of Eddie Coyle* (1973). That place was also the site of the attack on Ted Landsmark in 1976, one of the other signature media events of the busing crisis of the mid-1970s, and one that further elevated the city as a place of violent whiteness.

Landsmark was a young African American, Yale-educated lawyer who happened to walk into a rally against busing that had begun in various white districts of the city and, after a march, convened in City Hall Plaza on April 5, 1976. The specific reasons for a protest that day were the culmination of a search for a new headmaster at South Boston High School, which had resulted in the job being offered to an outsider, a progressive educator from Minnesota named Jerome Wynegar, and the remanding of the administrative oversight of the Boston schools from the school committee to the federal court—and of J. Arthur Garrity in particular. The tensions that triggered both the march and the assault were generalized, though inspired by these specific occurrences. Historian Louis Masur explains, "The protesters spotted Landsmark and turned on him. One went to trip him up. A couple of them yelled, 'Get the nigger.' A few of the antibusing protesters at the front jumped him. He was being kicked and punched. Another unidentified Black man hurried away from the scene. . . . The incident lasted maybe fifteen or twenty seconds. Landsmark's glasses were shattered and his nose broken. He was left drifting, bloodied, and dazed."[23]

While the event itself was emblematic of the racist sentiment animating the resistance to busing, the fact that a local newspaper photographer for the *Boston Herald*, Stanley Forman, happened to be there to capture the incident on film transformed it into an image of the city and nation that resounded throughout the world. Forman won both a Pulitzer Prize and a World Press Photo Award for the picture. As in the images of the Kennedy incident of 1974, the violence depicted is that of angry white people, with a large component of young males in the picture. The photo also shows the city as grimly utilitarian, charmless, featuring its most alienating architecture. In the context of the anti-busing moment, the site became identified with a racist white populist insurgency. Masur writes, "The image taken eighteen months into the battle over the desegregation of the public schools, crystallized Boston's reputation as a racist city."[24] That I can access

FIGURE 5. "The Soiling of Old Glory." Lawyer Ted Landsmark is accosted by participants in an anti-busing rally at City Hall Plaza in April 1976. —Courtesy Stanley Forman Photograph.

this image on my computer speaks to its persistence and powers of definition as it exists in the digital age. That it could appear almost instantly all over the world in 1976 speaks to the wonder of the reach of international wire services by satellite transmission, a system that was developed in the prior decade and that allowed for images and news packets to travel globally in a matter of minutes.[25] Such images speak to ways busing coverage defined a city in a clear and visually compelling way as a racist site, and that images such as those of the anti-busing rally on the Boston Common and of the assault on Ted Landsmark became memorialized as chronotopes that perpetually evoke place in emotionally powerful terms.

J. Anthony Lukas's *Common Ground* and Class Mobility

By the time J. Anthony Lukas's bestselling book *Common Ground: A Turbulent Decade in the Lives of Three American Families* (1986) appeared, the narrative of place and events was on its way to being established, as were the key images associated with the busing crisis. The book, which won the Pulitzer Prize, the National Book Critics Circle Award, the Robert F. Kennedy Book Award, and the American Book Award, largely recast in more detailed and nuanced ways narratives of the city that had been defined a decade earlier. The ultimate success of the book solidified them further. As of 1986, the school situation in Boston had reached a kind of stasis, so the book functioned more as an after-the-fact treatment than it did as a time-sensitive piece of journalism, even as it developed the story with deeper explanations and a greater range of personal dramas. The book's status and great popularity have made it the quintessential account of this historical period in the city of Boston.

Common Ground looks at the events of the mid-1970s ostensibly through the prisms of three families with different class and racial points of view on the busing crisis. First were the African American Twymons, who lived in the decayed but gentrifying South End of Boston in a recently constructed, subsidized housing enclave, Methunion, sponsored by the Methodist Church. The white and elite Divers featured Colin, a graduate of Amherst and Harvard Law School who worked for Kevin White, the mayor of the city. They were urban homesteaders—gentrifiers—who lived in an abutting area of the South End, a district of townhouses built in the mid-nineteenth century but long since decayed. The third family were the working-class McGoffs of Charlestown, a family that has been there for generations and who lived in a housing project and were avowedly anti-busing. This distribution of protagonists was promising and provided a sense of the city at a historical point when its population and even its built environment were beginning to change. Families like the Twymons or McGoffs would gradually feel more and more isolated in their communities as the gentrification of abutting real estate would prove to be, if erratic, ultimately ongoing. Far-sighted developers hungrily eyed the property that these families had called home for at least a few generations. For example, the Bunker Hill Housing Project in which the McGoffs resided was in the process of being recast as a mixed-income area in which subsidized units would stand beside market-priced residences.

Rather than following the dominant spatial meme as it occurred in mass media during the 1970s, Lukas changed things and moved his focus from South Boston to Charlestown. It is a distinct region but in ways even more homogeneous than South Boston, which is adjacent to the city's financial district. Charlestown is connected to the North End of Boston by a bridge, a fact that makes it seem even more self-contained than South Boston. The bridge is infamous for its role in closing off the return of those who have committed crimes in Boston. Indeed, this bridge is one of the visual conceits in the film *The Town* (dir. Ben Affleck, 2010). In the 1970s, Charlestown began to gentrify, a phenomenon that distinguished it from South Boston, which would not do so in any significant way for another fifteen years, but the distinctions between the gentrified zone of Charlestown and its housing projects were vast and stark.

Lukas's study morphs into a work that implicitly locates more involved issues around busing that daily or even weekly journalism did not and perhaps could not cover. As the book goes on, it largely moves away from the school issue to a more varied consideration of urban lives and the tensions of gentrification. But it does so almost seamlessly, so this reframing remains implicit and does not confront the predominant dynamics of the busing narrative. In a culminating scene, the crime that originated in the Methunion Housing Project, where the Twymons resided, spills into the world of the Diver family, as we see the clash between new and more prosperous residents and the residual poorer ones. Eventually, underclass youths from Methunion find the temptation of pregnable homes and upper-middle-class residents in their immediate vicinity too good an economic opportunity to pass up. When this crime wave spills over into the Divers' neighborhood, the two narratives have a period of overlap. Similarly, Lukas tells of Rachel Twymon's sister, Alva Walker Debman, attempting to buy a home on the other side of the racial red-line in the Codman Square region of Dorchester. Indeed, the BBURG agreement that declared the Jewish regions of Mattapan open to African American home buyers also stipulated that abutting regions, like the street where Debnam had purchased her house, would remain all white. Lukas wrote, "Not until rocks and bottles began crashing through their windows did Alva and Otis [her husband] realize they had jumped two blocks beyond the nearest Black family, ratcheting the level of apprehension another notch."[26] The Debnams experienced a nightmare of racial harassment, vandalism, and official indifference. Such impediments to actual integrated housing became part of Lukas's portrait of the extreme difficulty of addressing the disparity of opportunities caused by segregated schooling by altering housing patterns. It also provided a further picture of the perceived sanctity of neighborhoods and the means by which that perception was enforced with violence and intimidation, thus apparently confirming the narratives that prevailed in 1974 and 1975.

In the school-based narrative as it developed in the last portion of the book, we learn more about the public school in the South End that the Diver children attended, the Bancroft School, which was controlled largely by urban "homesteaders" like the Diver family. In their distinctly myopic view of integration, they employed their white privilege to control the school's curriculum and largely create school integration by allowing a shifting population of African American students to either accept the vision of its white parents' board or move on to another school. In the summer of 1974, Joan Diver received a notice from the schools informing her that her son, Brad, had been reassigned to a nearby school that was a more usual one for the district—poor, overcrowded, largely minority. At that point she and Colin employed their considerable political clout to have the assignment reversed, ultimately appealing to Judge Garrity and those who he had appointed to oversee the mechanics of school integration. In deference to the politically connected white parents—including the Diver family—the children who had been enrolled at the Bancroft were allowed to remain.

This is something of a transitional scene in the book and one that is definitional for the terms of the "new" Boston, since class and racial privilege ultimately will out. This "victory" signaled a shift in Lukas's narrative, as he subsequently showed us the power of entrenched racism and the entrenched and historically embedded nature of class and racial privilege. This began the narrative's turn toward a determinist reading of the post-1960s urban reality, where the hopes of a new and progressive vision of U.S. life gave way to the dystopic city of crime, conflict, and social isolation. The city the narrative leaves is one that is entrenched in its problems, riven by class, ethnicity, and race. In ways, Colin Diver is the hope of the book—a liberal and an antiracist who seeks to raise his family in a world where class and race are not the basis for geographic isolation. When he gives in to urban despair and migrates with his family to suburban Newton, it is a kind of judgment of the intransigence of the weight of history.

In this regard, Boston seemed an ideal urban canvas for his tale, a place captured by its history and imprisoned by its own recurring social dynamics—and their uncritical representation. Lukas's long and thoughtful rendering of the busing episode tended to buttress already powerful narratives of event and place with its descriptive content, even as it added complexity and historical depth.

Charles Stuart and the Soul of a Racist City

The infamous Charles Stuart murder case occurred not long after the publication of *Common Ground* and soon after the 1988 presidential race, which featured an advertisement picturing paroled African American Willie Horton as an image of Black criminality to accompany a cautionary tale for white people—set in Massachusetts, the home of candidate Michael Dukakis. That ad trafficked in the racist assumptions of criminality that were widely available in U.S. mass culture in the late twentieth century, as well as imposed them on a geography where such assumptions were, in the view of racists (or conservative realists), denied by a liberal populace. Such assertions brought the busing story back to the fore of news consumers. The Stuart murder tale built on the busing coverage and enhanced its story of space and race. But it introduced any number of complications as a matter of its bifurcated narrative.

On October 23, 1989, Charles Stuart dialed 911 to report the shooting of his wife, Carole DiMaiti Stuart, who was seven months pregnant at the time. Charles himself was also injured with a gunshot wound in his stomach. They were on their way home—but going in precisely the wrong direction—from a childbirth class at the Brigham and Women's Hospital in Jamaica Plain, not far from Fenway Park, and making their way through the mixed-race and mixed-income neighborhood of Mission Hill, which is close by the hospital and was either an idyllic vision of an integrated neighborhood or a deeply fraught racial contact zone where racial antipathies flourished and poorer residents always felt the pressures of imminent displacement by the more affluent. Stuart described his alleged assailant as a "six foot Black man with a raspy voice."[27]

In the next days, the Mission Hill sector of the city became a danger zone for African American men in their twenties and thirties, with Boston mayor Raymond Flynn declaring war on street crime, always a racialized act. In the following days, an African American man from Mission Hill, Willie Bennett, a thirty-nine-year-old ex-con, was arrested and charged with the murder. The initial events—as then understood—were well covered by the national press, as they fit a dominant narrative about African American inner-city violence and exacerbated latent and overt white racism and antiurban inclinations.

This story projects out into the emergent world of new media—mostly the rise of cable television—as it was defined in the late 1980s, and easily maps onto residual notions of place, containing many images that complement those that occurred with some frequency around the busing crisis of the mid-1970s. But in January 1990, a few months later, Charles Stuart, the "grieving husband," committed suicide by leaping from the Tobin, formerly the Mystic River, Bridge, apparently with the knowledge that he was about to be arrested for his wife's murder.

The two phases of this story *both* frame a narrative of place with a significant racist component: the story of Willie Bennett murdering a pregnant white woman, and the story of an ambitious white man killing his wife and selling the story to a credulous press and public before committing suicide. In the first instance, Boston, as in the busing story, is a place of racial antipathies where attempts to breach the divide lead to social disruption and violence. In the second, Boston is a racist city where unfounded narratives of Black criminality are easily concocted, consumed, and reproduced by a white populace and power structure. In the initial iteration, local stations referred to it as a "hellish crime" and featured clips of police officers questioning African Americans and searching vacant lots in the parts of Mission Hill that abutted public housing.[28]

The story was not only a highly visible local one: it also achieved significant national prominence for its sensational merging of place, race, and violence. On October 24, 1989, the story of a Black assailant murdering a pregnant white woman featuring footage of Mission Hill was broadcast on the network newscasts.[29] This event also achieved enhanced coverage as a result of the coincidence of Stuart's 911 call occurring on a night the television show *Rescue 911*, a reality-based television show that aired on CBS from 1989 to 1996, happened to be filming in Boston. Stuart became an instant television star, and networks, as a result of the reality television coverage, could avail themselves of that footage in their presentation of the story. It also was the source for a very quickly made made-for-TV movie, *Goodnight Sweet Wife: A Murder in Boston* (1990), though the production was actually shot in Chicago. The Stuart saga furthered the media narrative regarding place, space, and race in intriguing ways. It was initially a tale about uncritical assumptions of race and space: a white man and his pregnant wife are accosted by a man of color, and then, as the story unfolds, it became a tale about deception, domestic violence, and brutality—a man kills his pregnant wife for financial gain. Unfortunately, the second narrative never quite undid the first. Both, however, employed tropes of place that further developed those found in the coverage of busing.

By 1990, there was significant explosion in media outlets as a matter of the proliferation of cable television. Although *Rescue 911* was a network television show initially, it achieved much of its visibility and notoriety through its constant presence on various cable outlets after 1993. The reality format that inspired the show was a matter of the networks' response to competition from cable outlets, as the profit margins for shows such as *Rescue 911* were enhanced by the cheapness of filming on the street and not having to hire actors. The Stuart movie on the Lifetime Network further attested to the greater proliferation of televised material in a media world that included an ever-expanding number of cable outlets looking for provocative content.

The Stuart saga shows the tensions inherent in the cities of the eastern United States by the late 1980s, as minority communities, still beset by the impact of the post-industrial and neoliberal economy, found themselves too often as have-nots in an increasingly bifurcated social and economic world. In urban locales, these communities were increasingly feeling the pressures of gentrification. The white fear that fueled the initial understanding of this incident suggests the ways that the spatial sanctity of racially monolithic and then mixed neighborhoods, even in cities like Boston, was being breached by nothing less than a redefinition of centralized urban space. That is, gentrification in effect created a white and wealthy sense of proprietorship over the city as a whole. Mission Hill is a mixed-race community, including both a number of working-class health workers and public housing residents. It borders the Fenway area, which is not only the home of the Red Sox but also the site of a number of prestigious teaching hospitals—Brigham and Women's and Beth Israel Deaconess Hospitals, as well as Harvard Medical School.

The hysteria and bad judgment that defined the Stuart case related to the contemporary, racialized vision of rampant criminality that was focused around young African American men in urban spaces, a vision that led to all manner of aggressive policing, including the stop-and-frisk regime of Bill Bratton and Rudolph Giuliani in New York City from 1994 to 1996. Bratton had been the head of the Boston Police Department before arriving in New York. Notably, Congress passed the federal crime bill of 1994 with an eye to cleaning up U.S. cities, resulting in the incarceration of massive numbers of young men, and particularly young men of color.[30] The Boston police commissioner at the time of the Stuart case was Mickey Roache, who led a predominantly white force known for its own policies of arbitrarily detaining and frisking minority youths and other older Black and Brown men.[31]

Initially the media participated in the hysteria around the Stuart case, creating a version of the assault on due process that accompanied the contemporary arrest of the five adolescents in New York City known as the Central Park Five. The local coverage of the first phase of the story was unrelentingly racist, particularly by the Rupert Murdoch–owned *Boston Herald*, which called for death to the erroneously apprehended suspect, and a more general regime of enhanced policing of people of color. But the *Boston Globe* coverage was credulous, if less extreme. Both papers reported that, according to Boston police, a Black male had committed the crimes shortly after the Stuarts left a childbirth class on Monday evening in Mission Hill. Most Boston-area broadcast and print media immediately featured the story, and many ran spinoffs about the hunt for the suspect, the Stuarts, the Mission Hill area, violent crime in Boston, and the recorded 911 telephone call that Charles Stuart had made from his car to the Boston police.[32] National outlets also responded with credulity to Stuart's tale, again defining Boston as a place of intense racial antagonisms, particularly around issues of the apparent sanctity of white space.

As noted, the coverage of the story divided into two parts. On one hand, there was the initial coverage, from that October and November, when the presumption of an African American assailant was largely unquestioned. Those stories tend to emphasize the city's urban crime problem and the fact that white citizens were at risk for acts of violence by African American perpetrators. It also had a spatial dimension since it traversed the spaces of the abutting urban locale—Revere—and a farther northern white suburb—Reading—the Boylston Street shopping district where Charles worked, and the region around the Fens, the complex of Frederick Law Olmstead-designed parkland near Fenway Park and the hospitals. Of those places, the only remotely integrated zone was that of the Fens and Mission Hill, which abut Roxbury and Jamaica Plain. And that broader schematic of space reconfirmed the spatial information of the busing story.

Local stories immediately found Stuart's story credible and discussed the need for the reinstitution of the death penalty, the need for aggressive policing, and the proliferation of crime in the city. National headlines emphasized the city as a site for urban crime, with a late October 1989 piece in the *New York Times* beginning, "The slaying of a pregnant woman abducted outside a hospital here has focused national attention on a recent spate of street violence in a city seldom preoccupied with crime."[33] Almost all of these renderings emphasized Carol and "Chuck" Stuart as an all-American couple—attractive, successful, anticipating a great future. The implicit topic of this story, as it proceeded, was inner-city violence perpetrated by African Americans. One source attributed the reason for violence as urban "poverty and despair," while another focused on the largely African American regions of Roxbury and Dorchester (though Dorchester included both predominantly minority and predominantly white areas). In those earlier stories, the racial assumptions of white readers and writers largely went unquestioned, mirroring the attitudes of law enforcement officials who initially accepted Stuart's story—although this was partially a matter of Stuart's wounds, which were serious enough to warrant more than a month in the hospital—clearly not his intention when he inflicted them on himself. This Boston was recognizable as the place where racial divisions and strife created the busing crisis of the 1970s. Indeed, that reiteration of an extant narrative clearly contributed to the coverage of both race and place. Stuart employed assumptions of "white space" as central to his murder ploy, intentionally traversing a liminal area in order to give credence to his racially determined story of Black criminality.

And then there were those stories after January 4, 1990, when Charles Stuart placed an elliptical note in his car, declaring, "The allegations have taken all of my strength," never admitting to the crime, and then jumped to his death. In the 1990 version and beyond, Stuart was portrayed as a monster, a duplicitous man whose desires to transcend his background clouded his moral judgment and allowed him to commit a vile act. Those stories, rather than exemplifying the embedded racial antipathies of the city, commented on them and often added a discussion of the power of social class. And indeed, that recounting truly went viral: *Time, Newsweek, People* (it was the cover story of all three on January 22, 1990); network news show *Inside Edition*; the *New York Times*; and the *Washington Post* all featured the story.[34] But rather than treating the saga as a tale of institutional racism—media, politics, the police—these more widely encountered treatments largely focused on Stuart as a pathological figure. This is not to say that such broader critiques never surfaced; rather, they tended to appear on public television, particularly the local affiliate, WGBH, and in academic or low-circulation, long-form panel discussions.[35] Such treatments at times looked to broader issues of embedded racism in media, even as they maintained some focus on Boston as a place where such misidentification could and did happen.

As these subsequent stories emphasized, Stuart was from the white and working-class city of Revere, in the landing path of Logan Airport and abutting East Boston, the Italian American sector of the city largely exempted from Judge Garrity's court order. He never attended college and worked for a Back Bay furrier, Kakas and Sons, where he was given a view of a life of privilege and opulence that seemingly seduced him. He met his future wife while working in an Italian restaurant when she was a student at Boston College. Carol was from the more solidly middle-class town of Medford, and after college went to Suffolk Law School and worked as in-house counsel for Cahner Publishers in Newton—not far from where Colin Diver moved after leaving the South End. The aspirations of the murderer and his deceptions reiterated the moral of the busing story. In a contemporary telling of the tale from that November, *People* magazine published an essay, one among many, that bought Charles Stuart's story: "The Monday-night birthing class at Boston's Brigham and Women's Hospital ended just before 8:30, but Carol and Charles Stuart lingered. As the other couples filed out into the night, Carol said her usual friendly goodbyes. Like the 10 other women in the session, she was about seven months pregnant; the baby would be her first. Carol, 30, was eager to head back to her comfortable gray two-story house in the affluent suburb of Reading, Mass."[36]

As Margaret Carlson wrote in *Time* in a retrospective piece in 2001:

> By identifying the killer of his seven-months-pregnant wife as a "raspy-voiced Black man dressed in a jogging suit," Stuart tapped into assumptions about race and crime so powerful that they overwhelmed skepticism about his tale. His fabrication raised the curtain on a drama in which the press and police, prosecutors, politicians, and the public played out their parts as though they were following the script for the television movie that CBS would ultimately make about the case. Instead of suspicion, Stuart was showered with sympathy. The media apotheosized the couple as starry-eyed lovers out of Camelot cut down by an urban savage.[37]

The narrative Stuart tapped into was from the fabric of the world he knew: "Mr. Stuart's upbringing in Revere may also have played a part. 'Don't discount the way people think here,' said a customer at Reardon's bar. 'Racism is a fact, good or bad. We divide people up into groups, and you will notice no blacks live in Revere.'"[38]

The postmortem on the case was broadly about the functional racism embedded in white-led institutions and their willingness to believe Stuart almost without question, despite clues of his deceit that may have been investigated. The Charles Stuart case and the way in which the city and its institutions handled the case became a further explanation of the power of historically intransigent beliefs and prejudices to impact contemporary events. But unlike in the busing case, this judgment was far more explicit and far more a matter of commentary than news. Wrote Charles P. Pierce, a gifted reporter from the region, in *Esquire* in 2015: "Eventually, Charles Stuart's brother gave him up, and Stuart threw himself off the Tobin Bridge and drowned. That's the story I recalled today when I read the *Post* story—a story that plainly is meant to drown out the cries of a community for justice, that is meant to allay the night terrors currently afflicting the folks in the suburbs, that is meant to tell a comforting story and, in the telling, take the heat off what pretty plainly is a police department gone renegade."[39]

One of the intriguing aspects of the Stuart story is its particular mapping of racialized space. Arguably, the spike in crime in the urban United States, and the hysterical response to it, was a response to the ways in which "safe" streets became a precondition and condition for gentrification. For African Americans in the wake of the forces of gentrification, this was a nightmare of racist policing. Those who were unable to take advantage of the possibilities afforded by the civil rights movement of the 1960s and 1970s—fewer restrictions on housing, more access to quality education, increased outreach by white-collar employers—were increasingly beleaguered, harassed, and displaced.[40] In Boston, the hospital where Charles and Carol attended childbirth classes is in "white space," but it is close to an area that is coded as Brown and Black (Roxbury) or interracial or contested (Mission Hill). Mission Hill in the 1990 census was around 41 percent white, 26 percent Black, and 23 percent Hispanic, a place that remained integrated but which was clearly gentrifying and becoming whiter.[41] Indeed, Stuart began with the assumption, common in the era of stop-and-frisk, of the reappropriation of Henri Lefebvre's "right to the city" as a "white" right to the city. But rather than Lefebvre's dynamic locale of cooperative activity and open access, in this case it was a space of white dominance and exclusion, a regime where racial dominance became the rule.[42] Boston, as a place that had the image of beleaguered whites resisting integration, in effect "defending" their white spaces, was a perfect site for such a story. Writes Elijah Anderson, "For the larger society, from the nightly news and media reports of rampant Black-on-Black crime and at times from close observation of Black people in public, images of the Black ghetto loom large."[43]

The Stuart tale is one replete with markers that signify the socioeconomic changes of the 1980s and 1990s. While Charles Stuart, as a media representation, replicated many characters from journalism and fiction over a hundred years or so, and certainly since the U.S. economy boomed as a matter of industrialization, the specific elements of his story defined a post-industrial moment as well as Boston as a place. Stuart's modest origins in the abutting industrial suburb of Revere and his desire and need to transcend those origins took on a particular urgency as a matter of the stark divide between rich and poor in the late twentieth century. Stuart's Revere friends, when interviewed, talked about how fully he had separated himself from them, preferring the more middle-class regions of Reading. Stuart's mania for maintaining or even improving his chance at status and wealth became almost comprehensible within a world where opportunity and mobility became more and more circumscribed. It also revealed the ways in which race was employed as an apparent marker for class and criminality, and the ways in which that false marker had mass credence. However, as in the busing case and its spatial implications, racism, which is a historically embedded attitude, became magnified by the status anxiety.

The ways in which this aspect of the city's history became magnified and a kind of synecdoche for the city as a whole moves us back toward a consideration of the redefinition of the urban as it was occurring in the 1970s, 1980s, and 1990s, and the particularity of the Boston case. Although it is by no means my goal to mitigate the expression of racism that was at the heart of each of these news stories, a more macro-picture, one that is aware of how "Boston" became imprinted in the national imaginary, shows them as skirmishes in the ongoing battle between the local and often parochial dimensions of U.S. urban social life, and the reorganization of cities within the neoliberal vein, a reorganization that often left those local elements marginalized and relatively powerless over the long term. And in creating that marginalization, individuals and communities rebelled, often against those whose presence was far more of an effect of socioeconomic change and less a matter of effectively recognizing the root causes of their dislocation. Mass media generally contributed to this simplistic rendering of cause and effect.

In the case of Boston, deindustrialization was a key factor in the social disruptions of the later years of the twentieth century, since it left large populations of the city without adequate and ongoing employment—and it often left them without prospects for such employment. In Lukas's *Common Ground*, an incident that was not necessarily a matter of emphasis by the author but looms large in the broader historical picture that I am painting reveals the terms and degree of this anxiety. Previous generations of McGoffs had worked in factories or, more recently, in a bar that was primarily patronized by those who worked in the shipyard. But for the generation of McGoffs who were swept into the busing crisis, college—whether four-year or two-year—was the aspiration. Although not commented on, it is clear that aspirational hopes for an avenue toward social and economic mobility were potentially effectuated through higher education. Writes Lukas about Lisa McGoff after her graduation from high school: "It was time to move on, time to attend to other things. The first was college."[44]

This was clearly in response to the decline of industrial work and the further degradation of life's circumstances for those who had no such education. The McGoff family's life in the Bunker Hill housing project was made more and more chaotic by the economic decline of those who resided in such housing—the formerly working-class denizens of Charlestown—as an absence of work generated all forms of social chaos.

Interestingly, since it was the racial gulf between the Twymons and McGoffs that is central to the book, that the Twymons evinced similar aspirations and were beset by many of the same social issues, pushes against the typical narrative of the busing story. Rachel Twymon, the matriarch of the family, always had the success of her children in mind and always looked for opportunities for their advancement. When one son found his way to Tennessee State College in Nashville, Lukas defined him as the child who "best exemplified the bourgeois values that Rachel had sought to instill in her family."[45] As with the McGoffs, previous generations of the family found factory, retail, or domestic work. But for Rachel, there was a clear vision of the increased desirability, even necessity, of a college education for her children. This was accentuated by the sense of greater opportunities for African Americans in the wake of the civil rights movement. When she looked at the available options in the public schools, her sense was that K–12 education *needed* to lead toward the end-goal of higher education. It is an interesting contrast to the views of the Diver family, whose class privilege allowed them to see public education as an option and one that aligned with their liberal values, yet that the Diver family could also choose to abandon this system is exemplary. Their educational outpost, the Bancroft School, had already been shown as an island under siege, and perspicaciously valuing their hard-attained white privilege, they had no desire to have their children experience downward mobility as a result of their social ideals.

Busing as a phenomenon, then, became a social policy that exacerbated anxiety over education and housing. Rather than provide greater opportunity for advancement, the crisis primarily shuffled poor whites and poor African Americans from place to place amid a declining public educational infrastructure. It is unsurprising that Diver-like families—similar racially but wealthier—of the 2000s largely choose to send their children to private schools, in effect re-elaborating the neoliberal vision of the declining public sector and paying for the services their wealth affords them. The contemporary demographics of the public system confirm that few gentrifiers actually send their children to the city's schools. The tale becomes a kind of morality opera about race in the United States in which all parties are enlisted to play their scripted parts. Boston became a text on which contemporary political maps were drawn: for "conservatives" to rally for its resistance to federal intervention, it stands for entrenched values of self-determination, community coherence, and the "rights" of free association. For liberals, it stands for the prospect of social opportunity, the need to eradicate racism, the necessity of acceding to the rule of law. The media coverage largely replicated this drama through its very simple and temporally reduced vision.

David Harvey writes about the emergence of the neoliberal regime in the 1970s and 1980s as a restoration of class power, substantially through "accumulation by dispossession." He notes, "If the main achievements of neo-liberalism have been redistributive rather than generative, then ways had to be found to redistribute wealth and income either from the mass of population towards the upper classes or from vulnerable to richer countries."[46] But there is a far more involved economic tale that is less apparent: that of the strangling of public assets in the interest of lowering taxes on the wealthy. Indeed, a feature of neoliberal management in increasingly gentrified cities is to starve the sector of public education. As work and public services become increasingly unavailable to families, the gradual cordoning off of both available space and prospective opportunity for those in the process of being dispossessed may trigger any type of negative response. And it is difficult to say that any city experienced the transition to the knowledge economy, the decline of unionized work, and the phenomenon of gentrification more than Boston. But as that story remains largely untold, we are left with a static, sedimented meme to carry over into the later century: Boston is a place of working-class white authenticity and "tradition." And while that story redounds with bigotry and intolerance, it also seems to have a nugget at its center that seems oddly alluring, a kind of retreat from the vicissitudes of financial insecurity with a reified notion of ethnocentric space and community that adheres to notions of predetermined and "traditional" space. Perhaps this aspect of the Boston story persists because it signifies a kind of retrograde longing for a prior order.

CHAPTER TWO

Crime, Silence, and Southie

Priestly Abuse and Whitey Bulger

In the preceding chapter, we saw two distinct narratives of Boston in the 1970s and 1980s as spatially defining segregation. Indeed, considering the era of busing and the sensational Charles Stuart tale, the relative means by which those of Irish and Italian extraction—and who employed that ethnic identity as significant for their self-definition—inhered as a group and placed themselves in distinction from those of other backgrounds is striking. But such definitions take as their source not only a narrow cultural context; they also derive from the ways in which mass media employs these markers as embedded explanations of social events, and as media burgeons, the circulation of these tropes becomes more powerfully definitional for place. While these group definitions certainly have a salient sociohistorical dimension, they are not transhistorical facts, and when they are treated as such, they tend to rigidly calcify group definition, a practice that has significant implications for ideas of time, place, and space.

Part of the production of Boston is its relationship to and identification with Catholicism. This fact does not make the city distinctive, but it places its historical arc into a particular trajectory. Catholics came to the United States in large numbers in the 1840s and 1850s, as Irish and German nationals immigrated largely to cities in the northeastern United States and then to the Midwest. In Boston, the number of Irish newcomers far eclipsed those from Germany, who were much more heavily concentrated in other eastern seaboard cities, such as Baltimore, Philadelphia, and New York, with others migrating to what were then newer cities in the Midwest: Cincinnati, St. Louis, Chicago, and Milwaukee. Boston was proportionately the most Irish city in the United States, with a population that was roughly 25 percent Irish by 1870. In the late 1880s, a significant Italian population, mostly from southern Italy, also came to Boston, creating a city that was substantially Catholic, even if that group was bifurcated in cultural and sometimes linguistic terms.

In this chapter, I explore the related but distinct stories of priests sexually abusing young children, overwhelmingly boys, in Boston and its contiguous suburbs, and the saga of the gangster Whitey Bulger, a career criminal whose legend drew on a range of factors, many of which were manifestations of the mythologizing of a kind of South Boston ("Southie") parochialism and the facility with which this story, his story, could be plotted within the structures of a conventional gangster genre narrative. Whitey's story also gained visibility as a matter of the prominence of his politician brother, William, who went on to become president of the Massachusetts state senate. In any case, both the tale of abuse in the Roman Catholic church and the Whitey Bulger stories became major national foci—and, in the case of the church, an international scandal—as well as news events that were expressive of a place-bound vision of Boston that emphasized historically entrenched definitions of community. Both of these stories recapitulate elements of the previous chapter's conceptions of place. These include its insularity; the dominance of its white, Catholic ethnic communities; its casual exclusions; and at times overt, at other times covert, forms of racism.

In addition to place-based affinities, Whitey Bulger's story also touches on that of school integration and its resistance in telling ways. These activities include his firebombing of the John F. Kennedy birthplace in Brookline, Massachusetts, and the burning down of an elementary school in Wellesley, where federal judge W. Arthur Garrity resided. In a more politic way, William Bulger was also an implacable foe of busing but tried to avoid being cast as a fire-breathing racist in hopes of maintaining a viable political profile. Nevertheless, much of the ground-level organizing against busing in South Boston was through Bulger, a state senator at the time, and his office.[1]

In addition to exploring the recurring and evolving visions of place that arrange around these two news-based narratives, I also explore the ways in which "news" as a concept was in the process of morphing into a far more expansive and interactive entity as the analog age gave way to the digital in the early 2000s. Both stories sprawled inordinately after they became available to consumers via digital means, as well as became far more trenchant to a range of readers and apprehenders. Digital readers may experience a very different form of connection with these narratives, engaging and identifying with them in ways that are far more intimate and personal than their response to, say, Walter Cronkite reading the evening news. By the stories' digital nature and their pervasive availability through personal and mobile devices at any time, such narratives become personal and thereby affectively enhanced. This condition of apprehension, then, increases the impact of the news, creating a dimension of response that involves the reader/viewer not only in the content of story but also in its deep structure, which includes place. Through both their content and their mode of presentation, these two tales of sex, violence, and religion have become powerfully affecting and resonant.[2]

The city's status as a center of Catholicism is clear in the sexual abuse story and less obvious, but still present—and perhaps oddly so—in the case of Whitey Bulger. The association of Bulger with Irish ethnicity and South Boston certainly made his Catholicism something of a default condition. Bulger was a practicing Catholic until his death and the product of Catholic education until he was expelled from Catholic elementary school, where his teachers and school officials remembered him as difficult and surly. The association of Catholicism and urban gangsters in the United States goes back to the wave of Irish immigration in the mid-nineteenth century, and then became more pronounced with the massive immigration from Italy from 1880 to 1924.[3] Not incidentally, Bulger's legacy was as a decidedly Irish-Catholic gangster involved with other Irish-Catholic gangsters, as well as some Italian-Catholics and Jews. The Bulger story is also place-specific, if not in its full contours, then certainly in its associated geography. Upon his death, the first sentence in the *New York Times* obituary identified him as a "South Boston mobster."[4] While Bulger was not involved in the sex-abuse scandal in any way, his looming national presence during the early 2000s (as the abuse scandal became a fixture in the news) reminded readers and watchers of those stories of the impenetrability of the streets and alleys of South Boston, and the mysteries behind the vows of *omerta* that were definitional both for gangsters and priests.

The story of the priest abuse scandal in the Roman Catholic church primarily took place in Italian- and Irish-dominated parishes. And although its geography was sprawling and its victims from a range of class backgrounds, the visuals of the scandal tended to emphasize its working-class dimension as well as its situation in either working-class sectors of the city or industrial/working-class suburbs, such as Lynn, Salem, Quincy, and others. This emphasis had a rationale since the majority of cases did take place in less wealthy parishes. But that proportion is far from overwhelming.

Visually, the televised news and documentaries around these characters and events prominently employed the discrete spaces of the city and lent themselves to a strong association of a notion of Boston as *the* place of Catholicism and its devout, working-class parishioners. For example, in one of the early broadcasts after the first *Boston Globe* story on the proliferation of abuse in the archdiocese, airing on January 12, 2002, NBC featured Cardinal Bernard Law in the well-appointed media room of the cardinal's residence, wearing his robes and collar, and then cut to local churches of more modest stature. It also included brief interviews with reform advocate Phil Saviano and "alleged victim" (as captioned in the newscast) Anthony Muzzi Jr. Both were notable for their Boston accents, relatively modest dress, and ethnic backgrounds.[5] Such markers tied them to prior national stories of place, as did a subsequent *Nightline* (ABC News) feature in March 2002, including an interview with plaintiff's lawyer Mitchell Garabedian and abuse victim Patrick McSorley. Both were clearly "Boston," with strong accents and interviewed in modest environments. McSorley was both Irish and a product of the housing projects in Hyde Park, a locale included in the busing story.[6] Similarly, a CNN report from February 2002 showed the church of St. Julia's of Weston, a high-priced suburb but a decidedly modest church and street view of Route 20, not far from the border of much more working-class Waltham and I-95 (Route 128).[7]

The places pictured and the figures interviewed evoked those of the preceding chapter and became as ubiquitous as the city itself, part of its allure and definition. "Boston" as a media entity stands for the authentic city of entrenched residents and neighborhoods. If the modernist city represented the designs of planners and social workers to rationalize both housing and urban space in response to the flood of immigrants during the late nineteenth and early twentieth centuries, the regionally significant three-decker wood-frame houses that were so much a part of Boston and New England working-class culture represented the virtual antithesis of that rationalist design. These homes were wood, not brick, and subject to fire, deterioration, and all manner of blight. They proliferated in Boston and the surrounding region from 1870 to 1910, and their rehabilitation has been an aspect of the city's twenty-first-century gentrification.[8] Further, the massive public housing popular in cities like New York and Chicago during the early years of the twentieth century not only offered a vision of the administrative state's impulse to create orderly housing; it also offered a strategy for surveying and controlling the U.S. underclass, now housed *en masse* and subject to

FIGURE 6. A characteristic three-decker house in Boston's Hyde Park neighborhood. —Courtesy Boston Landmarks Commission image collection, Collection 5210.004, City of Boston Archives.

all manner of intrusions and control. The three-deckers performed no such social mission. They represent a market-driven response to the influx of immigrants, but one that contained none of the then-operative theories of social amelioration and control. As such, they stand as a monument to a more authentically working-class type of abode, one that while uniform in many ways also resisted more considered and intrusive visions of the administrative state. The images of this distinct, multifamily housing stand as a regional brand and a visual statement of working-class authenticity.

Such locales and characters are also central to the telling of the Whitey Bulger saga. This story, as covered in the mass media, had considerable temporal and chronological overlap with the story of priest sexual abuse: it was substantially a tale of the 1990s and 2000s; it featured South Boston; it included his connection to the Catholic church; and it was structured around codes of affiliation, loyalty, and secrecy—codes that resounded with the dictates of *omerta*, a practice that was definitional for the gangs of organized criminals in Sicily. This practice has its connections to the legalisms and unwritten tenets of Catholicism and was certainly connected to the devices of the church's insistence on maintaining the issue and rectification of the priest abuse scandal as a matter exclusively for that closed society. It is also a quality that seeped into Boston civic life, both in the cult of organized crime and in the overlap between the church and state.

It is intriguing and even paradoxical that the elevation of this code, which has its roots in the sixteenth century and which promotes and mystifies silence, occurred as a matter of the wide disclosure of the sexual misdeeds of priests and the rampant and avaricious criminality of Whitey Bulger. The code of silence was elevated by the disclosure of the acts that had not been—and should not be—revealed, acts that were revealed widely through a medium that is concurrently public and private. As such, the gloss of the code of *omerta* informing these stories oddly added an allure to the disclosures of their details. The internet as a medium, including its interactive dimension, fostered such a paradoxical mix of secrecy and disclosure. And indeed, Whitey Bulger was and is everywhere: from the many online news sources to newspapers all over the world; video newsfeeds from U.S. and international sources; sites such as the Mob Museum, the *Encyclopedia Britannica*, and Biography; and blogs like Lawnext and Mark Holan's Irish American Blog.[9] In all of these places his profile as a Boston gangster of boldness and wile, as a man of South Boston, and as a brother to the president of the Massachusetts state senate, William Bulger, is little in doubt.

As these stories grew in expanse, they fed on the responses and further information provided by often-anonymous digital consumers on all types of sites, including newspapers like the London *Daily Mail* and the *Washington Post*. Both Bulger and the various priests were visible figures in their communities, so subject to telling interactions with all types of Bostonians.

Bulger was a famous local figure in organized crime in Boston during the 1970s and 1980s, and a member and then leader of the violent and active Somerville- and South Boston–based "Winter Hill" gang. He became more prominent as a national figure after his brother, William, emerged as the president of the Massachusetts state senate in 1978. The Bulger brothers' stories had significant national resonance and became even more enticing after Whitey disappeared in 1994 and then when it became widely known—after 2000—that he had been an FBI informant after 1975. Bulger was on the FBI's most wanted list from 1997 until his capture in 2011. His FBI minder—and former fellow South Bostonian John Connolly—was arrested in 2000 and convicted of federal racketeering charges in 2002. Bulger was convicted of state racketeering charges in 2008 and later convicted of thirty-one counts of federal weapons, money laundering, and extortion charges in 2013.[10]

These are two distinct stories, that of the Bulgers and that of sex abuse within the church—both deeply Boston-centric—that have certain elements in common and have become somewhat definitional for the city over time and space. The visual tropes are striking in their similarity: that Boston is a world of narrow streets, decaying three-tiered wood residences, dark taverns, and almost unobstructed whiteness. This vision of the city, of course, is something of a caricature, but it is a caricature that has proven remarkably resilient. It is part of the definition of the city as both retrograde and tribal. The Bulger saga has, over the last eight or so years, taken on a life of its own, surfacing with great visibility intermittently. The last of these moments was in October 2018, when Bulger was violently killed in prison, and then in 2020 when his killers were apprehended.[11] Bulger's death coverage was consonant with the coverage of his life, with the same file footage from his various arrests featured. He was referred to as a mobster and killer but always noted as being of Boston. Like the film *Spotlight* (2015), based on the *Boston Globe*'s investigation into priest abuse, Bulger's tale has also been the topic of an explicit, fact-based Hollywood feature film, *Black Mass* (2015), starring Johnny Depp. The film is discussed in a later chapter, but it traffics significantly in the extant tropes of place. Further, Martin Scorsese's *The Departed* employs a mob kingpin who is explicitly modeled on Bulger, and the Showtime series *Ray Donovan* also employs a Whitey-based figure, played by James Woods. The family's patriarch, Mickey Donovan, played by John Voight, likewise has various aspects of his story that connect to the fact and legend of Bulger. There are also multiple documentaries of the Bulger saga.[12] Such a ubiquity suggests how these news stories fueled notions of place that reemerged in much more complex and resonant narratives of popular culture media.

The Most Catholic City in America Goes Digital

Boston Globe reporter Michael Rezendes—one of the Spotlight team that reported the priest abuse series of stories—noted in conversation with investigative journalist David Mizner that, as of 2001, the year before the story of the epidemic of sexual abuse of children by priests broke, Boston was proportionally the most Catholic city in the United States, with over half of its 3.8 million residents (this figure includes the metropolitan area) noting their church affiliation.[13] But that status became increasingly complicated after the revelations of persistent and rampant sexual abuse by area priests appeared in the *Boston Globe* in early 2002. These allegations had the impact of further disrupting an institution that was already in eclipse. A recent *Globe* article noted that Sunday mass attendance had declined from 70 percent in 1970 to 16 percent in 2015. Yet, the definition of place connected to certain conceptions of the church continues and to some degree defines the concept of this place—as it exists historically and currently in the national imaginary. And arguably, this association aided the media, correctly or incorrectly, in establishing Boston as the starting point for a cascading national and then international deluge of complaints about clergy misconduct, as well as defined the institutional structure of the church as complicit in allowing those who had been named to continue to operate within the ecumenical domain.

The sexual abuse scandal within the Boston archdiocese and its immediate environs is a story that defines—and is defined by—place even if that reference to place is accessed remotely and digitally. It is a dynamic tale that developed an exponential and affective presence due to the post-2002 technological sprawl. It emerged as a story from the relatively early days of the mass-digitization of news, which had the impact of vastly expanding the definition of how viewers/readers experience events. It had the electronic power to sprawl inordinately as a matter of its visibility in widely available and relatively participatory forms. It also developed a popular presence, nationally and internationally, that created a sense of institution and place which far eclipsed earlier stories.

It also possessed certain commonalities with the Boston busing narrative and the racialized/racist story of Charles Stuart, and so could prove somewhat reiterative and further refining in its expression of place. Like those earlier tales, the priest abuse story overwhelmingly emphasized the city as a place defined by its entrenched historical markers—its working class; its white ethnic population; its narrow streets; its wood-framed, multifamily dwellings; and its distinctive regional accent—all of which connected to its insularity. The abuse story gained significant momentum through its "placeness," as that geographic anchor provided a means of defining the concrete environs in which this most body-centric story occurred, developing narratives supported by images that are place-specific. Boston, the place that served as the default location of these events, is one that developed as a locale in the national imaginary as a compendium of certain temporal and material facts and their reification and dispersal through digital means.

Gillian Rose writes of the ways in which digital technology has eroded the efficacy of regarding the object of cultural studies analysis as "auratic," in a reference to Walter Benjamin's "The Work of Art in the Age of Mechanical Reproduction." Rose notes Benjamin's discussion of how technology alters an aesthetic object's cultural distinctness, its aura, through its technological means of increasing its reproducibility and so its availability.[14] According to Rose, the digital enterprise further erodes its means of regard and resulting consideration: "Over the past thirty years there have been profound changes in the processes and practices of cultural production, in the circulation and display of cultural objects, and in the processes of audiencing, participation and critique. A wide range of digital technologies has enabled these changes; yet, cultural geographers have had almost nothing to say about their implications for the creation of meaningful places, spaces and landscapes." Rose asks that we treat objects of cultural regard—including place—as part of a process of analysis that destabilizes the meaning of a given textual object. Instead, such places become dynamic aspects of synergistic media networks, networks that reduce the distinctions between users and producers, as well as between place and its representation. Writes Rose, "Once cultural production and reproduction goes digital, that object both dissolves and disperses."[15] In this case, that object is the projection of "Boston" as an urban entity with certain definitional characteristics. As it was projected digitally, it morphed into something that was both a resonant image of a dimension of its history and its then-present, as well as an entity that was a result of certain aspects of recurring narratives of place.

The "Boston" that we encounter in these stories of the Catholic church and its stewards gone deeply wrong seems oddly stuck in a temporality that fixes the date as a perpetual 1954, or maybe 1956. Indeed, the social formations implied by the video coverage and images in the multiple network television news stories—over fifty in 2002–4—reelaborate what had become recurrent chronotopes of place, thus in turn becoming more associative and emotionally evocative.[16] The housing, the neighborhoods, the dress, the relationships seem to be stuck in time and summoned by place. It is a world defined not only or necessarily by faith but also by the social comfort gained by living in ethnic enclaves that were formed decades before and that resisted the encroaching of new people. Indeed, such a demographic organization of population brings to mind the tale, recounted in the last chapter, of Alva Walker Debman's decision to buy a house on the other side of the racial boundary in Codman Square in Dorchester, only to be later driven out by her white neighbors. In the story of priest abuse, we gaze on the insularity and allegiances of that particular world as digitally projected, circulated, recirculated, and reproduced.

The historical narrative of Boston's large and influential Catholic population began with the mass migration of the mid-nineteenth century from Ireland and the further burgeoning of the city's Irish and Italian populations in the late nineteenth and early twentieth centuries. Both communities became ensconced as vital constituencies in twentieth-century Boston, and the spatial organization of the city to some extent organized around the ways that each group had formed its own churches and parishes. As newcomers continued to arrive, those places of Catholic worship served as magnets for settlement. For example, Irish settlements in Brighton and Charlestown burgeoned, as Italian settlements in East Boston and Revere (Charles Stuart's hometown) similarly grew.

But how did these definitions track with the more contemporary situation? How were they the reality of the post-industrial city? To what degree were they devices that enhanced the concept of the contemporary city and to what degree did they detract from it? In the later twentieth and early twenty-first centuries, such distinctions among ethnic Catholics were less absolute but still very much visible. In today's Boston, a city of high rents, soaring real-estate prices and property taxes, and a significant nonwhite population, housing is, as a matter of economic necessity, less ethnically homogeneous. Although these tales well organize around issues of religion and ethnicity, with each story including degrees of both considerations, we still need to ask: how may we push against these more easily arrived at tales to see the macro-socioeconomic narratives that may be extracted? Indeed, it is my view that Boston—in these selected tales—becomes a site for the imprinting of a kind of right-populist notion of "tradition," one that tracks with neoconservative plaints against its neoliberal mirror image. That is, as Boston changed into a post-industrial city defined by the financialization of its real estate, the shifting terms of its population, and the digitalization of work, there has been a pushback in the area where such a response is possible—the geographic and political resistance of those left out of this configuration of the new. And in that vision of stasis lies the resilience of certain values and attitudes. "Boston" thus becomes an entity that is far from the complex, multiethnic, and financially dynamic city that Boston has actually, but only partially, become.

Priestly Misconduct and the City

The Boston aspect of this story of sexual abuse in the Catholic church was not the first one that became public: the story had a deep structure that extended way beyond the later 1990s and early 2000s. Investigative reporter Jason Berry, working in New Orleans, covered a version set in rural Louisiana that began in 1983. It involved a parish priest named Gilbert Gauthe who was a serial abuser in the unincorporated parish of Henry, near Lafayette. Bishops had moved Gauthe around western Louisiana for some ten years, abusing numbers of children at each stop. Berry's exposé was published in the *Times of Acadiana*, a small, Lafayette-based newspaper, in 1985, after any number of national magazines had passed on the story. And while the story received some further national notices, it failed fully to resonate and to trigger a sense of larger crisis. Even with the publication of Berry's book, *Lead Us Not into Temptation* (1992), the issue of sex abuse by priests received shockingly little notice nationally or internationally.[17]

As Berry's book was being published, the case of Kevin Fitzpatrick also came to light and became the topic of a Boston television station's news report. His parish priest, James Porter, in Attleboro, Massachusetts—an industrial suburb between Boston and Providence—had repeatedly sexually abused Fitzpatrick. By 1992, Porter's crimes were the subject of primarily local and some national news programming. Nationally syndicated talk show host Phil Donahue devoted an episode to the topic in 1993 and included Jason Berry as a panelist, along with Father Andrew Greeley (a dissenter within the church) and Barbara Blaine, the founder of the Survivors Network of Those Abused by Priests (SNAP). Donahue allowed for a broad airing of credible complaints, and Greeley talked about the practice of moving "problem" priests from parish to parish, as well as the prevalence of abuse within Catholicism. Yet, despite ample evidence to the contrary, cases like those of Gauthe and Porter were treated by the wider press and the church as aberrations and discussed primarily in terms of specific abusers, rather than systemically.[18] And even as more and more cases arose, the decade between the Porter case and the Spotlight stories produced little insight into the machinations of the church in tamping down the ample evidence of its complicity in keeping predators from criminal prosecution.[19]

The issue of sexual abuse by Catholic clergymen largely—but not entirely—receded from the public radar for six years, although it turned out that many cases were being settled out of court during that time. Since the complainants were bound by confidentiality agreements, none came to light. In 1998, one of the Boston-based priests named in those agreements, John J. Geoghan, was defrocked. Geoghan had made the news two years earlier when a complaint against him was filed, but coverage was limited to a brief story on an inside page in the *Globe*'s metro section. In 1997, *Globe* columnist Eileen McNamara asked publicly: "If we take child abuse so seriously, where is the outcry?"[20] And even when Geoghan was laicized in 1998, the story still failed to pick up momentum. It was not until 2002 that the broader and systemic story of abuse and its coverup broke, largely through the persistence of a group of *Globe* reporters and editors connected with the Spotlight team. This story soon went national and international, arguably leading to a series of investigations into allegations of pederasty and the church's collusion with the accused to move them to other locales or to otherwise shield them from prosecution. Reported Rachel Martin for NPR in 2007, "Four dioceses have filed for bankruptcy: Portland, Ore.; Tucson, Ariz.; Davenport, Iowa; and Spokane, Wash. The Spokane Archdiocese just last week agreed to pay more than $48 million to settle claims. In California alone, settlement costs have exceeded $200 million. These are the hard costs; the long-term emotional damage is harder to quantify."[21] Immediately after January 2002, Boston became the visible incarnation of the epidemic abuse of children, mostly boys, from working-class families by the clergy, nationally and internationally. Ironically, as the news story circulated worldwide through digital recirculation, it also became increasingly a "Boston" story, though its dimensions and ramifications were inarguably global in reach and expanse. This story and the means of covering it became the source material for the film *Spotlight* (2015). The film won two academy awards, including Best Picture, and was nominated for six awards.

Part of the power of the story was its association with Boston cardinal Bernard Law, who afforded readers and viewers of the narrative an antagonist or villain, much as Louise Day Hicks served as an often-reviled media

FIGURE 7. Defense attorney Mitchell Garabedian questions Cardinal Bernard Law at an evidentiary hearing involving defrocked priest John Geoghan at Suffolk Superior Court, August 2, 2002, in Boston. —Courtesy 02080203817. AP Images / George Martell, Pool.

presence in the busing crisis. (Both of these figures also stood as heroes, unsurprisingly, to those who allied with their views.) Soon after the story broke, it developed an institutional focus, and again the association of the city with Catholicism fit the geographic template of the narrative. Law was both tied to place and emblematic of that place. He was seen in a range of stories but almost always in the same posture—either addressing the cameras with a show of contrition and resolve, or in action, walking through a congregation with crosier in hand, showing his status as ecclesiastical prince of the church. Law seemed to sum up both the mysticism of the church and its hypocrisy. The news stories repeatedly told of his failure to act on the complaints against priests during his tenure as archbishop. Again, the lavish settings of his cathedral and his almost princely robes defined a vision of Catholicism that tracked with a narrative of Boston as an otherworldly place dominated by an unaccountable clergy. Law became a story unto himself and was easily cast as the face (and body) signifying the problems of the Boston church—and the Roman Catholic church more generally. He was featured in an overwhelming proportion of the Boston-based clergy abuse stories covered in the national press throughout 2002, and appeared again intermittently over the next year, though he resigned from his post as archbishop in December 2002. After his resignation, Law moved to the Vatican where he served in various ceremonial posts until his retirement in 2011 and his death at age eighty-six in 2017.[22] But he remained visible. In a 2005 segment on Pope John Paul II's death, Law held a central role as a group protested his presence at the funeral, with the news story commenting on his place in the Boston church's sex scandal.[23]

Throughout the 2002 coverage, Law's sanctimony and legalistic defenses and apologies made him the nexus of the institutional crisis, as he was pictured addressing various publics. These stories almost invariably found Law at his residence in Brighton, which abutted St. John's Seminary, where many of the named priests received their educations, mere yards from Boston College. It is matter of some irony that in 2003, the cardinal's residence was sold—to Boston College—in order to raise funds to pay out the various settlements against the church in the many abuses cases adjudicated, as well as to manage the optics of the church as a bloated and out-of-touch institution.[24] He was also frequently pictured at the main Catholic cathedral in the city, the Cathedral of the Holy Cross in the city's South End. Each of these recurring visual tropes marked place and associated Law distinctly with that locale. All of these surroundings are ornate, lavish in a religious way, and indicative of a church insulated by power, wealth, and prestige from the consequences of its bad faith, not to mention its legal defense of the indefensible (almost sardonically, if coincidentally, captured in the cardinal's name: Law). Following the narrative of the church's insularity and corruption, the images often show protesters outside of these establishments, apparently unable to enter and make their specific complaints face to face, literally kept out of the power center of the institution.

The Investigation

Although the first coverage of priestly abuse in the Boston area came to light in 1992, the broader story did not fully break until 2002, despite evidence that might have made it far more visible much earlier. To some degree, the later and more resonant story emanated from the work of the *Boston Globe* investigative team, now memorialized in the film *Spotlight*. Those

FIGURE 8. The Cathedral of the Holy Cross, the Mother Church of the Diocese of Boston. —Courtesy Jana Corkin.

reporters—Matt Carroll, Sacha Pfeiffer, Michael Rezendes, and their editor, Walter Robinson—dug through the various dead-ends that had limited coverage since 1992. The meta-textual story of the story—or the story of how they got the story, as told in the film—is one with distinctly local dimensions, since it delves into the obstructive powers of the newspaper hierarchy, the courts, and the church as the reporters attempt to track down, interview, and follow various leads.

But beyond the Boston-area James Porter case, and the southwestern Louisiana case of the 1980s, there were other reported instances of abuse, and these cases also received national news coverage. For example, a 1988 feature focused on a case in Allentown, Pennsylvania, and a 1990 story on NBC's *Nightly News* reported on the burgeoning number of abuse complaints against Catholic clergy, with the voiceover noting settlements of over $300 million and pending cases in forty-three states. It went on to make the point that "no credible study" placed the number of abusers in the clergy above 6 percent or affirmed that abuse was more prevalent now than it was in the past. Rather, it argued that the climate for litigation had changed.[25] But given the facts of this report and the geographic range of locations where abuse was found—New York City, "a large city in the Midwest," and even Canada—why was this not a bigger story earlier?

The national story of sexual abuse by Catholic clergymen reemerged some two years after the NBC report, in the spring of 1992, when the Porter case came to light. Porter was accused of molesting around two hundred boys and young men in the 1960s and 1970s. A local television station in Boston—WBZ—broke the story in May 1992, and eventually Porter was tracked to Minnesota and then arrested and extradited. This case received significant national coverage, including the noted episode of the syndicated, nationally televised *Phil Donahue Show*. Interestingly, many of the reports noted the broader problem that Porter's accusation and ultimate conviction illustrated. Some three years later, in June 1993, NBC News reported that the church had spent $350 million in settlement fees for sexual imposition cases involving priests.[26] It similarly noted the existence of a church-sponsored investigation and a report on how to deal with such priests. These recommendations included a process of reporting to Rome and placing the priests in church-sponsored treatment programs. The NBC report observed that members of SNAP were excluded from participating in the study. Similarly, in August, some months before Porter's sentencing, an NBC report noted that 61 percent of all Catholics believed that sexual abuse by priests was a significant problem. On August 29, the *Globe* Sunday magazine ran a feature about Porter, marking an aggressive entrée by that regional publication into the issue of sexual abuse within the church.[27]

But for the *Globe*, under the somewhat conservative editorial guidance of Matt Storin, this story was a one-off, as follow-ups and broader institutional coverage never appeared.[28] It is also worth noting that the story focused almost entirely on Porter and North Attleboro, even though much broader and geographically far-flung reporting preceded it. In fact, the story cited one townsperson's fear that the Porter case would be defining for North Attleboro in the same way Lizzie Borden and Fall River are historically paired. The Porter sentencing in December of that year triggered a spate of local and national television news stories—although this event was only a perfunctory presence in local newspapers. These visuals largely confined themselves to the courtroom with nary a church in sight. This is indeed distinct from later coverage, which tended to convey the church as an institution, precisely through showing church buildings as edifice of a certain type.

The cases against the church went on in a scattered manner and with no sense of a burgeoning, systemic problem. In 1994, Tom Brokaw reported for NBC *Nightly News* on a scandal in Santa Fe, New Mexico, that was threatening to bankrupt the diocese. In 1997, complaints arose against Dallas priest Rudy Kos, which became a source of investigation for the four networks. Kos was eventually convicted and the church paid $23 million in a settlement, reached in 1998.[29] But after that report, the topic vanished from view until early 2002. In January, the story of John J. Geoghan, a serial abuser covering at least thirty years, came to public notice. The network coverage coincided with the publication of the first *Boston Globe* Spotlight team story. After that publication, the story of pederasty among the Catholic clergy was a persistent feature in the national news until 2014, and then afterward, with the death of Bernard Law in 2017, as well as with the release of ex-priest Paul Shanley from prison the same year. In those first years, the stories were almost uniformly about Boston, but they came to take on different geographies over time—Los Angeles, Philadelphia, and other locations, urban and rural. The story recently resurfaced with the revelations about Philadelphia archbishop Theodore McCarrick, but this has been an ongoing story, with few respites since the *Globe* series.[30] Indeed, McCarrick has now been criminally charged in the Massachusetts state courts.

Christina Mancini and Ryan T. Shields affirmed the importance of the story of sex abuse by Catholic clergymen in 2002: "Several accounts speak to the national prominence of the Catholic Church sexual abuse scandal. The *New York Times* extended front-page coverage to the story for forty-one consecutive days in 2002."[31] This attention was not unique to the *New York Times*. For example, in 2004, the *Boston Globe* created an online resource center that provided detailed information about ongoing sexual abuse in line with these accounts. Members of the public also appeared fixated on the story. In 2002, readers of the Associated Press ranked the Catholic church sex-abuse scandal as the third most important story of the year (overshadowed only by the number 1 and 2 stories: "the Showdown with Iraq" and "D.C. Sniper Shootings," respectively).[32]

Since virtually every story from 1988 to 1998 that covered abuse within the church considered, at least in passing, the larger scale of the issue, why did this more focused coverage fail to materialize before 2002? What role did the place-specific reporting play in the resonance of the Boston-based coverage? Is it a result of the media environment that existed as of early 2002? Certainly, the *Globe* coverage itself called for notice, as a result of its depth and frequency, not to mention its impact. As the Spotlight team editor Walter Robinson noted in an interview after the release of the film, "This is pre-Internet.... You may recall this from the film. When our visitor Phil Saviano ... mentions the Gauthe case, we didn't know. Back in the day, if there was a case in New Orleans, and there was another big case in Dallas, unless the *New York Times* or *The New Yorker* or *CBS News* descended upon that story and did it nationally, how would the rest of us have known about it?" The relative isolation of that era helped keep things quiet and made it harder for people to connect the dots. Robinson continued, "So in a way, the Church was more protected. The bishops and the cardinals said, 'Well, this is one aberrant priest.' And they actually said this—'We're no different than the Methodists or the Lutherans or the Boy Scouts.'"[33]

The Role of Boston

But the specifically Boston dimension, along with the burgeoning of the internet as a means of investigating the various cases and disseminating the range of incidents, provided the coverage with a kind of anchor that created narrative momentum, a forward movement derived in part from the association of sexual abuse in the church with a specific rendering of place, and a place with a certain media footprint at that. The originating locale in the resonant and ongoing story of abuse in the Catholic church was Boston, and it was the recurring terms of that city's representation that has defined most subsequent coverage. This means that the narratives and visuals that depict sexual abuse in the church have been either of Boston or places that are depicted as *like* Boston—such as Attleboro. These motifs include the presentation of the church as an institution shrouded in mystery and cloaked in silence, as well as abuse as a recurring factor in the lives of the boys (and some girls) of the working class. Growing out of these motifs is the depiction of the church as that which protects the culprits through institutional means, and the sense that all of this is embedded in the insularity of Catholicism. And while these aspects of the recurring story were far from unique to Boston, they easily grafted onto a resonant narrative of place and then were recombined in the coverage of other places.

When the *Globe* story broke in 2002, it turned out that its initial subject, Father John J. Geoghan, had been named any number of times in complaints to the various parishes and diocese where he had served since his ordination in 1962. But the church had long made it a practice to suppress those complaints and transfer the offending priest to another parish. By 1995, after Porter's incarceration, a number of Geoghan's victims had filed civil suits, and in July 1996 a story appeared in the *Boston Herald* titled "Mom Sues Priest for Alleged Sexual Abuse of Sons."[34] Still, there seems to have been little follow up. The Geoghan case proceeded, and by 1997 there was a second civil suit, one that was noted by *Globe* columnist Eileen McNamara on January 15, 1997.[35] But again, that story had little "bounce," and when Geoghan was defrocked the next year, the *Globe* covered it on June 6—"Cardinal Announces Defrocking of Priest Accused of Molestation"—the story failed to resonate.[36] That it fell flat is intriguing, considering its chronological proximity to the Dallas story. But there seems to have been little desire to uncover the extent of the problem and the role of the church in its persistence.

Despite the organizational intricacy of the Catholic Church, its regional and national leaders relied on the relative isolation of one diocese from another to shield the abusers within other parishes and dioceses. Further, this strategy scattered the various complaints through their use of confidentiality agreements, which meant that each complainant or plaintiff would have very restricted access to the details of all prior settlements. In the summer of 2001, McNamara returned to the Geoghan story:

> Columnist McNamara returned to the fray in mid-July 2001. The *Globe* had already reported that Geoghan repeatedly went on "sick leave" before reemerging at another parish, and in June 2001, during the discovery portion of Geoghan's trial, Law had filed a document that included an admission: in September 1984—before the alleged crimes had occurred—he had been warned about Geoghan. Without naming the source, he acknowledged receiving a letter alleging that Geoghan had molested seven boys. On July 22, McNamara wrote: "Will Cardinal Bernard F. Law be allowed to continue to play duck and cover indefinitely? Will no one require the head of the Archdiocese of Boston to explain how it was that the pastors, bishops, archbishops, and cardinal-archbishops who supervised Geoghan never confronted, or even suspected, his alleged exploitation of children in five different parishes across 28 years?[37]

McNamara's column led directly to the Spotlight team's investigation.

The reporters, however, were initially stymied by the limited access they had to the various civil suits the church had settled. This lack of access meant that no sense of the systematic suppression of victims' stories could readily emerge, nor could a sense of the broader whitewashing of such complaints. The standard confidentiality agreements that were part of those settlements walled off their details from the reporters, and thus from the public. But the seal on these agreements was lifted by a Boston Superior Court judge, Constance W. Sweeney, who decided in November 2001, amid the *Globe* team's investigation, that it was not in the public interest to maintain the secrecy of these files, and she ordered those cases unsealed. The result was a cascade of evidence that the church had known about these cases for years and had systematically protected both its clergy and its institutional reputation by keeping them from the public. This shift in legal judgment had the effect of opening up the story and making it one that could be reported in a far more systematic way, an event that had implications for other locales.

Judge Sweeney's ruling signaled a significant shift in the power and role of the Roman Catholic church, a shift that also had implications for the elaboration of place, and an elaboration that had much to do with the power, centrality, and even the social role of the church in Boston. Sweeney's ruling responded to the power of disclosure made available by digital means of dispersing information. That is, Sweeney's general disposition was toward transparency, which had been an emphasis in her judicial philosophy since ascending to the bench in 1986. By 2001, with the age of digital media emerging, such ideals of disclosure were becoming increasingly attainable.[38]

The existence of digital media effectively changed the nature of the concept of "the public." That view of an aggregated mass, now reimagined by the existence of the internet—and the digital information it dispersed to an ever-growing group—meant that the number of readers of the stories rendered possible by the unsealing of these previously confidential agreements had increased geometrically. But this fact also dramatically changed the conditions under which the stories could be read, in terms of both time and space, making them more compelling by allowing a more personal interaction with their revelations.

This court decision made for a sprawling story, one that would grow exponentially over time. Sacha Pfeiffer recounted in an interview for an article in *The New Yorker*:

> Once we got all these personnel files, he (Associate Managing Editor Ben Bradlee Jr.) started saying, "We can't just do these priest-du-jour stories anymore." There were horrific stories in the files. But at some point you just stop writing about individual stories. We began looking at larger issues. Why did it happen? What was the role of the laity, or the lack of the role of the laity? What's the psychology of the priests? Why did there seem to be more boys and men coming forward than girls and women?" (Some reasons: priests had physical access to boys that they simply didn't have to girls—in church, in their homes, on camping trips; and, chillingly, because more boys were targeted, in part because they were less likely to talk.) Poor families were targeted, too: mothers who needed help, children who needed care.[39]

Such images and narratives of working-class families in awe of the church successfully re-elaborated Boston as a place of entrenched neighborhoods and institutions, a place that as seen extensively in other media, including the coverage of the events noted in the previous chapter and in the growing tale of Whitey Bulger. Such a feedback loop of narratives tied to place-defining images speaks to the power of mass media to fix place as a conceptual entity.

Digital Media and the Spread of the Story

But beyond the investigative journalism of the *Globe* team, there is another story of dissemination and consumption. The emergent scandal of pederasty among the clergy morphed into a vastly larger mass event than the stories of the previous chapter—and ultimately spread in ways that the earlier incarnations of the story did not. In the period after the introduction of the internet 2.0 platform in the early 2000s, a technology that allowed users not only to view content but also to interact with it dynamically, internet content, including news, burgeoned, as transmission speed and online access increased dramatically. By the 2010s, the priest abuse story extended geometrically as a matter of the relationship between this type of story and the specific terms of digital modes of representation and apprehension now available, which included interactive message boards that provided latitude for discussion and further information regarding the misdeeds of clergy.

As an example of the reach of the story by mid-decade, consider a documentary film that initially aired on PBS. Indeed, the story of priest abuse in Boston had many media iterations, but a particularly affecting narrative was that broadcast on PBS's *Frontline* on January 16, 2007, and originally released in 2006, ironically titled *Hand of God*, directed by Joe Cultrera, whose brother Paul is the featured character. The parish priest, Joseph Birmingham, had repeatedly abused Paul in the 1960s while living in the working-class Boston suburb of Salem. Birmingham, who died in 1989, was accused of molesting at least fifty boys in a variety of locales and under three different cardinals: Richard Cushing, Humberto Medeiros, and Bernard Law.[40] This later treatment reaffirmed the reporting of the Spotlight team but does so in trenchant, emotional terms. This is an extremely intimate film by a director about a family member, featuring their home, their parents, and narrative accounts and photographs of other family members. It finds visual terms that replicate the role of the church in a community of a certain type and during a certain era, showing the edifice of the local church and photographs and footage of priests, Cardinal Law, and various high officers of the Boston archdiocese. The Cultreras were Italian and Catholic, parishioners in a church built by immigrants in 1925, a group of white, working-class men who mostly lived insular and modest lives. Eventually, the film becomes an investigation of the crimes of Birmingham and others like him, mostly in Salem. Cultrera's father talks about his unmitigated trust in the priest and his pride at seeing his son being driven in Birmingham's car. The visual medium affirms the specificity of place, as do the particular terms of the narrative. We are again in a working-class and ethnically distinct enclave defined by wood-sided, multifamily homes and the centrality of the Catholic church. This is an emotionally powerful tale, and one that builds on other related stories of its type and place. It culminates with the filmmaker being physically removed from the grounds of St. John's Seminary as he seeks an audience with the cardinal, an act that affirmed the church's imperiousness and lack of regard and sympathy for its victims.

It was not a film with a large circulation initially, relying on miniscule festival audiences and then the modest audience of public television. But as I rewatched this broadcast in 2020, I was reminded of the many viewers who have subsequently accessed this film on a variety of platforms—PBS On Demand, Amazon, YouTube—a fact that is so much a matter of the snowballing of the abuse scandal as a matter of its greater availability. This film is a living entity that remains as vital as when it was first released, even as it references a specific time and place.

Such availability is a testament to what has happened to mass media since the film was released and since the Spotlight story broke. Between 1998 and 2009, the number of internet subscribers went from 50 million to 1 billion, and then by 2012 that number had more than doubled again.[41] As Sacha Pfeiffer noted in an interview, the story of the prevalence of abuse and the related and perhaps more resonant story of the diocese coverup, were enlarged by the availability of digital platforms that circulated the news widely and led directly to more tips, which, of course, led to more stories. Pfeiffer went on to note that it was among the first of major news stories to circulate and grow in this fashion:

> We did really benefit though, because that was truly the very early days of reading stories online, and if we had published in the 90s, the only person that would have seen that story were the ones who would have got the *Boston Globe* home delivery. And instead, our story reached all around the country and across the globe. That meant that victims from all over the country were calling us, and verifying their stories. We were definitely not as technologically advanced at the time. But I think this was the first news story that went truly viral.[42]

This insight becomes important when placing the 2002 coverage alongside the glimmers of the story that had been surfacing for some fifteen years. Pfeiffer's comment about the internet bears scrutiny not only for what it meant about the immediate visibility of the story but also for what it suggests about the sprawl of the story both geographically and temporally, since details of the story could be read or viewed any place and anytime, as well as accessed in public spaces or personal spaces—even as the story's geographic hook linked it to working-class Boston.

But even before the advent of the internet, the personal (even agonizing) nature of the abuse scandal was addressed by the ways in which it was reported and researched:

> The first stories in the series included a telephone number at the *Globe* that people could call to report additional clergy sexual abuse, and survivors came forward in droves. More documents came to light, and the story grew and grew. "It kept tentacling," Pfeiffer said. "In the majority of cases, victims approached us. To explain: We began researching this issue in August 2001, and we published our first story—actually, package of stories—on the topic on January 6, 2002, followed by another package on January 7, 2002. A slew of follow-up stories came after that, as did another package of stories on January 31, 2002. With each of those stories, and with many of the nearly 900 stories on clergy sex abuse that have since been published in the *Globe*, we included what we call our "tip box," which lists two phone numbers (one to reach a live reporter, one to leave a recorded confidential message) and an email address so readers could get in touch with us to offer information and comments. . . . If we let several hours go by without checking our answering machine or email, dozens of unanswered messages and emails would have piled up—and I am referring here only to our general answering machine and email box, not our personal answering machines and email, which were also being flooded."[43]

The role of the relatively ancient technology of the telephone connects the coverage of the church scandal to that of the busing story—which fed on and increased in intensity as a result of talk radio. But in this case, the presence of internet technology created media accentuation and sprawl in a proportion way beyond that which was possible in 1974.

The way the story burgeoned in the 2000s makes it an example of a *type* of story that is specific to the age of digital media and that attests to the power of the internet. Since the home computer and high-speed internet connections were becoming more and more usual, the stories published in the *Globe* were available, or soon available, in some form to readers all over the world. In addition, social media platforms allowed for the extensive and perpetual discussion of the stories and the events they portrayed, as well as the introduction of related stories. Discussion boards provided a safe environment for a quasi-public elaboration of events that were particularly personal and which had been private. The fact that such forums could be accessed from one's private space was a particular feature of this then-emergent technology, allowing virtual selves to discuss events that had been disturbingly visceral.

By 2004, the dioceses or archdioceses of Portland, Oregon; Tucson, Arizona; Spokane, Washington; Davenport, Iowa; San Diego, California; Fairbanks, Alaska; Wilmington, Delaware; and Milwaukee, Wisconsin had all declared bankruptcy in response to civil litigation over sex abuse cases, and this did not include the larger cases in New York, Philadelphia, Chicago, Los Angeles, Oakland, San Francisco, and so many other U.S. cities. To limit the revelations to the United States neglects the subsequent uncovering of abuse in many nations of the world with a significant Catholic population—Ireland, France, Italy, El Salvador, Spain, Portugal, Chile, and the Philippines, for example. If one looks at the stories indexed by the term "priest sexual abuse" in the *New York Times* archives, there is no shortage of articles from the 1980s and many more in the 1990s. But in 2002, the number is almost incalculable, and the coverage continued in force for more than a year, finally diminishing significantly in 2005, numbering over two thousand for the time period. Events like the murder of John Geoghan in 2003, or the release of convicted priest and pedophile Paul Shanley in 2017, forcefully brought the narrative back to the fore of newspaper coverage. The life of repose and honor that deposed cardinal Bernard Law led in Rome intermittently also made news in the years following his leaving Boston, and then his death in 2017 led to a spate of coverage.

As I continued to research this story into the 2020s, it was far more available on the internet than the stories from the decades earlier that I analyzed in chapter 1. Further, it is far more *visually*—in pictures and videos—and narratively available, since its digital form lends itself to fairly involved renderings of incidents and their significance. There are also various documentaries available, some primarily informational but some deeply personal.

The video archive of local, national, and international news available on YouTube and other online sites is quite extensive, reminding us of the attention that this story garnered in 2002 and in the years immediately thereafter. Such resources include the Netflix series *The Keepers* (2017); *Unrepentant: Investigating Abuse in the Canadian Catholic Church* (VeraCity, City TV, 2020); *Deliver Us from Evil* (dir. Amy Berg, Disarming Films, 2006); and *Sex Abuse in the Church: Code of Silence* (dir. Martin Boudot, Premieres Lignes, 2017), just to name a few. YouTube is replete with news clips, short documentaries, international sources (*60 Minutes Australia*), podcasts, and so on.

But even more than that, the fact that I was able to access this footage in 2020 and beyond, and that timelines, charts, lists, individual testimonies, and independent films exist, all attest to the extent of this problem. This is clearly a story to which many people can connect in some way, shape, or form, even if they are not Catholic and even if they have never lived in any of the cities explicitly named in the coverage. It may be enough to know Catholics, to be interested in the institution of the church, or to be appalled by the contours of the narrative. The abuse story is, among other things, a tale of how the internet may create a sprawling horizontal expansion of a story.

Boston in the Digital Age

The public narrative of the epidemic of clergy sexual abuse tells of an institution that has lost much of its social rationale, as well as its moral center. But the journalistic coverage of sexual abuse by Catholic clergy in Boston also served to inscribe and reinscribe place. Coming as it did after the busing crisis and the Stuart murder case, both highly racialized, we can easily see the ways in which the restricted terms of "Boston"—a city seen as ensconced in the past and captive to a kind of tribalism that was definitional for its urban spaces—became a perfect canvas for defining a narrative which counters that of a world that has opened up digitally and geometrically, that is, a world where the local or regional has already been marginalized by the technology and practices that make trade of all kinds, including the exchange of information, a far-flung enterprise. For individuals living in an environment defined by a hope of continuity, that sense of a wider world filled with people, things, and knowledge not measurable in a small and traditional conceptual frame can erode a person's sense of safety. If one looks at the role of the church in urban America from the late nineteenth to the mid-twentieth century, it provided exactly that kind of comfort to new immigrants from Europe and the British Isles, and a generation or two of their descendants, emphasizing apparently immutable social bonds and timeless verities. The post-2002 crisis put an end to the era, although it was certainly already eroding by the 1960s through that period's cultural roil and the fact that immigrants from other places altered both the makeup of the church and the demographics of U.S. cities.

Looking at the television network coverage of the phenomenon of priests sexually abusing their young parishioners, it is striking how the story seems almost to originate in Boston in early 2002, although we know that its antecedents were up to twenty years old. This treatment of the scandal suggests the degree to which changes in information technology that emerged gradually in the 1990s had created both a sense of a wider world and a concurrent sense of the need to shut out that world, until it could not be shut out anymore. Boston became a site on which those tensions were mapped through the content of the *Globe* series and its resonant impact on wider news coverage. The number of Boston-based stories from the first six months of 2002 in the national media dwarfed mention of other locales. Certainly, part of this emphasis followed from the extensive reporting by the *Boston Globe*. But other local and regional papers were also on the story, even if they did not pursue it as doggedly.

The national coverage of the sexual abuse scandal marked it as a Boston story and focused on tropes of place that were ubiquitous in the events described in chapter 1. This coverage was initially tied to the prosecution of John Geoghan, who at the time of his trial was an aging, unprepossessing (or so his appearance conveyed), white man. In an early story, via CNN, he was shown in photographs at trial and in some older photographs with younger men at religious ceremonies.[44] Later on, fleeting interviews with plaintiffs tended to, following the emphases of the busing coverage, exude the markings of working-class origins through their dress and accents. In this early coverage, there were fully as many shots of courtroom interiors as there were of church interiors; accordingly, we have the confluence of two institutions, legal and ecclesiastical. Further, reports also showed at times a curbside view of the same types of streets and houses that populated the video frames during the busing crisis. For example, in an NBC *Nightly News* feature on February 9, 2002, an alleged victim, Bill Oberle, is depicted on the street in front of a framed three-decker house in a working-class district.[45] The house and the accent are reminiscent of the sounds and visuals encountered almost every night on the evening news in the early fall of 1974, when the busing story was a national fixture. Again, this architecture not only had a kind of local significance as a marker of family and neighborhood stability but it also developed a kind of national and international resonance as a marker of place and authenticity. Indeed, triple-decker houses were featured prominently in television footage of the priest abuse story and in films about and set in Boston.

As the abuse story broadened, it also became increasingly a story not of a priest or of priests but rather of the church as an institution; however, in that focus, in order for the stories to remain effective and sufficiently dramatic, there had to be a personal dimension that could serve as an emotional hook for audiences. This need for context led to a focus on the individuals who formed the institutional hierarchy of the church. As religion scholar Peter Steinfels notes, with a nod to Timothy Lytton, "The media thrive on personal drama, shocking events implying a larger trend or crisis, identifiable public figures, familiar settings and 'straightforward moral lessons' (p. 86) . . . The news media prize these as highly credible sources . . . and value an unfolding drama."[46] Thus, personalizing rather than institutionalizing was simply the stuff of affective AND effective journalism. In this particular story, that of Bill Oberle (and also of many others already noted), the drama emphasized the disparities of power between the clergy and the abused, as well as the institutional heft of the church. Such emphases well lent themselves to embedded narratives of place, as "Catholic" Boston had been effectively portrayed as the "most Catholic city in America," and as a place where "precincts" and "parishes" were interchangeable terms, a place where the hierarchy of the church had long had a powerful role in civic life. The priests we see readily became a means to articulating the centers of power that functioned within the city, standing for both themselves and the institution that credentialed them.

This means of defining the institution by its representatives and adherents was a strategy of personalizing the institutional tale. But the looming power that dwarfed that of these relatively minor actors was often invoked, affirming that there were victims who had been exploited and harmed by an institution dedicated to its own self-preservation. For example, the previously cited NBC story from January 12, 2002, invoked this larger institutional context, detailing the Vatican's response by showing documents that defined the church's position. The reporter, Dan Abrams, talks over the visuals of the treatise and notes that the protocols demand an immediate reporting to the Vatican where charges will be brought before a secret tribunal that will define punishment, again invoking the rite and tradition of *omerta*. The worst and most egregious of the offenders will, he reports, be excommunicated. Such coverage, of course, played to the broad contours of the church's image, its insularity, its secretiveness, its foreignness, its distinct hierarchies, and its institutional and ecclesiastical resistance to secular law. In a latter part of the NBC story, viewers were also introduced to Phil Saviano, a native of Worcester but a resident of Boston and an important figure in the local chapter of SNAP. Saviano's exact locale at the time of his abuse became moot as he emerged as a key testifier in the public case associated with the diocese in Boston, where he had lived since college. Saviano was an articulate spokesperson for his cause, calling for the church to open its files and its complaints to public authorities, so that those named might be tried.[47]

But more commonly depicted than figures like Saviano were working-class males who expressed their grief and frustration and even their departure from the church. They tended to conform both to ethnic assumptions about place and a notion of the average working-class Catholic man. This figure, who morphed from one individual to another over the life of the journalistic and digitally recirculating tale, tended to be even more visible in the Boston-based abuse stories than in narratives with different urban (and rural) locales. These men talked about their faith and their vulnerability. The church and its clergy acted as a kind of surrogate parent in working-class districts in and around the city. Indeed, in the most egregious cases, mothers told of priests coming into their single-parent homes and grooming their young sons, such as in the Dussourd case, where Geoghan would "put" the six boys to bed, showing up at bedtime in his clerical garb and spending time alone with them in their bedrooms.[48] This lurid tale, among so many, was perfect for the narrative of place that was so much a feature of the various network newscasts.

With minimal effort, I can find countless news reports, magazine features, personal testimonies, databases, and films that reiterated this scandal. And as I link to those items, I can engage in an act of private encounter with the investigation. In effect, the abuse story is a perfect vehicle for the structures of feeling made possible by the internet, a medium that allows for the public and private to conjoin in ways that were anticipated by television and radio but which expanded the realm of the private and the role of affective encounter in ways that far transcended those earlier media. In addition, the abuse story allows for a postmodern dialectic of place and placelessness to enter the equation, asking us to consider how their means of transmission and encounter impact and are impacted by their particular geographies of origin. While these stories are space- and time-specific (in their anchoring), the details of the allegations in Boston from the 1960s through the 1980s, as well as their presentation in digital form, allow them to also float beyond the limits of those specific facts of time and place. These events are perpetually recurring electronically. In contrast, for example, earlier iterations of this story, such as the Joseph Porter allegations in North Attleboro in the early 1990s, were available only to those watching the nightly newscasts and reading scant coverage in the local and regional newspapers. They could see them discussed on Phil Donahue, through the devices of syndicated television and the appropriation of the talk radio format by television. Such restrictions of reader/viewer point to the temporal and geographic barriers that were eradicated by the development and expansion of the internet.

But the internet must be contextualized as part of a continuum of technological change, and in particular change dating back to the emergence of television as a viable form of mass engagement in the 1950s. Seeing the ways in which television and related forms of technology had already begun at that time to change to cultural landscape, in his 1974 discussion of television as a medium, the late British cultural critic Raymond Williams coined the term "mobile privatization." By this, he meant the tendency of communications technology to increase the ways in which an individual could maintain their physical isolation while exploring—or at least encountering—electronic worlds that simulated a kind of movement, and at times fostered that movement (as in Williams's example of the private car).[49] But little known to Williams at that time, the omnipresence of mobile devices with access to an extensive electronic world of information and entertainment would further create a salience to his idea. Indeed, the "everywhere" and "nowhere" aspect of the ever-present digital world has both enhanced the fact of the private individual as well as made that entity's boundaries somewhat porous. As David Morley points out, Williams's emphasis on the "private" tracks well with the emergent technologies that have succeeded television, as these visual and interactive media have increasingly moved from the domain of the formal and quasi-public spaces of the middle-class home—the television in the parlor or living room, watched by the aggregated family—to more and more intimate areas, such as bedrooms, bathrooms, kitchens, and that these movements have tracked with the increased interactivity of those devices.[50]

Thus, the textual productions accessed through online platforms alter the relationship between text and context, between viewer and viewed, since the information, while static in its content, is a matter of the individual net-surfer choosing to view it in their own time and place and as a matter of their own individual frame of reference. This fact allows for the combination and recombination of these relatively inelastic materials becoming involved with other contexts to create a range of meanings. Further, the technological device that allows for this encounter with these networked materials is also variable and relatively mobile, ranging from an Apple watch to a large-screen, high-definition, "smart" television. The net surfer/reader/viewer has a degree of agency previously unknown in the world of news and information transmission. And that agency includes a kind of removal, but a relative removal at that, from apparent temporal and spatial constraints. As we think of the very personal and distinct events recounted on these many websites that catalog and describe priest sexual abuse, we are drawn into the dialectic of the medium that keeps this story alive and simultaneously, perhaps exponentially, adds to its power. While space becomes fluid and lends itself to new understandings, to see such technologies as eradicating either the space of reception or the space of representation is a misreading, a view that fails to take into account the inevitability of time and location, as well as the desire for such parameters as conceptual markers, as elements of the encountered narrative. Time and space remain part of the conceptual diagram, part of the conception of event and its spatiotemporal moorings. We remain situated both in the space and time of the story as well as the space and time of its apprehension.

In his excellent analysis "Media Studies, Geographical Imaginations, and Relational Space," Richard Ek works through the reorientations produced by changing technologies of communication, noting how our present state of virtuality allows us to develop plastic conceptions of space that are never really spaceless. He instead formulates a more complex vision of space that incorporates the digital in tension with the material: "A number of human geographers have begun to see space, place and time as co-constituted, folded together, situated, mobile and multiple. . . . Every locality becomes a site of intersection and juxtaposition of old and new spatio-temporalities embedded in complex, layered histories. Place is an open, hybrid meeting place. As a consequence, a global sense of place is needed, where places are imagined '. . . as articulated moments in networks of social relations and understandings.'"[51]

Such a complex formulation speaks to our vision of place and events, and the representation and transmission of both. As we encounter our electronic vision of the priest abuse narrative, the authenticity of the tale relies on its anchor in time and place, though its affective power may be experienced immediately. It is precisely the association of place that provides one parameter of comprehension. Indeed, that aspect of the story built on received notions of historical place and its resonant cultural markers. That the visual transmission of the story returned to those markers repeatedly suggests how significant they were both for content providers and consumers. Their prominence may be seen as an antidote to notions of placelessness, suggesting the need for a deeper, rooted structure of narrative, one that is of *someplace* and not simply reduced to its digital means of transmission. These narratives are accessible from any number of places, both mobile and fixed, but rather than decoupling the narrative from place, such access promotes the extension of networks. Writes Fiona Allon of contemporary technologies, "Rather than an annihilation of space . . . I want to suggest that such new technologies produce new spatialities and temporalities."[52] The "Boston" produced in this narrative is both of the present and the past, both of the near and of the distant, but in any case it contains material and historical presences that lend its digital footprint power and depth to accelerate a tale of individual transgression and institutional power and cupidity. That story is related and similar to that found in other locales and other times. It is a both a cognitive and affective means of creating a network of victims and their sympathizers, as well as a means of comprehending the particular circumstances of the stories being told digitally. Indeed, these visual hooks recirculate images and ideas that have emerged as chronotopes of place in the last part of the twentieth century and the first part of the twenty-first.

Whitey Bulger at Large

Such digital resonances, complete with their embedded representations of space and place in a world where those terms have become increasingly plastic and perhaps elastic but also meaningful in new and salient ways, connect us to the late twentieth- and twenty-first-century tale of James "Whitey" Bulger. This tale became newly visible when on June 23, 2011, the South Boston–based and Southie-identified gangster was apprehended. He had been one of the FBI's most wanted men in the United States for over twelve years and on the run for some sixteen. Bulger's cult in his home area of Boston—or more precisely, South Boston—is attested to in the many interviews that punctuated the news coverage of his saga and became further mythologized by that coverage.

James Bulger was born in Boston in 1929 and lived most of his early life in the Irish-ethnic enclave of South Boston. He became notorious in the 1980s as a member of the Winter Hill gang, a consortium of gangsters who combined the residue of two South Boston groups with a nearby Somerville-based operation. By that time, Bulger had done federal prison time for armed robbery and had already begun his role as an FBI informant. He employed his affiliation with the Winter Hill group to become *the* crime boss of South Boston, a title he retained until his disappearance in 1995. By all accounts, Bulger's disappearance was the result of a tip from an FBI agent, who informed the gangster of an imminent indictment. From 1995 to 2011, Bulger was nowhere to be found by law enforcement officials. But that is not to say that he was entirely out of the news.

Bulger surfaced in local news in the 1980s, but his visibility was further enhanced by the rise of his younger brother William, who was elected to the Massachusetts state house of representatives in 1969. In the 1970s, Bill was a young state senator from South Boston who took a public and vocal stance against forced school busing. By 1977, the younger Bulger was the Massachusetts senate majority leader, and by 1978 the powerful president of the state senate, a job he held until 1996. The fact of these two brothers living oddly parallel (yet divergent) lives in very distinctive sectors of the regional social and economic life enhanced the fame of both. Indeed, it was the conceptual hook of the brothers' relationship that was central to many of the early stories about Whitey.

The coverage of the Whitey Bulger story built fully on the Boston *mythos*. The priest abuse narratives required the collapsing of many places in the region into a convenient tale of working-class Boston Catholicism, since the incidents took place in a range of locales, some more prosperous than others—Newton, Salem, Watertown, Waltham, Quincy, and so on—but the

FIGURE 9. The Old Harbor housing project, home of the Bulger family. —Courtesy Landmarks Commission image collection, 5210.004, City of Boston Archives.

Bulger story had an authentic South Boston address and ethnicity. Whitey Bulger's family found their way to the Old Harbor (now the McCormack) housing projects (as featured in *Good Will Hunting*), and he lived there with his mother off and on until he was sentenced to nine years imprisonment in Alcatraz.

Even the story of the two brothers feels as though it was imported from a Warner Brothers film of the 1930s. That one brother should emerge as a political fixer and the other as a crime boss plays into the narrative of Irish American rogue politicians that was also part of the urban *mythos* as it existed in the twentieth century. The first of the mythologizing stories about the Brothers Bulger appeared in a four-part series by Christine Chinlund, Dick Lehr, and Kevin Cullen in the *Boston Globe*, published September 18–21, 1988. In that series, the *Globe* featured the parallel ascension of the two brothers in their chosen areas of expertise. This narrative traded heavily in the lore of place: the *Globe* began the first article of the four-part series with a geographic metaphor: "On the first day of school in 1948, when students spilled out of the Old Harbor tenements in South Boston, Bill Bulger set off in the opposite direction, walking out the back side of the project to Andrew Station where he caught a streetcar to Boston College High School and a decade of serious study."[53] Boston College High School is one of the elite, Jesuit-led Catholic prep schools in the city, a school that still requires Latin and Greek and that sends almost all of its graduates to college. This dichotomy between one brother embracing a scholastic tradition and answering the call of politics and the other embracing a life of crime is not necessarily one endemic to Boston but it is one that easily traded in the *mythos* of urban place.

The national coverage of Whitey Bulger and the brothers, a far less comprehensive and myth-making take than the later *Globe* story, appeared in a brief item in the *New York Times* in 1987, a year before the far more extensive *Globe* story. The story sat for a number of years and then got picked up again after Whitey was indicted in January 1995. This indictment led to his disappearance, but at the time of a 1995 story in the *Times* and the contemporary feature on NBC *Nightly News*, his removal from Boston was not yet known, although he seems to have vanished in late December. The NBC story was dated January 13 and the *Times* story was from the 16th. Both pieces dug into the parallel lives of the two brothers, focusing on their ethnicity (Irish), neighborhood (South Boston), and larger city environs (Boston). The visuals of the video narrative borrowed much from the busing story and anticipated that of the church sexual abuse story. The cameras roll to show the same houses that had stood in to mark the working-class contours of place in the busing story; they would subsequently perform the same narrative function in the reporting on clergy abuse. The narrator indicates this is a "Boston" story and refers to the "hardscrabble Irish enclave" and the "mean streets" of South Boston, as the visuals show a gritty and clearly down-at-the-heels urban neighborhood. The scene shifts to a church front, and then into a food pantry affiliated with that place of worship. Men and women interviewed on the streets reveal a certain respect and fondness for the criminal, making him into something of a Robin Hood figure, again emphasizing the regressiveness, distinction, and isolation of place.[54] Bulger, despite his overt criminality, remained (to a degree) a somewhat sympathetic figure for those who had been (or believed themselves to have been) left behind by contemporary life.

Bulger appeared on the TV show *America's Most Wanted* in September 1995, and then again in April 2014; on *Unsolved Mysteries* in November 1996; and on the FBI most wanted list in 1999. Such shows traverse the same media path defined by *Rescue 911* in the Stuart case, providing cheap and high-profit programming for network outlets, and then extensive opportunity for secondary cable outlets owned by the same media companies. Such practices had the effect of making characters like Bulger almost ubiquitous on the small screen.

After Whitey's disappearance in 1995, the story lay fairly fallow for a number of years except for the national crime investigation shows, until the trial of his partner in crime Steve "the Rifleman" Flemmi, whose testimony revealed that FBI agent John J. Connolly Jr., another son of South Boston and the handler of Flemmi and Bulger as informants, had given the pair in effect carte blanche. In return for tips on the criminal doings of the Italian mob, mostly based in Providence, Rhode Island, Bulger was largely immune from prosecution. This resulted in Connolly being charged and convicted in 1999, and then Bulger being charged with multiple counts of murder in 2000 as a result of testimony arising from the Connolly trial. The Connolly story also fit the narrative of place and space developed in the many iterations of the Bulger story in that it referred again to insularity and a kind of tribalism derived from place and ethnicity and organized around the loyalties and *omerta* associated with the church and organized crime. When the Whitey story truly became a national phenomenon, the Connolly side of it became an important piece. A 2002 story on CNN investigated the Bulger brothers angle and noted the FBI co-conspirator's tale. The occasion at this point was the subpoena of William by a congressional committee.[55] After 1995, Bulger resigned from the state senate and became chancellor of the University of Massachusetts System, a post from which he would step down after his appearance before Congress.

But it was only after 2001, when Republicans took over control of the national legislative branches, that the story burgeoned. Bulger had been on the FBI's most wanted list then for over two years, and the state had a Republican governor, Mitt Romney, who was no friend of the former senate president. When Bulger testified with immunity before the congressional oversight committee in 2003 and admitted he had spoken with his brother in 1995, the calls for his resignation began and continued until he resigned as chancellor in November 2003.

Whitey was ultimately apprehended in Santa Monica, California, in June 2011 and convicted and sentenced in June 2013. By that time, his legend had only grown. While the elements of his specific narrative that lent themselves to mythologizing—as a Robin Hood, as an FBI informant, as a bad brother among the pair of two star-crossed brothers—had already been exhausted, his sheer ability to evade the law became a dominant part of his story in his last years of freedom. The tale of Whitey Bulger received a further boost from the way his story lent itself to extant narratives of criminal complexity and intrigue, dimensions that employed place and space strategically and connected that association to a vision of Catholic Boston offered in the coverage of priest sexual abuse. Further, the Bulger story proliferated and expanded its mythological imprint through its rapid recycling and recirculation—indeed, its near pervasive accessibility—through digital means. Although it is important to make a distinction here: the Bulger story was not one of a mushrooming mass of victims engaged in finding themselves in the digital imprint of the case. Rather, Bulger was a celebrity whose story fascinated its viewers and resonated with a large public, for various reasons, including its apparent reiteration of the Robin Hood trope, in which a working-class criminal disperses his gains through his impoverished community, a truly idealistic and largely false rendering of the Whitey narrative.

Bulger became an archetype of the urban criminal though the intricacies of his case. That his case was Boston-based and involved the FBI, the Italian mafia, a highly visible and prominent politician brother, as well as the fact that he was sixteen and a half years on the run, further elevated it in the variegated media world of the 2000s. Bulger, as a figure and as a myth, was widely available in news stories and documentaries, all of which emphasized the "mean streets" of Boston—and particularly of South Boston—and the code of *omerta* among the thugs of that region. The widely available videos and longer- and shorter-form tellings recount the same stories with the same emphases in slightly different terms. Indeed, there were thirty-five network newscasts that contained a Whitey Bulger story between his arrest in 2011 and his trial in 2013.[56] Thus, though plastic, the Bulger stories were also elastic, returning to its original place in the larger urban myth of South Boston. When Bulger died in late October 2018, his notoriety was confirmed by the sheer mass of attention his passing received. His obituaries employed the resonant terms of Boston-ness as shorthand for telling his story. Indeed, the first paragraph of his *New York Times* notice is emblematic: "James (Whitey) Bulger, the South Boston mobster and F.B.I. informer who was captured after 16 years on the run and finally brought to justice in

2013 for a murderous reign of terror that inspired books, films and a saga of Irish-American brotherhood and brutality, was found beaten to death on Tuesday in a West Virginia prison."[57] That Bulger remained the essence of a South Boston criminal speaks to the ways that place had become a trope for a certain kind of residual urban criminality, and the ways that criminality was tied to notions of authenticity. Indeed, *that* iteration of place is the *essence* of place, a definition that we can trace to all manner of narratives.

The coverage has odd echoes of the priest abuse stories in its portrayal of the corruption of regional, Catholic-dominated institutions—the FBI and the courts—and the power of the abusers to mitigate the controls that apparently were entrenched in the system. At the point of Bulger's death, a terse reiteration of the resonant terms of his legacy occurred for the week or so the story remained an "event." The coverage was truly far-flung, including various international venues, as the Reuters video feed was regularly picked up and recirculated in Europe and Asia.[58] The stories all focused on his presence as a figure from "organized crime," but they also included references to Boston and South Boston, employed as a kind of shorthand or signpost.

The local coverage in particular played up the Boston/South Boston angle. Although at the point of his death Bulger had not been in Boston for some twenty-three years, his association with place took the form of either stand-ups from his former gang headquarters in Somerville, or streetscapes of South Boston, redolent of the romance of working-class, insular, and Irish Catholic Boston that were so much a part of the priest sexual abuse and busing sagas. Many of these newscasts featured interviews—either with law enforcement officials set in Boston or with the families of Bulger's victims—that conformed to a certain prototype of place, including framed three-decker houses, regional accents, and working-class interviewees.[59]

Bulger's constant fame after 2002 has been a matter of his ongoing presence through digital media. As in the case of the Spotlight stories, the perpetual presence of news stories and documentaries about Bulger made his tale widely available. In addition, various discussion boards (focused on criminals and criminality) are sites for ongoing consideration and speculation concerning his deeds and locations. After the domestic terror attacks of 2001, the FBI developed digital surveillance and search capabilities, and Bulger's image and criminal profile widely circulated, including on Twitter and Facebook feeds.

Bulger's transience and unknown location in ways made him the perfect internet object. Since he was literally no place, the placelessness of internet resources conformed to his status. Since he was nowhere, he might be found anywhere, and his virtual presence was the only clear rendering of his existence. And his spectral presence contributed to many Whitey sightings in disparate places. But in a dialectical fashion, and one that connects to the story of the Roman Catholic church, the more a story floats free into placelessness, the more a corollary sense of located-ness becomes an entrenched and arguably necessary part of the story. Both of these stories lent themselves to a kind of narrative shorthand that was enacted through visual and virtual media. And while the characters featured—Whitey Bulger and Bernard Law, in particular, along with various priests who had their infamous fifteen minutes of notoriety—became part of the story, the recurring and more resonant aspect of the narrative was that of place, of Boston, or South Boston, which ultimately served as a synecdoche for the entire city. Such a marker became definitional for a feedback loop of place and incidents that occurred there: Boston is the dominance of a corrupt Catholic church; Boston is a place of insularity and criminality; Boston is a place of tradition and resistance to change.

In her discussion of the connection between place and placelessness in our characterization of the contemporary rendering of the urban, Myria Georgiou offers elucidating insights on the ways in which the existence of digital modes of representation provides a reconfiguration of place that enhances its vivid qualities while diminishing its material essence. She notes that visions of "the city" as an entity have long included visions of the common aspects of cities, as well as the unique dimensions and conceptions of each. Those embedded notions have been dramatically magnified and to a degree skewed, however, by the existence of technologies that have drastically redefined the virtual aspects of place. Writes Georgiou, "The distinction between the place and its image is anything but clear and the crossover between the place and its mediated image has come to shape the city both as a place and as non-place. What media do on a daily basis is to reaffirm the identity of the city as an ambivalent location between the real and the virtual."[60] Indeed, these tales refer both to Boston and to "Boston." And while their typicality and representational efficacy may be disputed, they retain the power to define place in the realm of mass culture through their strategic and salient reincorporation of aspects drawn from preexisting narratives.

In this case, we can see a recurrence of impervious and resilient working-class culture, informed by the persistent power of religion. Such a vision of stasis and "tradition" easily provides a template for future renderings of the city. Such emphases point to the contemporary fetishizing of a vision of place that is connected to notions of class and authenticity. It also suggests how the structures of feeling connected to "Boston" include a residual definition of working-class, Irish, Catholic culture as a matter of its status in the eclipse of the industrial and the emergence of the post-industrial. This view is both a reaction to the dislocation of post-industrial life and a means of understanding the new urbanism as a return to an imaginary idyll of an indefinite earlier time, but which seems a temporality lodged in the pre-automobile era of the twentieth century. As such, "Boston" is easily reified and employed in this narrative.

SECTION II
Sports and Mass Culture

IN THESE next two chapters, I discuss the relationship between the gentrified, post-industrial city of Boston; the media projection of that city; and the role of a highly visible sector of commerce and entertainment—professional sports. In chapter 3 I focus my discussion on the Red Sox baseball team and in chapter 4 on the Celtics basketball team. For many it is difficult to say or hear the word "Boston" without thinking of the Red Sox. Fenway Park has become a ubiquitous part of the city for tourists. And though the Celtics name and arena do not have quite the same resonance, the team remains an important aspect of the city's brand. The success of this aspect of a city's commerce—professional sports—is an element of the broader re-elaboration of the city in the 2000s, one related to the burgeoning of film production, proliferation of high-end restaurants, building of office towers and luxury apartments, and explosion of real-estate values over the last thirty or so years. All of these—including professional sports—are "clean" post-industrial businesses that have the dual impact of burnishing a city's brand as they create commerce. Commercial sports are also an important vector of the city's economic success, as well as an important transmitter of a city's meaning and definition in national and international markets. They are a phenomenon that enhances the allure of a city by creating and/or further developing a highly visible but ultimately small and nonproductive industry that redounds to the benefit of the city as an entity; however, those benefits, while economically significant, substantially emerge from the effects of branding and its relative visibility rather than as a direct result of the activity generated by the teams. Major league sports provide an unmatched means for promoting a city and a powerful device for articulating its brand in a distinct manner.

The name "Boston" appears in the news in relation to baseball, basketball, and hockey almost every day of the calendar year. Such persistent notice affirms the status of Boston as a "major league" city. This centrality of the teams' brands speaks to the place of professional sports in the neoliberal city and the location of the city of Boston within that international regime. These matters are products of the broader sociocultural economic environment of the post-industrial age, an era that attests to the powers of digital communications, including marketing, and which depends on the financial reach of elites, including team owners and well-heeled fans. The public relations and marketing arms of sports teams relentlessly promote the franchises and their home, increasing the synergistic impact of one on the other.

The contemporary city, and indeed the contemporary economy in the developed world, is driven by consumption. Cities have succeeded in part because the urban entity—which is the sum of its meanings and materialities, its experiences, its possible experiences, and its associated fantasies—becomes the object of consumption and association. Such a vision of a consumer society fits with the phenomenon of team affiliation in professional sports, as individuals invest emotionally and economically in their teams and associated symbols. This link between consumers and the object of consumption connects with Keith Hayward's view of the ways in which contemporary consumer culture has fundamentally altered subjectivity. Writes Hayward, "Consumerism instills the mistaken belief that identity and self worth can be constructed through the display and celebration of consumer products." And such a sense of identity also has spatial implications, as that consumer society is doing no less than "contributing to the substantial and situational reconfiguration of the post-industrial city."[1] Sports teams and their arenas are important place markers and aspects of civic life in the city and its region, a significance that points to the ways the economic nature and role of urban locales has changed in the late twentieth and early twenty-first centuries.

Both of these teams have intriguing historical legacies connected to race, legacies that are involving of place but which seem to be fading from their range of contemporary associations. Yet, just when these associations of long ago seem to be vanishing into the deep past, an incident will occur that reminds us of how the racist narratives of place and of teams remain available even if submerged. The brands of these two Boston teams are lodged in a narrative of the past that includes incidents and dispositions that were a matter of team, place, and organization that would seem increasingly irrelevant.

Perhaps the persistence of this history emerges from the ways in which place and team have employed the tropes of history, legacy, and authenticity as part of their branding. That is, the persistence of certain strategies—logos, notions of tradition, connections to place—connect the teams to whiteness as a matter of their association with Boston, a place that derives its contemporary brand from notions of authenticity connected to urban, ethnic whiteness. Perhaps such notions of "team" necessarily dredge up that always-available history, even as explicit referents are relatively rare.

CHAPTER THREE

Branding Red Sox Nation and Its Homeland

Wearing Red Sox

One evening in early October 2018, during game one of the Red Sox–Yankees playoff series, as I looked at the filled stands of Fenway Park replete with Red Sox hats and jerseys, I saw a passion for the team affirmed by the recurrence of the brand associated with it. On a more analytical level, I found a recurring act of identification through consumption, a need to belong to Red Sox Nation by purchasing and displaying its artifacts. I also saw an articulation of urban space that denotes a "safe" zone, a place within a city. This zone is that of fandom, a space that enlarges and also circumscribes the terms of dress and behavior expected and allowed, and the fact of paying to be within it enhances one's sense of belonging. Correspondingly, that zone has its virtual component which allows for related acts of affiliation and consumption in countless places through digital platforms around the world, through the auspices of any number of streaming platforms and digital devices. One need not physically attend the "shrine" in Boston to feel affiliated. Within our largely fragmented social order and often-atomized sense of self, group gestures of belonging provide an important adjunct to this purchasing of physical entry into this "nation," and belonging to the active fanbase of a sports team can create a deep and irrational attachment. The concept of Red Sox Nation was a term tossed off by a *Boston Globe* writer, Nathan Cobb, to explain the geographic dissonance experienced by those situated in the regions of Connecticut where *both* New York baseball, in this case the Mets, and Red Sox fans abound.[1] In coining the term, he provided a sense of the depth of the identification of this "imagined community" of those who identify with both the Red Sox and with Boston.[2] And the wearing of Red Sox–branded regalia necessarily feeds into narratives of place.

The Red Sox regional presence, which formed the basis for their later national presence, has been historically enhanced by local media—newspapers, radio, and later television (both over the airways and cable) and streaming platforms. The Red Sox have been available on radio since 1926 and have employed an extensive network throughout the region since after World War II. Prior to 1938, there were no restrictions on the wattage of AM radio station transmission, so powerful stations could broadcast over an extensive region. Historically, Red Sox broadcasts have been highly rated and lucrative for the team. Similarly, from 1948 to 2006, some numbers of Red Sox road games were available through broadcast television, not only enhancing team revenues but also substantially building the team's brand.[3]

The team's media presence affirms the city's status as a locale for professional sports, as well as the sports media's outsized role in U.S. culture in the digital age. The presence of a major league sports franchise can produce significant economic gains and visibility for a city. A beautiful new ballpark in the central business district is far preferable for city-branding to an office building. Indeed, the link between a city's major league teams and its brand is clear.[4] As Mark Goodwin explains of the post-industrial city: "In this new world, the emergence of style as identity and consumption as a form of self-definition have gone hand-in-hand.... The selling of an urban lifestyle thus becomes part and parcel of an increasingly sophisticated commodification of everyday life in which images and myths are relentlessly packaged."[5] The Red Sox are an important commodity *in* the city of Boston and important one *for* the city, as they help define the thing called "Boston" through their ubiquitous media presence; conversely, the branded city helps to define the team. The Red Sox draw fans to town to see the team, to tour Fenway Park, or even to venture to the Fenway area to *look* at the esteemed ballpark. The *sense* of the team that circulates in mass culture through all types of media grafts on to a conception of place that is connected to the city's brand. Indeed, that vision—traditional, historic, authentic—maps on to a vision of the city where school busing was resisted, that spawned the iconic figure of Whitey Bulger, that became ground zero in the Catholic church's sexual abuse scandal, and that has supported racially and ethnically homogenous neighborhoods, even as the contemporary Red Sox also undeniably feature stars from all over the Caribbean, including players from Venezuela, Aruba, Puerto Rico, and the Dominican Republic.

In contemporary terms, the enhanced role of finance capital has made the city increasingly a playground for the rich. The city is not only an engine for the consumer-driven economy of the twenty-first century; it is also a symbol of that economy. And part of its symbolism and sense of centrality is consumable sports. A group of prominent sports sociologists assert, "Within the context of a creeping urban homogeneity, major sporting events, new stadia, and other sports-related experiences have become among the most effective vehicles for the advancement of internally and externally identifiable places."[6] Indeed, far-flung consumers employing technological means of apprehension readily associate teams and stadia with places.

Metropolises that had largely flourished as a result of their prominence in an industrial mode of production were in decline by the 1950s to the mid-1970s. Locales such as Boston, Cleveland, Pittsburgh, Detroit, and St. Louis lost wealth and population in a dramatic fashion. Such cities attempted to devise new paradigms for urban success, systems based on light industry or nonproductive enterprise in the areas of information, finance, real estate, and health care. As the dominant model of work shifted, so did the distribution of the nation's population, and indeed that shift in population density proved anticipatory for these looming economic changes. The sociologist Mark Gottdiener placed the high period of suburbanization in the United States as 1950 to 1965, a time when "suburban relocation developed into a mass movement primarily as a consequence of attractive supply-side features made available to the majority of citizens, who happened to be white."[7] But by the end of the century, many of the inner cities that had largely failed in the 1960s and early1970s were thriving again.

Boston's fortunes in the twenty-first century exemplify this ongoing demographic ascension. It is far more affluent than it was in 1960, though that relative wealth is both spatially and racially disparate.[8] It is notable that within the city, its major sports facilities are next to and easily accessible from the most gentrified of urban neighborhoods. As Boston has seen a marked and continual increase in wealth since 1980, the consumption of its professional sports-related commodities—tickets and merchandise, as well as electronic subscriptions through electronic media—has also grown. In the late twentieth and early twenty-first centuries, in-person revenues, though important, were often superseded by those from other sources: media sales, subscriptions to sports networks, advertising revenues through partially or wholly owned networks, rights fees for broadcasts or rebroadcasts, and merchandising. The relative success of a team in competition is more important for how it affects the team's brand than as a value in itself. Pricing structures for actual attendees may reflect more about the desired makeup of the crowd and their ability to pay than a calculation based on the actual cost of fielding a team and managing a stadium.[9]

Branding the Team, Branding the City

The fate of the Red Sox and Fenway Park as urban enterprises tells us much about the status and condition of cities in the twentieth and twenty-first centuries. Baseball itself is very much a game with strong ties to the past, and those connections are often a matter of emphasis. Many who have written about it define its pastoral associations and rhythms: a game played not according to a clock, one that may take an indeterminate amount of time. Further, the game allows for any number of quirks in that playing field, as the outfield and foul grounds take on the contours of the ballpark, which traditionally took on the shape of its urban setting. There was a moment in the 1960s, 1970s, and 1980s when those idiosyncratic spaces were replaced by multisport stadia—as in Washington, DC; New York (Shea); Atlanta; Pittsburgh; Houston; Cincinnati; St. Louis; Oakland, California; Seattle; and Minneapolis. By the 2000s, only the cash-strapped Oakland As still played in the "concrete donut" (and it looks like they will not be playing there for long), as those stadia came to be called. In baseball, they were replaced by the retro parks, which had far smaller seating capacities, asymmetrical designs, and seats much closer to the field—something on the order of the remaining stadiums from the earlier twentieth century, Fenway Park and Wrigley Field. Such stadia intentionally invoked an earlier urban moment and aesthetic.

Professional sports in general are emblematic of the shift to a substantially urban culture, since it was the concentration of population and the growth of leisure time that went with industrialization and city life that created the possibility of professional, spectator sports in the late nineteenth century. But baseball in particular affirmed that shift with an embedded nostalgia for the pre-urban moment, and it has been that affirmation that is vital to many of its popular cultural incarnations, including films like *Field of Dreams*, *The Rookie*, *Bull Durham*, *Trouble with the Curve*, and so on. And, of course, the ultimate civic symbol of baseball's past is Fenway Park.

But the heightened status of this stadium as a symbol of the nostalgic heart of the sport—and the city—is a relatively recent occurrence, and therefore significant as a marker of cultural change.

Until the late 1970s, Fenway Park was widely viewed as a place with a certain charm but also a number of drawbacks. It was well known for the intense discomfort of its seats, the narrowness of its concourses, the primordial state of its restrooms, its limited seating, and its many obstructed views. Although the location made the stadium, as it had in 1912, a place that could be relatively easily reached by public transportation, access by car and then parking were a nightmare and quite expensive. The neighborhood was light industrial, with the stadium hemmed in by Boston University and Kenmore Square to the northwest, the large concentration of hospitals and medical buildings—including Harvard Medical School—to the south, and the Massachusetts Turnpike to the immediate north. As of the late 1960s and 1970s, the abutting Lansdowne Street was home to a range of rock and dance clubs, along with industrial lofts. Similarly, the streetscape of Brookline Avenue, directly across from the ballpark, also had light industrial spaces. There was a diner, a bowling alley (candlepins!), and a dry cleaner. Such modest environs provided a sense of historical continuity and context.

Since in this pre-gentrification era there was no particular value added either to the antiquated ballpark or to its region, its status as a practical consideration was much in doubt during the 1960s, when Red Sox owner Tom Yawkey possessed no great attachment to either the location or the structure. He declared to a *Globe* reporter in 1967 that he would move the team from Boston if a new stadium wasn't approved by the city.[10] That possibility of declaring Fenway outmoded and unprofitable and replacing it continued intermittently through the 1970s, 1980s, and 1990s. Indeed, Fenway in the regional, if not national, imaginary once stood for the convoluted state of Boston and Massachusetts politics, and the utter impossibility of getting things accomplished. In the 1990s, as the team languished, Fenway seemed finally on its last legs. But again, it was not quite moribund due to that difficulty of getting a replacement built. Said one developer to a *Boston Phoenix* reporter in 1998: "First, you have to consider the inertia and negativism that is native to Boston." Another commented, "Look how long it took to replace the [Boston] Garden [the arena that was home to the Celtics, Bruins, and traveling rodeos; see chapter 4]. Remember the years of squabbling about a convention center? And don't forget the fumbling and farce that surrounded the Patriots' bid to build a new stadium."[11] In a compromise that recognized the relative hold Fenway had on the regional imagination, a plan was put forward to build a new Fenway Park on what was essentially the same site, but having the amenities and earning capacity of a new ballpark. These included larger seats, better sightlines, larger concourses, greater parking capacity, and more luxury boxes. Indeed, this would have been a ballpark like those that had recently been built in Baltimore, Cincinnati, Detroit, and San Francisco, among other places. As of 1998, in the last years of the John Harrington regime of team management, this new construction looked like all but a sure thing. But the ambivalence of Boston mayor Thomas Menino won out, fueled to a degree by a "save Fenway" movement.

In 2002, after the purchase of the team by a syndicate comprising the media-savvy investors John Henry, Tom Werner, and Larry Lucchino, the Red Sox recommitted to their current ballpark and the team got behind enhancing its brand as a living museum of baseball. This strategy proved an astute reading of the contemporary cultural and economic environment, and fully appropriate to values of the moment associated with the "urban." The brand of the city at this point was becoming more and more articulate and increasingly visible. Not only had the news stories noted in the previous chapters already found their way to the public eye; so had the many of the television shows and films featuring Boston previously noted—including Academy Award winners *Good Will Hunting* (1997) and *Mystic River* (2001). By attaching the team to the ballpark and the larger idea of the city as a rooted place and authentic site of working-class culture, the ownership group built on the paradoxical state of branding a place with its embedded connection to white, working-class ethnicity as it gradually ceased to be such a place. Baseball as a commodity is a perfect device for nostalgia, as Fenway Park is a perfect synecdoche for that emotional form of recall. As Daniel Rosensweig notes of retro ballparks, they offer a commodification of the past.[12] Such a treatment of regional and national history is commensurate with the goals of place branding, offering "not only functional benefits but also added-value features. Strong brands must have an added value in the minds of consumers. . . . The added value is rather related to the subconscious and emotions, is about loyalty and that loyalty is the key of brand building."[13] One need only attend a Red Sox game in any venue to see the degree of emotional identification with the brand. Fenway Park epitomizes the significance of stadia in the allure of baseball, as

FIGURE 10. Fenway Park, October 5, 2018, as the Red Sox play the Yankees. —Courtesy Jana Corkin.

Benjamin D. Lisle explains: "The stadium is where relationships in place and across time are anchored and staged, where people experience a version of 'the public' uniquely."[14] Indeed, Fenway Park emerges as a chronotope for a certain vision of place.

The riddle of marketing the post-2000 franchise has been to maintain the efficacy of the terms of the brand, even as some of its embedded meanings cease to be contemporarily germane. The ballpark has been carefully modified but with the goal of maintaining its recognizable historical features. Subsequently, the team has added a number of premium seats by utilizing new visions of vertical space—on top of a wall, on the roof of the concourse, and on the field, and have been allowed to use the abutting Jersey Street (formerly Yawkey Way) as a locale open only to ticket holders, as a kind of concourse but one external to the stadium. But the judgment of the meaning and value of the brand signifies a distinctive view of the baseball business, one that largely did not exist in the era before the 2000s, when digital technology allowed for the marketing of the game, team, and place through devices like the streaming MLB.com application or the digital presence of ESPN. This perspective sees the team in terms of pure marketability and recognizes the greater value of its virtual brand over the apparent benefit of greater seating capacity, luxury boxes, and concession sales. When the Red Sox are nationally televised or internationally streamed, it is not just the game that is being highlighted but also the ballpark and the city, and the way in which they are covered becomes part of the value of that exposure. Sociologist Michael Ian Borer explains the social meanings and significance of the Red Sox stadium:

> Places can be both functional and symbolic. Places can provide an anchor, a foundation, or a "mnemonic" device for shared experiences between people in the present, past, and future. "Mnemonic" devices, either as ideas or objects, help individuals retrieve or preserve memories. Public places as public symbols can do the same for communities. They can act as reminders to people in the present about people, events, or ideas from the past. Public places as public symbols can do the same for communities.... Places endowed with meaning for one generation, whether implicitly or explicitly, provide meaning for the next, thereby providing a bridge between the past and future that binds people together.[15]

This living symbol is not only redolent of history and memory; it is also history in itself, a relic from the time when professional sports were emergent. But the power of this living symbol extends way beyond its immediate group of consumers. It also extends to a far larger audience, one that has been virtually and digitally exposed to this symbol through the devices of mass media, a body of representational devices that not only picture this object but also provide a resonant, received narrative of its meaning and significance. And that meaning evokes a social continuity and affirms the power of certain symbols of the past to structure the present. Indeed, in 1999, when the Major League Baseball (MLB) All-Star Game, an important annual ritual, was at Fenway, Kevin Costner, not coincidentally the star of *Field of Dreams*, narrated the introduction for the national audience in terms that perfectly couched that ballpark's nostalgic dimensions. As the broadcast went on, so did the reverential treatment of the team, the park, and the city, bringing on revered icons of the past to tears and resounding applause. This document persists digitally on the internet so that such a tribute need not be lost to time.

In the many national and international broadcasts and digital streams from Fenway Park since the mid-1990s, and certainly in the era of reverence that accelerated with a force after the acquisition of the Red Sox by the media savvy Henry-Werner-Lucchino group after 2002, the ballpark and the city have been nostalgically couched in an image of both baseball and the city. The terms of reverence often applied to the stadium employ quotes from John Updike's famous *New Yorker* appreciation of Ted Williams's final game in 1961, a source referenced by broadcaster Bob Costas in a PBS documentary on that legendary Red Sox player, streaming on the PBS app as part of the *American Masters* series.[16] Updike famously called Fenway a "lyric, little bandbox of a ballpark. Everything is painted green and seems in curiously sharp focus, like the inside of an old-fashioned peeping-type Easter egg. It was built in 1912 and rebuilt in 1934, and offers, as do most Boston artifacts, a compromise between Man's Euclidean determinations and Nature's beguiling irregularities."[17] Updike, a transplant to New England, invoked nostalgia where many at the time only saw decay.

Fenway, when portrayed during a game, whether streaming or on broadcast television, is often visually couched in a shot taken from a drone, a blimp, or a tall building, containing sweeping views of the park from the north, from the Cambridge side of the Charles River, invoking Harvard and MIT, and then through the historically resonant Back Bay, to the ballpark that stands just outside of Kenmore Square and near Boston University—though BU gets significantly fewer mentions than the Cambridge institutions. These national broadcasts and streaming videos also frequently provide visual evidence of the "New Boston," showing viewers, often with comment, the city's signature skyscrapers, the nearby Prudential Tower and the abutting John Hancock Tower. These buildings signify a contemporary vitality that complements the decidedly backward-looking emphases of history and tradition. These emphases define a kind of solidity that is a strong part of the city's brand and one that also connects to its major tourist sites, including the Freedom Trail and its universities.

The Fenway region has undergone massive redevelopment in the last ten or so years, which has had the effect of drastically changing the environs of Fenway Park. This development will continue, with more than one large project planned. Such a rebuilding of the region has a range of possible and actual ramifications for the ways in which one encounters the Red

Sox and the broader context of the regional experience. As of 2023, the area has shifted significantly in scale and therefore density, with the addition of over a thousand rental units and significant commercial expansion along Boylston Street to the south and east of the ballpark. The Pierce, at the intersection of Brookline Avenue and Boylston Street, is a thirty-story building with one-bedroom apartments starting at $850,000. The nearby Fenway Triangle is seventeen-floors with one-bedroom units renting for just under $3,000 per month. These newer constructions are in addition to the mixed-use development on the nearby former Sears site, as well as development in Kenmore Square and a proposed building over the abutting Mass Pike. In addition, a huge new mixed-use project led by the team and their major concessionaires, the D'Angelo family, was announced earlier that summer:

> A development group led by the Red Sox shared its most detailed vision yet for [a] 2.1-million-square-foot project set on sites around Fenway. It envisions eight buildings in four spots along Jersey Street, Brookline Avenue, Van Ness Street, and behind the park's left field "Green Monster" on Lansdowne Street. They would be filled with nearly 1.7 million square feet of office space, about 216 residential units, as well as restaurants and stores on refurbished streets. . . . It's the latest large-scale development pitched for the booming Fenway neighborhood, this one centered around the park that remains its biggest draw.[18]

The Fenway region is far from the sleepy neighborhood of the city that it was historically. As the camera pans over the wall, the viewers now see not just the signature Citgo sign—a piece of nostalgia itself—but also new, large, luxurious buildings. Such images are somewhat at odds with the sense of the team as a purveyor of "tradition."

Yet, such identification with tradition is clearly at play for fans trooping out to Fenway wearing retro-looking Red Sox caps, fans that will fill the video projections from the park. Part of the burgeoning of the city and its sports team results from a decidedly neoliberal take on the city's history of racism and ethnic exclusion. That is, racial exclusion can be dismissed as a byproduct of the market-based economy; those who are not white *can* participate in the city's offerings, if they can afford to.

As cities—including Boston—shifted from engines of production to consumerist models of attraction, sports became a key commodity in marketing place, participating in an environment for the massive gentrification that occurred in the 1990s and 2000s, which placed communities of lower socioeconomic status in a precarious position, and allowing the neoliberal "triumph" of market forces that resulted in not only some of the most expensive real estate in the county but also sports teams with some of the most expensive tickets. The neoliberal sports complex functioned as a kind of catalyst for gentrification that included the eradication of minority regions. As Barry Bluestone and Mary Huff Stevenson affirm, "The region may have a fascination with sports, music, and fine art, but one is apt to encounter a sea of white faces at a Red Sox or Celtics game, a Boston Symphony event, or an opening at the Museum of Fine Arts."[19] As gentrification continues apace, that sea is unlikely to become significantly more diverse.

Professional Sports and the Neoliberal City: Fenway—and Other—Parks

Because the region was even then a sizable and prosperous one, Boston was the location of a charter team in the American League when it was organized in 1901, though the team was not finally named the Red Sox until 1907. But its subsequent, and more recent, fate shows that the synergies that create success for a franchise also impact the broader enterprise of the city, rolling the conceptual associations that accrue to a particular franchise into a more generalized definition of a city. In their melding of sports with a larger conception of a city's brand, Fenway Park and the Red Sox are aspects of the twenty-first-century urban lifestyle, a transitory entity that is ever subject to alterations and enhancements but which, when connected to a specific place, may take on aspects of the embedded meanings and symbols of the recent, and not so recent, past. Fenway Park serves as an iconic symbol of a ballpark, a symbol that finds its way into all manner of media productions, including television and feature films. When we look at the many new ballparks built after the construction of Camden Yards (Baltimore) in 1992, all have aspects of the Boston ballpark, and all attempt to build on the nostalgia that surrounds the game of baseball and to affirm that these new structures are connected to that of a place like Fenway Park. In Baltimore, Pittsburgh, and Cleveland, for example, the job of marketers has been to sell the new as though it were old; in the case of Fenway Park, the job is to sell the old as the contemporary.[20] This gesture is of course in keeping with many aspects of the allure of Boston, a place marketed through its history but experienced for its contemporary amenities. For example, as one walks the Freedom Trail, it is appealing to stop at a well-appointed and commodious restaurant for lunch. One need not be subject to the smells of the Haymarket, an open-air market replete with ripening and rotting vegetables and meats approaching their expiration date, as it existed in 1935 in order to appreciate the city's deep historical roots or the significance of that region of the city.[21]

The sports industry is an element, among others, that appropriates a vision of the urban that shifts from the moment of mass urbanization around the turn of the twentieth century, to the 1950s city of production, to the twenty-first-century city defined by regimes of greater inequality and the power of consumption, where those who can afford to pay for them have access to any number of privatized services. Such a city is defined by its amenities; it is a place where work may take place in any number of regions and places, including in one's home. Such a definition undoes the earlier spatial order: suburbs retain aspects of their place in the 1950s organization of urban regions, but they are increasingly fraught with economic uncertainty and resources stretched to their maximum, as well as with a sense of their limits due to the absence of urban accouterments and the removal of some affluent residents.

From midcentury on, professional sports have served as a kind of bellwether of urban life. As a team finds itself failing, a decision is made to relocate either to another city or to the outlying regions of the urban area, depending on the relative features and status—both social and economic—of the urban region at that moment of change. Professional baseball requires a certain density of population, a level of affluence, and a generalized interest in the sport. During the 1950s, for example, professional baseball teams—the reigning sport of the era—increasingly migrated from decaying urban zones to greener pastures, sometimes in locales beyond the city center or in areas remote from the neighborhoods where the older stadia were built, and sometimes for new locations in cities outside of the urban Northeast.[22]

The case of the Red Sox and their ballpark provides a telling example of the shifts in urban scales of value that took place in the post-industrial era. In the early1960s, the Red Sox were a failing franchise in a failing city with poor attendance and a losing team. Fenway Park, as noted earlier, rather than seeming a treasure and marketable asset, was to the team's owners, the Yawkey family, and the fanbase an aging albatross that virtually assured failure on the field and discomfort for those who attended. Indeed, in the summer of 1967, a season that would mark a major shift for the team's fortune, as it came from out of nowhere to compete in the World Series, Tom Yawkey announced that he was looking for a site outside of the city of Boston for a new stadium: "'With a new stadium,' Yawkey said, 'this club would be a financial success. There's no doubt in my mind. Without one, it cannot be. And if I were disposed to sell; or something happening to my health, the person who took over the club would find it almost impossible to exist financially in Fenway Park.'"[23] The contrast of these assertions with the current fate of the ballpark and the team is stunning. Such a clear distinction between then and now suggests radically different cultural notions of value and its expression in marketing.

This earlier era of movement, investment, and disinvestment contrasts with that of the last decades of the twentieth century and the earliest of the twenty-first for many cities of the East and West Coasts, and to a lesser degree those in the Rust Belt. In this later period, the gentrified, somewhat depopulated cities of the United States became the sites of a resurgent and highly lucrative professional sports industry. By the last years of the twentieth century, the formerly working-class entertainment of professional athletics had been transformed into yet another domain primarily reserved for economic elites, with ticket prices, parking, and concessions spiraling upward. Boston serves as an excellent example since it was the city in the country with the greatest shift in average income and among the most gentrified by the beginning of the 2000s. As of 2015, the cost of attending a Red Sox game, including concessions and two tickets but not including parking, was just over $350.[24] The price of the average ticket alone had increased by 500 percent since 2001.[25] In juxtaposition, the average annual wage in Massachusetts, a reasonable geography for the broader fanbase, was just under $45,000 in 2001 and was $59,000 by 2013. For those in blue-collar occupations, such as in the installation, maintenance, and repair occupations, the pay was more modest: around $53,000, a small rise from $47,840 in 2001, and for those who worked in production, it was only $39,000, again up modestly from $35,760 in 2001.[26] Teams that had formerly played in the suburbs or at the extent of urban locales, after the 1970s almost all moved back to the city. Those who had been in the city rededicated themselves with new ballparks and arenas in areas that could be more broadly developed as entertainment zones—though often at the expense of the public.[27]

Prior to that in the 1950s, 1960s, and early 1970s, this decline in the fortunes of urban-based sports franchises coincided with a larger trend in urban despair. The nadir of the twentieth-century phase of the urban enterprise in the United States can be, as a matter of convenience and visibility, dated to October 1975, when the *New York Daily News* affirmed that the city of New York would not receive federal money to repay its bond obligations, and thus would begin to slide into default. The famous headline read, "Ford to City: Drop Dead," but to some degree that moment defined a symbolic low point; by later that year, the forces that would lead to a dramatic restructuring of many older cities in the East and West, and ultimately even some in the middle of the country, were already arrayed.[28] These forces would become definitional for the U.S. economy in the last part of the twentieth century and the beginning of the twenty-first, and included the luring of white-collar jobs back to the city through the use of tax incentives, abatements, and other economic incentives to attract developers. Cities also underwrote the creation of infrastructure to support financial services and information-based enterprises.

And the rebirth and blooming of professional sports in the city occurred as the urban enterprise changed and prospered. The post-1975 period marked an era of increasing deterioration and privatization of city services, a strategy that resulted in a two-tiered system of schools, police services, garbage collection, and certainly housing. In Boston, though the parks system expanded with the culmination of the Big Dig, the broader lack of investment in infrastructure led to increasingly dysfunctional schools, roads, and public transit.[29] Such a system emphasized a citizenry that could either pay for what it wanted or a demographic that had few housing choices and simply had to take the services available to them through public devices. By 1980, this trend away from suburbanization was clearly visible for those who could afford to be part of a gentrified city; properties ceased to add value based on their distance from city center. That trend began to reverse, and value was increasingly added by a property's proximity to a city center. This trend continues today.[30]

The resulting city demographic, then, is both wealthier and poorer than it was as of 1980, with the middle class largely leaving urban neighborhoods for suburban because the cost of improved urban space in cities as diverse as San Francisco, New York, Miami, and Philadelphia is just too expensive for most families. The social dimension of such an economic shift has resulted not in a greater number of whites necessarily living within city limits; rather, the shift is to greater numbers of *wealthy* whites inhabiting those enclaves, as poorer whites are increasingly migrating to the suburbs, as are wealthier Hispanics and African Americans. Thomas B. Edsall, in a piece published in February 2015 in the *New York Times*, wrote of the broader emphasis of recent data on gentrification and urbanization: "The nation's urban centers are changing rapidly. Blacks are moving out, into the suburbs or to other regions of the country. Poverty is spreading from the urban core to the inner suburbs. White flight has slowed and in some cases reversed. Nationally, Hispanics have displaced blacks as the dominant urban minority."[31]

Why have those with the means to live elsewhere returned to the city centers of certain locales? Clearly the momentum of such a macro change in consumer behavior is at least suggestive of a shift in cultural ideas of value and attraction, including the perceived, and then actual, value of specific spaces and the symbols that define them and which in turn they define. By the last two decades of the twentieth century, just after the busing crisis, as urban space within certain locales was in the process of being gentrified, a reappropriation and reforming of that space took place. It rejected the simple idea of the desirability of the "new" and the terms of the American Dream that had been associated with suburbia, and replaced it with a scale of value derived from a sense of the significance of attaching one's self to symbolic capital that boasted of history, tradition, spatial limits, and contiguous amenities. In effect, it selectively valorized a late nineteenth- and early twentieth-century moment of U.S. urban history, a time when cars were just being introduced to urban life and the city functioned as a space of social exchange and relative comfort. Such a shift in value and such a "reading" of the past almost necessarily involves a sepia-toned celebration of baseball and its symbols that speaks to that earlier historical moment.[32]

Professional sports are a cause of gentrification, and their enhanced economic success also results from that increase in the value and status of urban spaces. Such success in the 2000s derives from sports' widespread media presence and multifaceted marketing. It is intriguing that part of the massive transfer of wealth from the middle and lower tiers of the distribution ladder upward to those who are at the top of that scale has included the large-scale subsidization of professional sports teams.

Boston has not subsidized stadium construction in the same way, though it does have a fairly new arena (opened in 1995) in TD Garden, home to the

Bruins and Celtics, abutting the old Boston Garden. This did receive some federal and state subsidies as a matter of its mixed use as a transportation hub related to the Big Dig, along with some local property tax abatements. The Red Sox have also benefited from a deal with the city that allowed them to take abutting parcels through eminent domain and pay relatively light property taxes. Nevertheless, compared to cities like New York, Baltimore, Denver, or Cincinnati, Boston's public largesse to its sports franchises has been relatively meager.[33]

In the year 2019, just prior to the Covid-19 crisis, we were in something of a golden age of sports—at least in economic terms. If we look at the vast revenues of Major League Baseball, the National Football League, and the National Basketball Association, as well as the astronomical player salaries, there can be no doubt that sports as an industrial—or, indeed, post-industrial—phenomenon are flourishing as they never have before. Since the 1980s, with the rise of cable television and free agency—when a player is allowed to receive bids on a relatively open market for their services, after a certain term—professional and elite-level college sports have expanded exponentially in interest and revenue. According to Plunkett Database—a reliable provider of global market research—the overall economic activity in the United States from sports is $500 billion, while the worldwide figure is $1.5 trillion.[34] This figure has grown dramatically in the last three decades. MLB's attendance statistics reveal that the average crowd at a game in 1960 was around 14,000 and in 2015 it was over 30,000.[35] Similarly, the average value of a franchise grew from $376 million to $523 million in the recession-marked period from 2006 to 2011.[36] When we think of international brands such as Nike or ESPN, it is clear they have been defined by professional sports and have become iconic for the post-industrial age, further linking sports commerce to the scale and terms of digital commerce more generally.

Race, Boston, and the Red Sox

Boston, as detailed in earlier chapters, has a legacy of racism that has found its expression and dissemination in a variety of visible narratives. The story of the Red Sox intersects with those narratives. As the brand of the city and that of the team co-mingle in the digital age, the legacy of the past remains embedded in concepts of team and place. The case of the Red Sox is one with broader implications for understanding the increasingly gentrified, post-industrial city, and the city that was the site of, and is known for, various acts of racial violence and exclusion. The team has furthered a notion of the city, a city where the keywords "tradition" and "authenticity" assert a conception of place. But can those terms be emptied of their racist content, especially when the device for employing them, a key symbol, is a team with a vexed racial history? I would argue that this area—agreement on racist policies and exclusions—is part of the associative glue between team and place, making the city of Boston both the home of busing and of the last major league team to integrate.

The Red Sox as a franchise and brand, like the city, are deeply associated with racist acts and intentions, a tag that is part of the city's historical legacy, one that connects the team to the busing crisis and the Charles Stuart case, among other related matters. Although the team has also largely, though not completely, emerged from the cloud of this association in more recent times, this legacy remains just below the surface. As discussed in previous chapters, contemporary perspectives on place are an amalgam of materiality and conceptual projections, now often digitally conveyed. These include marketing, history, and invented traditions of place as well as the presence of a number of these elements in the virtual firmament. In the case of the Red Sox, the various tropes that have increasingly come to define post-industrial Boston are very much operative. Some history here is illustrative.

In his excellent book about race and the Red Sox, *Shut Out: A Story of Race and Baseball in Boston*, journalist Howard Bryant details the poisonous racial history of the franchise, including that of the Yawkey family. He traces this legacy back to the relationship between Tom Yawkey and his foster father, Bill, and the looming and decidedly bigoted figure of Ty Cobb. It was Cobb who initially suggested that Yawkey use his inherited fortune to buy a team, and Yawkey did so in the midst of the Depression in 1933. Bryant points out that the three teams most resistant to integration and then to signing and developing talented African American players—the Red Sox, Tigers, and Phillies, the last three major league teams to integrate—all had in common a connection to the Ty Cobb Tigers of the 1910s and 1920s, and to their owner, Walter Briggs.[37]

The Red Sox remained an all-white team until 1959, when they signed Elijah "Pumpsie" Green, becoming the last of the major league teams to integrate, a choice that had lasting results for the team and the city. Indeed, one of the explanations for the failure of the Red Sox in the 1950s and 1960s was their lack of willingness to sign African American players and retain them. This was a result of the racism of the team's ownership and management, as well as its fanbase and broader civic situation. Reggie Smith became the team's first African American player of significance in the late 1960s. Just prior to Smith's emergence, in 1966, African American pitcher Earl Wilson, a young talent, was summarily traded to the Tigers after protesting a spring training incident where a bartender in Lakeland, Florida, refused to serve him. The stories of African American players and their trials with the team and with the city are legion. Players from Earl Wilson to Reggie Smith to Jim Rice to Tommy Harper found Boston and Fenway Park a distinctly toxic environment. In the 1970s, as the busing crisis simmered, there are no recorded instances of that conflict coming into the ballpark. It largely remained a backdrop. But its presence and what it signified about the city was by no means lost on players of that generation. Anecdotally, African American players have told about feeling unwelcome in certain places and parts of the city, with one of those places being Fenway Park.[38]

The Red Sox of the mid-1960s had seen little recent competitive success. It was the very embodiment of an organization built to fail. Yawkey apparently had little strategic sense or pressing desire to build a viable franchise that could remain a competitive entity over time. In 1967, as Dick O'Connell, a forward-looking figure in Red Sox management, took control of the team, the Red Sox almost miraculously competed for and then won the American League championship. That O'Connell saw fit to change the culture of the team and actively seek out Black and Brown players was based on a reading of a market on the rise. If we look at the opening of the Prudential building two years earlier and the reemergence of the Red Sox, we can plot the city's increased success and the team's return to relevance. Subsequently, the Red Sox have largely remained a competitive team and an economically successful one for most years since. After drawing only 652,000 fans in 1965, they have drawn over 2 million since 1990 and over 3 million in recent years. These changes in fortunes largely occurred as the team's value increased, as did its ability to contract better players in the era of baseball's free agency after 1976.[39] Such changes in fortune led to a shift in the conception of the city's brand and contributed to the broader re-conception of the city through various media.

In the world of baseball, in broader demographic terms, the Red Sox became more integrated as the city did, and as they became more integrated, they became more successful on the field and at the counting-house. As the team prospered from the 1970s to the 2000s, it developed a significant Afro-Caribbean presence, from the Cuban-born Luis Tiant in the 1970s to the teams of the late 1990s and 2000s that were anchored by the Dominican stars Pedro Martinez, Manny Ramirez, and David Ortiz. All of these post-1967 occurrences suggest the ways in which broader social change impacts that of sports. As the city became more diverse, so did the team associated with it. But this is not to say that the vexed racial history of the team ceased to play a role in its image. The Red Sox remain associated with that history, and to some degree that history is embedded in its brand.

But even as this legacy seems to have waned in the 1990s and 2000s, this was nonetheless at the point where economic conditions and the spatial terms of gentrification made Fenway largely inaccessible to many people of color for economic reasons. Those who can afford a few hundred dollars to attend will largely find an environment that is not overtly hostile and a team that includes any number of Black and Brown players. The Red Sox organization does not tolerate overt expressions of racism at Fenway and to some extent tries to sanitize the team's troubled past. One recent issue has been the renaming of the street abutting the ballpark, Thomas Yawkey Way. Some have objected to the honoring of the former team owner's legacy of racism, and in 2018 the name reverted to the previous one, Jersey Street.[40] The community relations portion of the Red Sox organization is actively involved in supporting a health center in Roxbury and a fund that supports African American youth baseball.

By all measures professional sports have thrived inordinately since the Reagan era, benefiting from the policies of neoliberalism that redistributed wealth to those who were already wealthy. This is emphatically true for the Red Sox. More broadly, the age of cable television, digital transmission, new ballparks (often publicly financed), and all manner of media saturation involving professional sports has led to a geometric rise in team value and revenue. If we look at sports as part symptom and part cause of the neoliberal moment in national and international culture and economics, all of this makes sense. The runup to this moment began just at the visible moment of inexorable decline of the U.S. city and its connection to the national and international industrial economy. One of the aspects of the story Elihu Rubin tells of the dawning of the "New Boston" is its ushering in the as-not-yet realized post-industrial milieu of Boston in 1965, as the Prudential

Center opened and ensconced a major insurance company as a pillar of the emergent economy, while also remaking the city's landscape with a major office and retail development in a formerly declining sector of the city—and one within walking distance of Fenway Park.[41]

But as 1965 provided a link to the city's future, the year 1967 provides us with a confluence of events that both revealed the state of the city and suggested the broader state of urban America. The dawning of the neoliberal moment in U.S. urban history had a distinct racial component, indeed a racist component. The reemergence of the city in the later 1970s and beyond was explicitly a turning away from considerations of racial and class equity. After the civil unrest of 1965, particularly the Watts Riot in an African American neighborhood of Los Angeles, subsequent summers brought the fear and expectation of further racial unrest. To some degree that unrest was not realized—until the summer of 1967 when Newark and Detroit erupted. In June of that year, in Boston's Roxbury neighborhood, a group of African American women, known at the time as Mothers for Adequate Welfare, were demonstrating at the social services office for an increase in benefits. When they were denied, they came back and locked themselves into the office building. They were soon removed. In response, the neighborhood erupted.

The Harvard University student paper reported on the event: "The violence of the evening left Blue Hill Ave. in a shambles. Storefronts were smashed. Apartment windows were broken. Businesses were looted. Two buildings were burned. The next day officials estimated the damage at $500,000."[42] The visible racial tensions in the city were a fairly recent phenomenon, though the racism that triggered disdain by white residents for African Americans was not. As the second Black migration took place in the late 1940s and 1950s, Boston's population of racial minorities grew significantly. Its African American population went from 3.1 percent in 1940 to 16.3 in 1970, and around 25 percent in 1990.[43] This increased African American presence had the impact of exacerbating extant white racism and affirming an environment of segregation by race but also by class.

Racial inequities in the context of Boston became part of the stasis and "tradition" connected to the city's brand. The profusion of white faces is a prominent aspect of the social environment at Fenway Park. It is also the virtual environment that millions of viewers encounter on their various electronic devices. The ways in which "tradition" is invoked in the celebration of these teams affirm a kind of pride in the deep roots of the city's decidedly racist and ethnocentric past. But how are these visions of tradition invoked, and how are they also sanitized—at least on the surface?

Image Is Reality: Sports, Media, Information Capital, and Red Sox Nation

Sports marketing fundamentally changed in the 1990s. This was largely as a result of the innovations and interventions of Nike and its founder, Phil Knight. In his analysis of the role of the image of Michael Jordan in the rise of the international Nike brand, the historian Walter Lafeber writes of Knight's latching on to the idea of sports marketing because of the ways in which competition creates winners and losers, and marketing a winner provided a ready entrée to a mass audience. Other athletic merchandise companies followed Nike's lead in the 1990s, including the Boston-based Reebok and New Balance Brands—both of which have been sold to multinational corporations as of this writing. But neither achieved the prominence or exhibited the marketing savvy and innovation of Knight and Nike, so Nike stands as the exemplar of the breakthrough of sports-related international branding and marketing. For Knight, and then for many others seeking the imprimatur of a "winning" image, that connection to an ultimately worldwide audience was powered by the same devices that allowed for its shoes to be made in Japan—and then Korea, and then Vietnam—and sold in the United States, and then the North American continent, and then Western Europe and Asia. These devices included satellites, computers, shipping containers, and all manner of international modes of trade and communication. Michael Jordan became a figure who both embodied the marketing power of sports and transcended that commercial force.[44] And though Nike's marketing breakthrough was, as noted, more inflected toward basketball, its methods and success had implications for all major spectator sports, including baseball.

Within the regime of what David Harvey has termed "flexible accumulation," or neoliberalism, successful locales are far less place-bound than they were in the industrial age. That is, they operate largely in the stratosphere of interregional and international exchange and in the circulation of products that are often immaterial—such as Nike's marketing of its distinctive logo—but that are expressive of capital wealth.[45] And the more each place is someplace but no place in particular, or no place in particular at all, the greater the incentive to put a stamp on a locale with a resonant and affirming image emblematic of a similarly positive narrative. But that stamp is also largely a matter of the virtual world. In a digital age, accouterments of place are a matter of its conceptual resonance and can be affixed to an apparently concrete object. It only follows that, as the city has succeeded, the economic value and footprint of the Red Sox has exploded since 1990. The Red Sox as of 2015 were valued at $2.1 billion. In 2002, they were valued at $426 million. This proportional increase far outpaced the average growth in value of a MLB franchise.[46]

The burgeoning of the sports enterprise in Boston was part of a larger economic growth of the industry that accompanied the rebirth and accelerating gentrification of certain older U.S. and Canadian cities. If we think of professional sports as aspects of the information age and the neoliberal/nonproductive economy, then their explosion in value in the 1980s and 1990s makes perfect sense, and their continued growth in the age of digital media in the 2000s was also predictable. As the fate of cities was reaching its bottom in the mid-1970s, the rebirth of world cities was very much tied to their connection to global information systems.

The story of sports and the post-industrial moment includes equal parts global trade and communications innovations. In addition to being a time for the rebirth of the Red Sox, the 1970s were a moment where a communications revolution took place that included the transmission of information globally through the use of satellite technology. As it was for the city more generally, the digital revolution was transformative for professional sports and the reach and definition of each team's brand. From 1976 to 1980, cable television, then a fledgling and largely money-losing industry, began broadcasting through communications satellites, with sports as an important component. The pioneers of this application of satellite technology included HBO, owned by Charles Dolan, who would go on to found Cablevision, and Ted Turner who founded TBS, TNT, and CNN. Not coincidentally, Dolan would become the principal of Madison Square Garden (MSG) cable, and his son would become the owner of the New York Knicks. Turner would use his station substantially as a means to broadcast his sports teams, the Atlanta Braves and the Atlanta Hawks. The Braves were the first nationally available team, programming via satellite transmission in 1976. In 1979, the Cubs, owned by the Wrigley family at that time, became another quasi-national team, transmitting games via satellite through the auspices of WGN, a broadcast entity of the *Chicago Tribune*. In 1982, following the financial model of Turner, the Tribune Company bought the team.

To see the burgeoning of sports media as vitally connected to the explosion in world commerce that marked the 1980s and 1990s requires no large leap of the imagination. Those very same satellites that were transmitting the Braves to homes in Boise and Walla Walla were also allowing a clothing entrepreneur in Manhattan to call in his order to a factory in Central America, and would later provide the device for sending via fax and then email a highly specific dress design. It would also allow for expedited shipping through the use of advanced weather tracking and GPS systems.

In effect, sports as a commodity exponentially grew and became global through the same deregulated, technology-saturated environment as securities trading. The growth of superstations WGN and TBS in the late 1970s relied on a bet that sports as a commodity could be enhanced through new technologies and then resold to advertisers for a geometric gain. This view was not simply a shrewd judgment; it also reveals a business strategy that placed sports on a developing multimedia platform amid other entities held by these diversified communications companies. The culmination of this trend toward international sports broadcasting and the decline of the local is the emergence and burgeoning in the 1990s of ESPN, now owned by the Disney Company. ESPN began as a small cable presence in 1979, with obscure programming and limited broadcast hours. By 1984, ABC had purchased the network for $227 million. By 1987, it was available in 50 percent of all U.S. homes. In the 2000s, it carried major sporting events, such as the NBA and MLB playoffs. The Red Sox also featured as a regular broadcast on ESPN, and even more so since 2004, particularly when they play the Yankees. Such a presence enhances the national and international visibility for both teams and thus adds to their relative success.

Since the late 1970s, the Red Sox have become active participants in the production and dissemination of their games, and therefore their brand, through electronic means. In many ways, these electronic transmissions of games and news are a furtherance of the media explosion that began in the 1920s when Red Sox games were transmitted on radio through local carriers who paid the team a rights fee. From the late 1940s to the 1980s, the Red Sox were carried only on local, over-the-air stations. By the early 1990s, the majority of games were exclusively on the New England Sports Network

(NESN). As of 2006, the Red Sox broadcast was only available through subscription to NESN, via cable or by streaming subscription. With the shift in the technical dimensions of the medium came a commensurate alteration of its range of dissemination. What also changed was the fiduciary relationship between the team and the network.

This change in the scale of the team's financial fortunes and the means by which revenue has been enhanced followed from a shift in ownership that resulted in a significant alteration in business strategy. After the Jean R. Yawkey Trust (the bequest of Yawkey's wife) sold the Red Sox to investment entrepreneur and hedge-fund operator John Henry in 2002 for $380 million, the team underwent a significant modernization in all aspects of its operations. The Henry syndicate included media mogul Tom Werner and brought on Larry Lucchino, a former partner of Bennett and Williams, a prominent Washington, DC, law firm, as its managing partner. As of today, the Fenway Sports Group, the umbrella organization created when the Red Sox were purchased, also owns Roush Fenway Racing, an Indy Car concern; the Liverpool soccer team; and NESN. John Henry himself recently bought the *Boston Globe* from the *New York Times* syndicate, which was also a minority partner in the purchase of the Red Sox in 2002.

NESN, however, was not the creation of the Fenway Sports Group. It came into existence in 1986 but its immediate impact was limited by the constraints of cable television in the 1980s. As of 2016, NESN has 4.1 million cable subscribers and was named by *Forbes* magazine as the thirteenth most valuable sports brand in the world. Indeed, part of the allure for the Henry Group in purchasing the Red Sox was the existence of AT&T-installed broadband cable throughout New England and NESN as part of that region's basic cable package. "We were late to that game, frankly," NESN CEO Sean McGrail said in a 2014 interview. "The old [Red Sox] ownership group wasn't in love with that idea. They just didn't understand it and hadn't really embraced that as a transitional method for NESN to really expand our reach."[47] It wasn't until the Yawkey Trust took over the team and ceded their management to businessman John Harrington that the value of NESN was clearly perceived. For the Henry Group, its enhancement is one of the group's central business strategies.

By the early 2000s MLB had launched its own streaming service, MLB TV, a remarkably successful service that today counts for the overwhelming number of viewers of the sport. Baseball fans can access every game being played from virtually any place in the world that has sufficient bandwidth, as well as earlier games, which are archived. As of 2023, MLB has sold rights for broadcasting and digital transmission to streaming services such as AppleTV, Hulu, and Peacock, further enlarging the reach for the digital broadcast of games—which are now broadcast in English and Spanish. This expansion of the sport's digital reach has led to a greater international following, including in Europe and Asia, as well as Mexico and Central and South America. Such a dissemination of the game electronically has in turn inspired successful events such as the World Baseball Classic, and spawned international games in places like London and Mexico City. The World Baseball Classic originated in 2006, and MLB became a sponsoring entity in 2013.[48] As of 2023, it has prospered in a variety of international locations and drawn fans to its broadcast and digital transmission through Fox Sports.

Not only has brand visibility—and profitability—for the Red Sox been enhanced by their own media outlets; the Red Sox have also benefited greatly from the rise of ESPN as the definitional media outlet—and an increasingly international one—in sports from the mid-1980s onward. When ESPN was founded by two New England–based entrepreneurs and built its headquarters in Bristol, Connecticut, it was difficult to imagine how closely linked it would be to the newspaper of record in the region, the *Boston Globe*. In the earlier 1960s, the *Globe*, like the Red Sox, was a relatively modest enterprise. It had a middling rank among the city's many papers and was thought of as an entrenched voice of the city's largely Catholic—and predominantly Irish—community. All of that changed with the hiring of Thomas Winship as its editor in 1965, a job he kept until 1984. Winship was substantially responsible for making the *Globe* into a liberal and national paper. His leadership saw the paper move away from its parochial roots and develop not only in-depth coverage but also a breadth of emphases, including in sports. And of course, the enlarging and enhancing of the *Globe* as a regional and national, and to a lesser degree, international newspaper was materially involved in both its investigation of sexual abuse in the church and of Whitey Bulger. Such reach and visibility further emerged from the availability of the newspaper through digital means and an online readership that has increased over time. As of 2023, for the modest price of a digital subscription, the digital version of the newspaper can be accessed from anywhere in the world, and the *Globe* claims over 200,000 digital subscribers.

In the early 1970s, Winship began to remake and expand the paper's sports section with the hiring of two young writers, former interns Bob Ryan and Peter Gammons. Both would go on to long and glorious careers: the former as the Celtics beat writer and columnist, and the latter as the Red Sox beat writer and columnist. And as the *Globe*'s sports page became a national standard, its writers and editors increasingly found their way to the fledgling cable sports network, where they continued to emphasize Boston sports and the Red Sox in particular.

The team's close relationship with the burgeoning ESPN enterprise only helped its, and the city's, visibility enhancing the team's national and international prominence. Such visibility has led to greater success and prominence. The Red Sox and Fenway's frequent appearance on national broadcasting venues enhances the city's brand. As of 2023, it is the third most valuable MLB franchise with a valuation of $4.5 billion.[49] It is also among the most visible teams in baseball, dominating—along with the Yankees—the national broadcast schedule. By one measure, the Red Sox have frequently been on ESPN's Sunday night baseball broadcast the maximum number of times allowable—by contract—per year (five times), and they appear on Fox for the Game of the Week the maximum number of times per season (twelve). Moreover, this does not include appearances on the MLB Network or in the postseason. While this data forms a backdrop for a larger measure of team and city success, it suggests that nothing enhances a brand more than the reiteration and embellishment of its core qualities. Although the Red Sox have been largely successful competitively in the last two and a half decades or so, their brand remains relatively undiminished, as does their visibility, when they are less successful. The current success of the Red Sox and the city of Boston provides two structures on which hang a postmodern narrative of place, one that employs elements of the city's historical past but negates certain aspects of it in order to reduce it to key terms that make it both authentic and attractive.

In broad terms, then, the success of the associative branding of the Red Sox has resulted in a kind of mass identification dubbed "Red Sox Nation." In ways, this title is the ultimate marker of the franchise's brand and the success of the various platforms employed in disseminating it. It is common to see a baseball game in Tampa or Baltimore or Toronto at which the sheer volume of Red Sox–branded regalia far eclipses those dressed in the garb of the home team, or to hear cheers for the visiting team drown out those for the locals. One part of the explanation is Boston's large student population, so that transient and brief Bostonians identify intensely with the team of that city. But this is only a partial and perhaps not very satisfying definition. For a broader view, there is a kind of resonance in the ways in which the team evokes place that feeds off notions of tradition and authenticity that we could see in other public evocations of place, including the news stories discussed in chapters 1 and 2.

This branding goes beyond the games themselves and finds its way into films, television shows, and journalism. Films such as *Field of Dreams* (1989), *Money Ball* (2011), *The Town* (2010), *A Civil Action* (1998), *Fever Pitch* (2005), and *Good Will Hunting* (1997), among others, employ the ballpark as an important location, trading on its visibility and iconic, authentic Boston-ness. And even when it's not there, it is invoked repeatedly, as in Clint Eastwood's estimable *Mystic River* (2001). Television shows with Boston connections almost all pay homage to the Red Sox and Fenway Park: *Ray Donovan, Cheers, Boston Legal, St. Elsewhere*. It is also the site of a range of works of fiction—*Murder at Fenway Park* (Trey Soos, 2017), *The Prince of Fenway Park* (Julianna Baggott, 2009), and *My Most Excellent Year: A Novel of Love, Mary Poppins, and Fenway Park* (Elizabeth Bush, 2008), among many, and iconic journalism by John Updike, Stephen King, Doris Kearns Goodwin, John Cheever, David Halberstam, and nationally visible sportswriters including Peter Gammons, Bill Simmons, Bob Ryan, and Charles Pierce.

The Red Sox, despite the economic scale of the game—salaries, ticket prices, overall team payroll, overall revenues—maintain a kind of working-class association due to their historical legacies and their associations with place. While Boston is depicted through the visual iconography of neighborhoods and three-decker houses, Fenway Park serves as a kind of baseball equivalent of such housing in its age, placed in what was formerly a fairly unprepossessing, largely light industrial neighborhood of the city, and associated with a past that includes its status as a place habituated by white, working-class fans. Explain Greg Ramshaw and Sean Gammon in their wider discussion of sports heritage as a marketing device, "Like other forms of heritage, sport draws from many sources including history, nostalgia, memory, myth and tradition in order to meet the demands of the present, which may include the establishment of roots or traditions, the creation or re-articulation of identity, or even the need for economic or social rehabilitation."[50] In a world in which image is all, and image is ephemeral, the rootedness of an authentic place (Boston, Fenway Park), a stalwart and previously struggling franchise, and an apparently focused and faithful working-class fanbase has a powerful emotional appeal. And that appeal translates into a mass of digital images that represent association and affiliation with the team. Images of the Red Sox and Fenway Park are disseminated widely in the digital stratosphere, all the while maintaining an apparent anchor in Boston, at a place that is bound by the Mass Pike and Kenmore Square.

CHAPTER FOUR

Race and Celtics Pride

In this chapter, I explore the relationship between the Celtics, another of the city's signature professional sports franchises—one currently substantially composed of African American players and African American coaches—and the recurring idea of "Boston." The Celtics on one level should have little to do with the negations connected to racism embedded in the city's brand, and the related image of the city as it developed over time and over a variety of technological platforms, or with the vexed legacy of Tom Yawkey's Red Sox. Yet, areas of conceptual overlap exist and raise a number of questions regarding associations, residual definitions, and motivated behavior. This overlap is largely a matter of media emphases on those aspects of Celtics-related iconography and narrative elements that fit the dominant definition of place. And since place is, in contemporary terms, a matter of its terms of mediation, then the impact of "Boston" on the team inevitably leads into these parameters of definition.

This chapter explores the associations between team and city, how they emerge and evolve, paying attention both to a broader social context and the situation of professional basketball in the range of national and international entertainments. It also considers the ways that context and brand enlarge through the devices of digital media. I show how connections between place and brand take in a range of factors, both historical and contemporary, to create an image of a team and a place that cannot fully escape from legacies of ethnocentrism and racism. I trace the origins of the team, as well as its significant choice of a name, and show its emergent image and connection with the residual image of the city. Finally, I explain how the neoliberal incarnation and dissemination of the team's brand retransmits elements of the team's and city's legacy.

The Boston Celtics and the Boston Red Sox share their associations with their named locale, drawing meaning from its apparent solidity as a "real" geography. And though each team has its own discrete history, the power of the "Boston" part of the team's name has involved the Celtics in a narrative of racial exclusion and casual racism that migrated from the naming of place and the shadow of the more overt racist practices of the local baseball team. The Red Sox and Celtics have very different histories and trajectories—ownership, resonant stars, fanbases—yet that they are associated so easily suggests the power of place as a conceptual marker steering a social narrative, and the enhanced power of place in a marketplace defined by digital branding. In the case of Boston, the meaning of place emerges from its historical icons, its ambience and architecture, its connection to Catholicism (as well as a more historically embedded Calvinism), and its vexed legacy and practice of racism. Such associations also suggest the ways in which the multiple mass-media devices of urban branding may affix meanings to highly visible entities—and how those meanings can recirculate to define further iterations of place. Such connections of image, or entity, and meaning result in a circulation of associations that is both reflective *and* generative.

In mass culture, the ideas of tradition and authenticity are often connected to notions of whiteness and racial exclusion, since the narrative of place frequently finds those ideas as aspects of a racially exclusionary usable past. In sports, beset by a history that includes discrimination and segregation (like professional basketball and Major League Baseball), when we venerate an earlier epoch, the racial narrative of exclusion inevitably creeps in. Spectator sports emerged in the era of industrialization. In the context of Boston, these notions of ethnicity are connected to a reading of tradition that privileges whiteness.[1] The emergence of the Boston Celtics as a "white" team (at least relatively, in National Basketball Association terms) in the late 1970s and 1980s easily involved it in a racial narrative that connected to matters of place and had the effect of marking the team's brand. Boston is a place strongly identified with elaborations of white ethnicity that link back to the later nineteenth and early twentieth centuries. This is not to say that the city's attraction as a place of deep historical meanings *necessarily* includes elements of racism, only that without a conscious effort to repel that aspect of its history, it will remain barely beneath the surface.

The images of the city partially produced through coverage of Boston's major sporting events often show pictures or sites such as the Statehouse, the Old North Church, Paul Revere's house, or Harvard and MIT, revealing a city of history and distinction, emphasizing its place as a historical center of the United States. These images that fill out coverage of games since the 2000s also show a city that is prosperous and booming, a city of construction cranes, of new glass and steel skyscrapers. Such images and their persistence suggest the repositioning of sports within the neoliberal moment, a moment from which Boston has benefited and that has been definitional for the recrafted city. Such digital images are not usually or necessarily a matter of focused advertising campaigns. They tend to rise up in the media ecosystem as conventions, associating place with certain words and images, creating resonant chronotopes. They strongly emphasize a kind of conceptual shorthand that easily leads to broad associations and assumptions about place, and therefore also serve as adjuncts to urban branding. But residual definitions of place remain, providing an image of a city well lodged in previous decades, defined by earlier social values and decidedly different demographics. The furtherance of this anachronistic definition occurs as its visible sports teams—also part of the neoliberal vision of culture—can be seen on all manner of digital devices—phones, tablets, laptops, televisions—playing before mostly white fans who watch the relatively Brown and Black teams on the field or court. This spectacle not only points to the ways in which a multicultural ideal reifies embedded concepts of diversity while uncritically sweeping away important notions of class with distinctly racial—and historically racial—implications; such images also have the impact of affirming their own bracketed social reality.

The ways in which "tradition" is invoked in the celebration of the Celtics affirms a kind of pride in the deep roots of the city's decidedly ethnocentric past. But how are these visions of tradition invoked, and how are they also sanitized—at least on a surface level? As baseball's national presence embodies a kind of Americanness, branding it as a sport that reeks of nostalgia and assumptive tradition, it lends itself easily to embedded ideas of place that are evocative of an idealization of an earlier time. But professional basketball has its own cultural and historical narrative, one that the Celtics both fall within and without. Basketball has been historically associated with urban life and its place as a center for recently arrived ethnic populations, as well as for African Americans leaving rural or small-town life. Arguably, its place in the mass culture of the United States has been linked to its international allure, that is, basketball's visible participants since the 1970s—African American and now international, but overall proportionately Black and Brown—make it, in one sense, the sport of a different narrative of the United States, one that can ultimately emerge as that of an anticolonial and antiracist vision of nation.[2]

Of course, this is an unrealized ideal, but the visual presentation of that ideal can be read into the image of an NBA game, and through that reading, especially in contemporary terms, basketball stands as a paragon of progressive policies and values among professional sports. Indeed, as the nation experienced significant social turbulence in the summer of 2020 after the murder of George Floyd, the NBA, including its leadership, were at the forefront of the protests. In an internal memo, league commissioner Adam Silver stated, "I spent the weekend watching the protests around the country over the deaths of George Floyd, Ahmaud Arbery and Breonna Taylor. As a league, we share the outrage and offer our sincere condolences to their families and friends. Just as we are fighting a pandemic, which is impacting communities and people of color more than anyone else, we are being reminded that there are wounds in our country that have never healed."[3] Such a presence for the league and the game speaks to significant changes in the world and in the United States over the last forty or so years, and in more pronounced terms over the last twenty. That the sport has such a notable place in the post-2000 world would have seemed unlikely seventy years ago, and similarly unlikely even in the last thirty. Professional basketball is neither "the national pastime," and thus associated with a preindustrial ideal (baseball), nor "America's sport," a game with industrial and militaristic contours well-suited to television (football). Basketball's presence on television remains relatively limited in comparison to these other major sports, and its fanbase is far narrower, yet its presence in the United States and in international sports culture is indeed significant, easily eclipsing baseball and football as an international game, and thus decidedly outside of narrowly nationalist visions of sport. It is a sport that celebrates its diversity but which, at least in the United States, is also commercially constrained by it. The marketing issue for the NBA has long been whether it is too Black and Brown to garner a mass audience. The Celtics (in their Boston market) have been expressive of these issues, and the franchise's means of addressing and resisting them is revealing as well as intriguing.

Basketball's Past

The National Basketball Association (NBA) did not emerge as an entity until after World War II, in 1949, long after the establishment of the two major leagues of baseball and the entrenchment of the National Football League, and it did not become a truly successful sports organization until the David Stern era in the 1990s. Prior to the emergence of the NBA, basketball was decidedly a niche sport. It developed as an urban game, suited for limited spaces and requiring limited equipment—just a ball or something that could be used instead of a ball, and a hoop, or something that could be used instead of a hoop. In this regard, it is more like soccer—at least, as it exists in almost every country except the United States—than like baseball, which needs gloves, bats, and much more space. Since basketball emerged as an urban game in the early twentieth century, it has been played among working-class populations, primarily by white ethnics and African American communities, groups that were overrepresented in urban America in the 1930s and 1940s, never fully connecting with a predominantly white, more prosperous, less Catholic and Jewish mass audience. Indeed, in this era of burgeoning world and national antisemitism, basketball suffered by its association with Jewish players and fans. Wrote one commentator: "Easy to learn and inexpensive to play, basketball attracted young Jewish children. All that was required was a ball or rolled up rags, and a goal. Thousands of Jewish children played the game morning, noon, and night. A distinct style began to emerge—more running, passing, and cutting to the basket. Soon thereafter, basketball was being referred to as a Jewish sport."[4] This designation was a means of marginalizing the game, as well as defining it as one that was endemically connected to an often-disparaged ethnic group. Such associations are instructive as we see basketball later defined as a game suited to and played by African Americans, a definition that would present its own impediments to achieving a mass audience in the United States. The prevalence of segregated teams in a sport that seemed to break down such barriers shows the ways in which the sport challenged the assumptions of segregation through the affirmation of white and Black bodies engaged in precisely the same activities, even as it also affirmed racist practices of the era. The first integrated college teams occurred in the late 1940s and gradually became more usual in the 1950s, with the integrated teams of the University of San Francisco in 1955 and 1956, featuring future Celtics players KC Jones and Bill Russell. But integrated teams did not become the rule until after the passage of the Civil Rights Act in 1964, and then only after an all African American team from Texas Western won the NCAA championship in 1966.[5]

In the 1930s and early 1940s, professional basketball was primarily a barnstorming concern, one dominated by the New York–based Original Celtics, the New York Rens (or Renaissance), and later the Harlem Globetrotters. The Globetrotters, owned by entertainment impresario Abe Saperstein, formed in the mid-1930s in Chicago and played outside of the Northeast region dominated by the Rens and Celtics, mostly in the South and Midwest. Significantly, the Celtics were the white team, featuring a number of Jewish players, and the Rens were African American. This bifurcation was reflective of a society defined by segregation, much as baseball had its segregated leagues. The designation "Harlem" for the Globetrotters, who had nothing to do with New York, was a sign to let bookers and fans know that the team was African American. The New York Celtics, an earlier team, were disbanded in 1918 shortly after the United States entered World War I. A related team later emerged as an American Basketball League (ABL) franchise in the later 1920s known as the Original Celtics. They began barnstorming after 1930 with the name denoting a white team, mostly of ethnic German, Jewish, Irish, and Italian Americans. Boston was a stop on the tours of the 1930s and briefly had a team in the 1920s incarnation of the all-white ABL, called the Whirlwinds, though by the end of that one season the team had moved out of the Boston Arena, with a capacity of five thousand or so, to Somerville and a decidedly smaller arena. The associations of the game and its predominant players help us to situate the history of basketball within a broader cultural context, one that was decidedly racist and ethnocentric, and also antiurban. That is, although the sport did eventually branch out into rural areas, it was largely considered a city sport played by city people. As such, the sport both lived within the contours of the racist and ethnocentric social mores of the time *and* pushed against those norms as a result of its status outside of dominant white, Protestant norms.[6]

The NBA began as a modest enterprise, beset by a range of financial challenges. Its immediate predecessor, the Basketball Association of America (BAA), was designed to compete with and then supersede the preexisting National Basketball League (NBL), and, as a means of promoting its financial stability and ultimate success, included as its principals men who owned arenas and hockey teams in many of the major cities on the East Coast, including the Celtics' owner Walter Brown, the Philadelphia Warrior's owner Eddie Gottlieb, and the New York Knickerbockers' owner Ned Irish. The merger between the NBL and BAA brought from the NBL the Indianapolis, Minneapolis, Rochester, Syracuse, and Fort Wayne franchises, all of which—with the exception of Indianapolis—were destined to survive, in other forms, into the twenty-first century.

The NBA's audience was limited and its gradual success did not begin to emerge until the cultural and demographic changes of the post–World War II-era—expanding wealth, expanding leisure time, the beginning of the Baby Boom, a lessening (in ways) of racial and ethnic boundaries—created conditions that allowed for its commercial growth. Then more dramatic, post-1980s cultural and economic shifts in all of these areas made it an important sport for that time. These factors again included the further rise of leisure time for middle-class Americans, the upward mobility of white ethnic populations and some African Americans in the civil rights era, and the gradual urbanization of an increasingly moneyed class that was in the process of gentrifying certain U.S. cities. Indeed, in the 1980s and beyond, an affluent class grew and spent increasing amounts of money on spectator sports—including professional basketball.

The growth of mass-media platforms from the 1950s on—radio, television, cable television, digital platforms—helped to enhance the sport's visibility. In the 1950s, the Celtics, and the NBA more generally, were broadcast through local radio stations. In Boston, that was the 50,000-watt WHDH—which also carried the Red Sox—owned by the *Boston Herald*. At the time, radio was considered more a matter of marketing than of income generation. This arrangement was similar to that of other teams in major markets—the Knicks, the Philadelphia Warriors, the Pistons, and so on. Local television entered the picture in limited ways in the early 1960s, and then national television in the later 1960s. But the airing of national games remained quite limited, creating space for cable broadcasts in the early 1980s. As an index of the limits of the NBA's media presence, in the 1989–90 season CBS broadcast only sixteen games. In 1987, CBS broadcast the first live, pre-finals-round playoff game. It was not until the 1990s that the NBA finals were broadcast live at night as a regular, annual occurrence.

While the NBA ascended gradually with initial limits on both its media presence and the demand for that presence, it has thrived as a global sport in the digital age when restrictions on audience and ideas of affiliation have become more elastic. It is the U.S.-based sport most connected with international digital branding and urban lifestyles, major consumerist lures that have been a boon for the sport since the 1990s and beyond. Indeed, the association of basketball with international hip-hop style can be seen in the branded regalia that pervades China, other parts of East Asia, Europe, and even parts of Africa.[7]

The NBA became a truly major sport in the United States when it became an international one, a phenomenon that worked concurrently with the emergence of Nike (as discussed in the preceding chapter) as an international brand associated with Michael Jordan. This was also at the point where globalized trade became ensconced fully in the U.S. economy, and major U.S. cities, thanks to that economic activity, became increasingly the home of international populations. The point of departure for the new NBA can, as a matter of relative accuracy and convenience, be placed in 1992, when NBA players were for the first time allowed to play in the Olympics. The so-called U.S. Dream Team, which dominated the competition, opened the door to the internationalizing of spectator sports in general and defined basketball, along with soccer, as the central sport in that trend. Currently, there are 108 foreign nationals playing in the NBA out of 450 roster spots. The Olympics clearly catalyzed this trend, but the game was already moving in the direction of internationalization when Croatian guard Drazen Petrovic debuted in the NBA in 1989. Portland and Seattle drafted the Lithuanian Arvydas Sabonis and the German national Deltef Schrempf in 1985. The first European player to wear an NBA jersey was France's Hervé Dubuisson, who played for the New Jersey Nets in the summer of 1984 in nonleague games.[8] All of this movement toward internationalization was, by design, incremental, culminating in the 1992 organization of an NBA overseas division with an office located in Hong Kong. As sports historians Steven J. Jackson and David L. Andrews write,

> Peopled with specialists in business, marketing, and international relations, the NBA International's brief was to mobilise relevant media and commodity flows in order to cultivate the league's visibility overseas, and thereby hopefully increase the revenue derived from the global consumption of televised games and licensed products. NBA International is structured and organised around regional offices, situated in Geneva, Barcelona, Melbourne, Hong Kong, Mexico City, and Miami, through which television and licensed merchandise deals are negotiated. In terms of television contracts, the majority have been signed with national networks in individual countries, such as the 54-game deal recently signed with Television Azteca in Mexico. The NBA has also signed a number of strategically important regional deals with satellite and cable distributors such as Star, ESPN International, and SkySports. In total, the 1995 NBA finals were broadcast to 160 different countries.[9]

Andrews sees the proliferation of European and Asian players in the NBA not only as an effect of globalization but also as a cause. Writes Andrews, "Within many countries, the NBA's residual Americanness is conjoined with local interest derived from the presence of their local players within the league."[10] In ways, then, the post-Olympics marketing of the NBA is a model for all sports. It has conjoined a vision of the United States that can include, or even welcome, individuals and ideas from without.

In June 1985, I was wearing my Celtics logo t-shirt as I traipsed through Vatican Square. Although I certainly was aware that the Celtics were in the midst of a finals series with the Lakers, I did not know that I would run into any number of Bostonians and Celtics fans at the Vatican. I was soon suffused with inquiries into whether I had seen the game last night and of the prospects for the team. I then learned that the games were available in the dead of the night on Italian television. Steven Jackson and David Andrews explain,

> "In those days, there was a young TV executive called Andrea Bassani, who is now the TV director for Euroleague," recalls Terry Lyons, the NBA's vice president of international communications and a league employee for the last 26 years: "His father was a pilot for TWA so Andrea had flight privileges which meant he was able to fly across the Atlantic,

come to our office in New York, grab a few tapes and fly back to Italy where they would air them the next night. That was our first international TV deal and it is fair to say technology has advanced since then!"[11]

As of 2023, the NBA League Pass was available in over two hundred countries, and games could be streamed from virtually anywhere. This is a far cry from the beginning of international broadcasts in the early 1980s and the occasional game overseas.[12] But those occurrences were certainly precursors to the 1990s explosion of the league as an international entity.

All of this points to the burgeoning of the NBA as a commodity under Commissioner David Stern and the connection of the sport to a vision of cosmopolitan capitalism. Stern employed the devices available to latch onto the zeitgeist of neoliberalism, noting the "fit" of his league for the cultural moment. These means included the technology that allowed a commodity to employ a global network of promotion and dispersion, technology that was a matter of the development of digital media, as well as its implementation in global markets. Stern himself has explained how he and others in the NBA leadership began attempting to think of the league not simply as a sport but also as a "major entertainment and consumer goods company."[13] As an economic entity that integrates spectacle and consumption, the NBA is definitional for the elaboration of an epoch that conjoins the marketing of place and placelessness in equal dimensions. It also serves as a political marker that asserts a certain narrative of U.S. culture, one that is on its face decidedly inclusive and liberal, but as it has transpired over time, one that need not require African American team ownership.

The NBA's in-person and even remote costs are far out of scale with most non-Western economies and unattainable even to so many fans that live in geographic proximity to NBA arenas; still, the league promotes varying levels of buy-in, from hats to jerseys (at a range of prices) to digital transmission packages and actual in-person attendance. Such a range of consumer experiences places NBA franchises well within the postmodern economy, a realm of exchange that relies not so much on fixed space and object value but on the dissemination of symbolic capital through devices that express place even as they can be understood as placeless in a virtual world.[14] As individuals in the actual world and in the virtual world adopt players and teams to root for, they are—as a matter of necessity—drawn into matters of place. And the more each place is someplace, or no place in particular, or no place at all, the greater the incentive to put a stamp on a locale with a resonant and distinct image that is emblematic of an affecting narrative. In a digital age, accouterments of place are a matter of their conceptual resonance and the way they provide resonant meanings to an apparently concrete object. The "Celtics" have a presence that both transcends place and concurrently repackages place as an associated conceptual entity, a brand. Yet, that brand contains elements of contradiction, both as a marketing entity that denotes team and as one that denotes place.

The Case of the *Boston* Celtics

The Celtics originated in 1946 when the BAA coalesced. Their name, as the story goes, came from a discussion between owner Walter Brown and publicity director Howie McHugh, who considered various possibilities including the Unicorns and the Whirlwinds, a nod to the 1920s ABL team. Brown chose the Celtics in deference to the original barnstorming team and the proliferation of people of Irish extraction in the region. The name advertised the whiteness of the Boston-based team, which was not distinct or unique at this time since the league was segregated. But the name's ongoing associations with a vision of whiteness to some degree remain. The name, of course, was fateful. It played fully into regional assumptions of heritage and identity, and melded perfectly with the broad national and international vision of the city in which the team resides. Although Brown and McHugh could not have predicted the many more national associations between the city and its Irishness—the Kennedy family, the Bulger family, Louise Day Hicks, and so on—their sense of the centrality of the city's Irish American population in its national presence proved to be uncanny. The name, as had that of the earlier barnstorming team, attempted to rebrand the game, marking it as not simply white but also moving it conceptually from its associations with Jewish and Southern and Eastern European players and organizations, as well as from African Americans.

When the BAA merged with the NBL to form the NBA in 1949, the Celtics were part of that transaction. Until 1955, the team played in the decidedly downscale and low-capacity Boston Arena. That Brown maintained his primary facility, the Boston Garden, for his A-list property, the Boston Bruins

FIGURE 11. Boston Garden and North Station in 1929, just after it opened. —Courtesy Creative Commons.

hockey team, tells us a lot about the basketball team's status in the city. The Boston Garden, a significant upgrade over the Boston Arena, was one of Tex Rickard's facilities, modeled after Madison Square Garden and opening in 1928. It was built for boxing and hockey but was almost immediately used for concerts, religious revivals, and political events. When the Celtics moved in, it was showing signs of age and the contiguous neighborhood was in decline. By the time the facility closed in 1995, it was filthy, crumbling, and decidedly uncomfortable. As *New York Times* columnist Harvey Araton wrote after the Celtics' last game at the arena: "Dimly lit. Poorly ventilated. Cubbyholes with hooks. Splintered benches. Ripped upholstery on the trainer's table. Peeling walls. Two showers. One sink, toilet and urinal. Go ahead. Play ball. To walk inside Boston Garden is to stumble into a Jack Finney novel. It is a treasure chest of champions, of memories that remained open a bit too long. It has not aged well. It is not quaint, like some Back Bay brownstone. Over the years, the Garden grew shabby, stodgy, downright scary when players gasped in stifling heat."[15]

As the Celtics succeeded over the years, the Garden developed a kind of legendary status. Broadcasters and journalists would invoke its rats and substandard mechanics. Indeed, in a 1988 Bruins hockey playoff game, the ice was all but invisible to TV viewers because of the fog generated by the humidity and heat of the day, the ice, and the terrible ventilation. But television audiences didn't have to suffer through the entire game, since a power failure brought it to an early termination.[16] The arena's lack of adequate heat and its absence of air conditioning, its cramped and filthy visitor's locker rooms, and the idiosyncrasies of the parquet basketball floor made it a facility teams hated to visit, and it was often cited as a factor in the team's success and as a means for the team's coach and general manager, Red Auerbach, to exercise his wiles.

The team's claim to fame and the definition of its "tradition," however recent, is largely based in its remarkable success from 1957 to 1969, when it won eleven NBA championships. Still, even during that time, the team was a stepchild of Boston sports, a lesser tenant in the Boston Garden. And that facility always lacked both the convenience and relative charm of Fenway Park. Boston Garden was built atop the city's North Station train station, which in 1928, when the arena opened, might have associated it with the glamor of train travel during that era. The site also included a hotel, originally the Hotel Manger, later called the Hotel Madison in 1958 after the Boston and Maine Railroad purchased it. But by the time the NBA became ensconced as a league, train travel in the United States was on a downward trajectory. Whatever contextual glamor the hotel and train station provided in 1930, it had long vanished by the 1960s. Needless to say, as train travel decreased, the hotel became increasingly empty and seamy, and the station a forlorn and grimy locale.

The neighborhood that housed the Boston Garden was a nether district within the city. The residential area immediately contiguous to the Garden, the West End, was the site of the first major urban renewal project in the city during the late 1950s, under the leadership of Mayor John Hynes. This district was a thriving but decidedly working- and lower-class neighborhood. Hynes and the Boston Housing Authority, and then the Boston Redevelopment Authority, decided surreptitiously to replace the existing neighborhood in one grand development, building a total of five residential high-rise buildings and displacing thousands. This area—known throughout most of its life as Charles River Park, but then renamed the West End

Apartments by its new owners—became even more remote from the North Station area as a matter of its scale and design, in effect making its residents far less urban meanderers in the Jane Jacobs sense and more members of a discrete region, largely dependent on their cars for mobility. The Garden was in a kind of urban no-man's land. Prior to the 2000s, the immediate vicinity of the Garden was under the Causeway Street trestle of the Massachusetts Bay Transit Authority (MBTA) tracks—dark, dank, underdeveloped, and unappealing. The Garden, and now the TD North Garden, sits by a major artery and the entrance to the Charles River basin, and so is cut off from neighborhoods to the north, west, and, to some degree, east. Even though the North End, now a major entertainment and restaurant district in the city, is not far, it is not in the immediate environs of the Garden, and it is beyond at least two major surface roads and a maze of secondary streets, so in its own distinctive environment. Today, however, in keeping with the city's boom in development, even the area around the Garden is flourishing.

The old Boston Garden became part of the team's brand and has to a degree remained so. It was not, however, part of the brand in any charming way, as Fenway Park would become for the Red Sox. Rather, it was more like Fenway without the allure: gloomy, cramped, and dirty. As Fenway Park had at one time been a symbol of the city's dysfunctional politics, which could not manage the logistical demands of funding and building a new stadium, so the Garden served as an even brighter beacon of that failed system.

But as time went on, and as the team reemerged as a powerhouse in the 1980s, a rare NBA team led by white players, the old Garden gradually became part of the media story of the team and a reiteration of an extant story of place, a perfect venue for a team associated with notions of working-class whiteness and residual notions of authenticity. This hallowing of place mostly took place, as it did in the case of Fenway Park after the 1970s, as post-industrialism increasingly hollowed out cities and neoliberalism began the process of recreating them as living theme parks. In this case, Boston Garden—and the Celtics—became a token of nostalgic whiteness as the NBA was just reviving in the 1980s. Such grittiness also became part of the team's brand. As folklorist Simon Bronner wrote in 1998,

> The Celtics and Lakers battled for the National Basketball Association championship three out of four years between 1984 and 1987. To heat up the rivalry, the press portrayed the Celtics as the team of old, playing in

the antiquated, dark and dingy Boston Garden in the traditional setting of old New England. It harped on the social virtues of the Celtics' teamwork, work ethic, and naturally a winning tradition. The dowdy digs of the Boston Garden and the plebeian reputation of Boston fans roused feelings of heartiness and pride in old-fashioned values.[17]

This environment was an aspect of the white, ethnic identity of the team, its embracing of tradition, and its "lunch pail" associations: the idea that the team comprised hard-working grinders with a notable lack of flash, that it succeeded because the sum was more than the combined individual value of its parts. Bronner continued, "The introduction of that game on television built up the 'mystique of Celtic tradition'; in 'ancient Boston Garden' against the 'jubilant Laker Express' and 'bright lights of Los Angeles': At a time of rapid mobility when economic shift from manufacturing to service and information translated into an image of decline for the East and boom for the West, the press found a story other than the outcome of the games."[18]

But gradually, the environs that Bronner noted and that many celebrated began to change. In 1983, the Hotel Madison was imploded. In 1995, the Garden was replaced on a site abutting the old location by a new version, complete with a corporate name, variously called the Fleet Center and later by other names, but now known as the TD Garden. In a nod to nostalgia, the signature parquet floor of the old Garden was moved to the new, but it was eventually replaced by a new parquet floor in 1999 as the NBA moved to standardize its arenas. The multiple championship banners and retired uniform numbers also made the trip to the new arena. However, the new arena altered the narrative of place to some extent.[19]

After 2004, when the Causeway Street trestle was eliminated as part of the Big Dig project, the neighborhood began to improve. As a result of the general boom in Boston construction and in the central city, the area around TD Garden also improved and is currently the site of several high-end retail and residential developments.[20] Indeed, the parent owner of the Garden, Delaware North, has become a major regional developer: Delaware North and Boston Properties formed a partnership to develop over 1.5 million square feet of mixed-use retail, office, hotel, and residential spaces, and an expansion of TD Garden on the 2.5-acre site: "This significant investment in development brings substantial improvements to North Station, transforms the area into a revitalized destination and provides major

FIGURE 12. Banners above TD Garden commemorate the various successes of the Celtics teams and players. —Courtesy Jp16103, CC BY-SA 4.0, https://creativecommons.org.

economic impact for the neighborhood."[21] Thus, the image of the Celtics as a "traditional" concern is a matter of what residual icons can be associated with a very different entity from the shoestring operation that operated out of a facility that was rarely filled and mostly uncomfortable. These icons include the championship banners and the retired jerseys hanging from the ceiling, the name "Garden" for the arena, and the parquet floor. They are the stuff of the visuals of the new arena and a feature of local and national media coverage.

As the city boomed, so did the team's financial fortunes. Yet the image of the team as a refuge for white players persisted. That the team boasted from 2017 to 2020 one of the few white stars in the league (though he was often injured), Gordon Hayward, may be incidental, but it is also redolent of an embedded narrative of place and team. Hayward's prominence as a free-agent acquisition might also have stemmed from the fact that most African American stars preferred not to bring their talents to Boston.

The Face of the Sport

As the received history of place reflects on the team, so the history of the team informs its role in defining place. During the first phase of NBA history, the Celtics emerged as the signature team of that relatively new league. An important part of this story began with the NBA integrating in 1950, when Sweetwater Clifton, Earl Lloyd, and Chick Cooper signed with the Knicks, the Washington Capitals, and the Celtics almost concurrently. That the Celtics were one of these teams seems to run counter to usual narratives of place. And while none of these players became stars, the league did set itself up to become the organization that it has become with this historic act of integration. The turning point for the team—and arguably for the league—came with the signing of Bill Russell in 1956, after the conclusion of the Melbourne Olympics. From 1957 to 1969, the Celtics won every NBA title but two, missing out only in 1958, when Russell was limited in the NBA finals by an ankle injury, and in 1967, when the aging team lost in the conference finals to the Philadelphia 76ers, led by Wilt Chamberlain. The existence of a team that became known as the New York Yankees of basketball created an identity for both the team and the league. It also created a team that, like the Yankees, other teams and their fans would love to hate. The team of that era featured any number of Hall of Fame–bound stars alongside Russell, including Bob Cousy, Bill Sharman, Sam Jones, KC Jones, Tom Sanders, and Tom Heinsohn in the earlier days, and then John Havlicek and Bailey Howell in the later part of the dynasty. The number of African American players on this list besides Russell—Sam Jones, KC Jones, and Tom Sanders—would seem to counter the embedded racist narrative of place and the resulting narrative of team. Yet, it does not fully do that.

Red Auerbach was a defining presence for the team, both on the court and in the media. He coached the team from 1950 to 1966, when he also served as general manager. He continued in that role until 1986, when he largely stepped down from his role in day-to-day operations. From 1986 until his death in 2006, he was the team president and vice chair, but those roles were to a degree honorific and became more so as he aged. The sight of Auerbach courtside was definitional during his coaching career and an identifiable aspect of the team's identity for fans of a certain depth. Subsequently, he could be found in a seat in the arena's upper loge at midcourt, always in the same seat. Since the league was a relatively dim presence in local and national media, few saw him. Images and video do exist and have found their way into any number of sports documentaries, including the recent Netflix production *Bill Russell, Legend* (dir. Sam Pollard, 2023), and the three-part ESPN 30-for-30 documentary *Celtics/Lakers* (dir. Jim Podhoretz, 2017). He was portrayed by actor Michael Chiklis in HBO's series *Winning Time* (created by Max Borenstein and Jim Hecht, 2022–23).

As a coach, his hectoring presence was emblematic of both the league's tolerance of characters and his competitive zeal. He instituted the fast-paced game that has become the norm in the more contemporary NBA, as well as a team that had no dominant scorer and whose best player—Russell—was a defensive stalwart. Auerbach was not above the casual racist remark uttered from time to time. Still, for the era, Auerbach succeeded because he operated in a professional world that he defined as largely transcending racial boundaries and which *relatively* did. As historian Aram Goudsouzian writes,

> This Celtics family transcended race, as whites and blacks shared professional respect and personal ties. Russell had once been the lone African American maintaining personal distance, but he became the team's standard-bearer for racial cooperation. He developed friendships and exchanged praise with his teammates, and he lauded Red Auerbach as a perfect coach. Other Black players followed him onto the Celtics. Sam Jones and KC Jones replaced Sharman and Cousy in the backcourt, and Satch Sanders started at forward. When Willie Naulls joined the team in 1963, Boston became the first franchise to play five blacks on the court at once. As the civil rights movement compelled national attention, the Celtics represented integration in action.[22]

Indeed, Hall of Fame African American coach John McClendon, who had coached Sam Jones at North Carolina A&T and who preceded Auerbach's international outreach by conducting basketball clinics in Africa during the 1950s, served as something of a model for the Celtics coach.[23] Yet, despite Auerbach's innovations and a playing style derived from the programs at historically Black colleges and universities, the Celtics nevertheless became involved with the city's reputation for racism.

But this association of team, place, and racism does have some justification. For the Celtics, the Bill Russell era was one of excellence but surprisingly low attendance, averaging between 7,000 and 8,200 paid patrons in the Boston Garden (the capacity was 13,909 in those days) during most of the Russell years, and not consistently getting over the 10,000 mark until after the 1972–73 season, with a very competitive team that featured John

Havlicek, Dave Cowens, and Jo Jo White (two white stars and one African American). Around Boston in the 1960s, the lore was that the difficult ticket to procure was one for the Bruins. Whether this occurrence was primarily about race is hard to say, but the concurrent issues concerning race and the Red Sox, and race and the city, make it difficult to minimize. While the Celtics were the first NBA to field an all African American starting five, subsequently the team also had the reputation of being race-conscious in compiling its roster: as the sport became increasingly African American, the Celtics were often whiter than the average team, a fact African American and white onlookers certainly noticed.[24]

Arguably, a key aspect of this association between bigotry of the place and of the team stemmed from the Bill Russell era and the persona of Russell himself. The phenomenon of Russell presents an interesting dimension of team and its city identification, since he was the face of the team on the court during its best days, as well as a civil rights warrior from the early days of the movement and an important public figure over some sixty years. His career included stints as an NBA coach and a broadcaster. He always spoke out clearly and often bluntly on matters of racial solidarity and pride. That he was a prominent figure prior to the league's national television presence—and decades before satellite transmission and streaming media—did limit his impact. Still, Russell's media presence and uncompromising personality enlarged him as a figure whose influence extended beyond a narrow base of sports fans.

Russell became a national celebrity as a college player for the University of San Francisco, where he led his team to two consecutive national championships. As a Celtic, he was a means of transforming both the team and the league, providing a presence as a force in the structure of the game and in society. While suited to a life of activism by means of his personality and upbringing, Russell became intensely interested in pan-African solidarity as he began doing international goodwill tours with the NBA. A visit he made to Liberia in 1959 (as a member of a State Department–sponsored tour) led to investments and an abiding curiosity in the African continent. After that time, he rarely missed an opportunity to assert his Blackness and racial pride.

Such sentiments and public postures were ahead of their times, and though Russell prospered and succeeded, his public image was far from endearing to a predominantly white fanbase. Russell was among the first outspoken African American athletes in a major spectator sport, preceding figures like Jim Brown and Mohammed Ali. As a so-called race man in the late 1950s and 1960s, Russell's role and reception may be difficult to understand from today's perspective, since his views made him a deeply problematic figure in white America and particularly in Boston. And that friction with local figures, including sportswriters, and with the Celtics fanbase was instrumental in defining the Celtics within the domain of regional racism.

Russell's emergence as an activist was a gradual occurrence. But the spring of 1963, when Martin Luther King Jr. organized his March on Washington, also marked the beginning of Russell's full visibility. He was among a group of NBA players who participated in that event. Prior to that time, Russell had alienated many in the city's press core by lambasting the city's embedded racism, once asserting to a reporter, "Boston is the most racist city in the country."[25] Reporters found him erratic—one day endearing, another day hostile—which did nothing to cement a warm relationship with a city that certainly contained many who were unwilling to accept him as a full human being. In 1963 and 1964, extended profiles of Russell came out in national magazines, one in the *Saturday Evening Post*, one in *Sports Illustrated*, and one in *Sport* magazine. In those very candid conversations, he expressed his disdain of white people, his support for the Nation of Islam, and his refusal to be nice to children or sign autographs.[26]

His resolution not to sign autographs, and his general unwillingness to do local events to promote the team, led to a sense of estrangement between the player and the region. Further, rather than deciding to live closer to the city, Russell chose to live in the white and Catholic—predominantly Irish and Italian—suburb of Reading (where Charles Stuart later lived), which even today has almost no African American families. Writes Aram Goudsouzian, "Russell and his family did integrate a neighborhood in the suburb of Reading, and in 1963 the town gave him a testimonial dinner, which so touched him that he wept. Yet when he considered moving to another neighborhood, a protest petition circulated. Once, the Russells found their home vandalized: beer poured on the pool table, trophies smashed, 'NIGGA' spray-painted on walls, and feces on their bed. Russell later called Boston 'the most rigidly segregated city in the country.'"[27] Russell was seen by a white fanbase and press as aloof, arrogant, and largely hostile to the white crowds that attended Celtics games and followed the team. And as he became an increasingly notable national figure, his negative experiences and bad feelings about living in the Boston area became an increasingly visible story, one enlarged by the racism of the Red Sox organization and the city's resistance to integrated schools.

It would be a deft conceptual act to distinguish absolutely between the franchise and the city in which it played. But those distinctions largely went unelaborated. Instead, the stories of other Celtics in that era facing housing discrimination and overt racism further added fuel to the fire. KC Jones was the subject of racist exclusion when he went to buy a house in the suburb of Framingham, and Tom Sanders faced similar hostility during his own housing search, deciding finally to settle in Roxbury. None of this was at all mitigated by the fact that Bill Russell became the first African American head coach in the NBA and the first African American team leader in any major sport. But given the team's name and its place of business, the divided legacy of the Celtics increasingly tracked a trajectory that moved parallel with or at least toward that of the Red Sox.

Subsequently, after Russell's retirement in 1969, he immediately left the city for the West Coast and what he hoped would be a budding career as an actor, much in the vein of his friend Jim Brown. But as that career failed to materialize, he soon was back in basketball as the coach of the Seattle Supersonics. From that platform, he continued to call out the city of Boston, which in 1974 was going through its very public civic crisis regarding school busing, asserting, "I expected what's happening in Boston."[28] Although he limited his direct comments about the team and the city, it was clear that he had not experienced a significant change of heart, and in 1975 he rejected the offer of induction into the Basketball Hall of Fame in nearby Springfield, Massachusetts, describing it as a "racist institution," noting (correctly) the role of people like Abe Saperstein, the longtime owner of the Globetrotters, who he felt had insulted his intelligence when he left college and considered joining the Globetrotters, and Adolph Rupp, a close friend of Red Auerbach's who as coach at the University of Kentucky fielded segregated teams until 1969. As of 1972, when he at last agreed to have his number retired, Russell requested it be done in private, with only a few ex-teammates in attendance on that day, March 12, 1972. A *New York Times* article recounted, "Reporters asked Russell why he wanted a private ceremony. 'You know I don't go for that stuff,' he said of the fanfare."[29] While this story took a significant shift in the 1990s, the impact of Russell's view and anger further defined the city and the team.

The immediate era after Russell's retirement was a fallow one for the franchise, but the team was soon back in the national conversation as a contender for the NBA championship. What was different this time, however, was that two of the core players, and arguably the featured younger player, were white. This came as the league was becoming increasingly African American. According to historian Adam J. Criblez, "As the 1970s began, the NBA consisted of fourteen teams composed of roughly equal numbers of white and Black players who made a salary, on average, of around $35,000 per year. Within the decade, the league expanded to twenty-two teams and was populated by more than 70 percent Black players with annual salaries 500 percent higher."[30] Indeed, in 1975, a *New York Times* writer estimated that the league was approximately 75 percent African American.[31] Race continued to be an important aspect of the relative visibility of professional basketball, as the nation's deeply conflicted views on the matter played out in a number of ways through public attitudes and comments about the most racially diverse of all major sports.

The championship Celtics teams of the 1970s and the 1980s were notable both for their success and for their relative whiteness, particularly the 1980s teams. The Celtics won the NBA title in 1974 and then again in 1976. Those teams featured Dave Cowens, John Havlicek, and Jo Jo White as mainstays. The rosters were roughly half white and half Black in this era when NBA rosters became predominantly African American. So, the team, as a whiter version of an NBA roster, easily mapped on to the racist city seen on the news with the busing crisis. The 1976 team traded Paul Westphal, who went on to his own stellar career in Phoenix, for the African American Charlie Scott, theoretically making the case for color blindness. But even by then it was whispered that the team's fanbase "required" a white star or two.

The connection of team to place, and the "brand" of Boston, did not help mitigate these accusations. The naming of the team by Walter Brown and Howie McHugh, it turned out, *was* fateful. By identifying the team with the region's reigning ethnic population, the owner and publicity man assured that the Celtics would maintain a public presence that could, and ultimately would, be connected to the insular populations of certain working-class neighborhoods, places where that name would be most elaborative. Would it have been different if the Celtics had been called the Unicorns? Unlike the Red Sox, who did not take on a name associated with Irishness, the Celtics have not been so much a part of the city's white ethnic fabric, save for the prominence of Jewish supporters, including a disproportion of season ticket holders, and management: Red Auerbach; legendary broadcaster Johnny Most; the owners of the Celtics training facility on Cape Cod and "Friends of Red" Jan and Jerry Volk; and the current owners, the Grousbecks.[32]

Auerbach's connections in the Boston Jewish community also positioned the team and its fanbase. Since Auerbach's family stayed in Washington, DC, during the basketball season, Auerbach developed a network that reflected his social comfort zone, attending any number of weddings, bar and bat mitzvahs, and events at Jewish civic organizations. His informal "Friends of Red" included any number of prominent Jewish businessmen. Yet, the relative absence of Celts among the Celtics did little to insulate the team from having their brand impacted by negative associations with place. As a matter of branding and associations with narratives of place, the team's name has been influential in creating perceptions and further associations. Indeed, at a Red Sox game, it is common to see the Celtics' color—Kelly green—adorning a t-shirt or a cap with the Red Sox logo, suggesting the close conceptual relationship between the two. So, the team took on a meaning as a matter of name and local context, and as time went on, the association of the Celtics with a kind of whiteness and racial exclusion became a kind of norm.

The Larry Bird Era: The Celtics and the Great White Hope

The 1980s teams were even more successful and even whiter, especially within a league that was by then overwhelmingly African American. These rosters included not only Hall of Fame players who were white, like Larry Bird, Kevin McHale, and (briefly) Bill Walton, but also more complementary players such as Danny Ainge, Greg Kite, Scott Wedman, and others. Indeed, a truism of the NBA in that era was that teams needed a certain presence of white players to be viable financially, and that it was not among the best players that race became definitional but rather those further down the roster. Although Red Auerbach always defended his roster choices as color-blind, the unstated NBA policy about race and roster makeup does lend at least some suspicion to those choices. And for some, the whiteness of the team was evidence enough of racist practice, especially when associated with the place and legacy of the

Red Sox. The fact that the team's fanbase was geographically centered in a city where race and racism, inside and outside of sports, has a long and visible presence apparently provided further evidence that these choices were not based simply on talent. These Celtics teams took the court as the league began to prosper as a result of the marketing of the Larry Bird/Magic Johnson rivalry, one with an embedded racial dimension. The central narrative of an increasing NBA media presence featuring the Celtics and Lakers further accentuated the whiteness of Boston's franchise. The proportion and visibility of white players fed into the Bill Russell and Boston Red Sox narratives of Boston as a place of distinctive bigotry.

There were various affirmations of this narrative that emphasized the centrality of the team. For example, Harvey Araton, a noted basketball journalist of longstanding reputation, has written scathingly about the Celtics front office's motivations in compiling the teams of the 1980s, both in a book and in various essays. In a piece written just after Auerbach's death in 2006, Araton explained, "Auerbach's team fell from its progressive perch, from a reputation in the 1960s as the Black team in a white sport to being considered by many as the white team in a Black sport. A remarkable transformation, and in true Auerbachian fashion, executed in the interests of doing whatever it took."[33] In Spike Lee's excellent film on race and the city *Do the Right Thing* (1989), he dresses a lone white gentrifier (played by John Savage) in the Bedford-Stuyvesant neighborhood of New York, where Lee's dramatic and effective commentary of race-relations is set, in a Larry Bird t-shirt. This filmic strategy affirmed an association that was well known, but Lee's strategic employing of this character provided a mass-culture accelerant, especially at a moment when the visibility of the NBA and the availability of films in analog home formats were both becoming widespread.

In 1987, after losing a crucial playoff game to the Celtics in which Larry Bird made a key steal at the end of the game to protect a small lead, Isiah Thomas, also a Hall of Fame player and the leader of the Detroit Pistons of that era, asserted that if Bird were Black, "he'd be just another good guy." This further fueled the sense that Boston's sporting public had a deeply embedded racism, and explicitly stating what many in and around the league thought but would not say. This comment came in response to that of his teammate Dennis Rodman, who "said in the locker room that Bird was 'very overrated' and that he had won three straight most valuable player awards only 'because he was white.'"[34] As sports columnist J. A. Adande reminds us, such sentiments were all but unquestioned in certain quarters. He writes, "When Spike Lee took a guest editor role at *Spin* magazine in 1990, he ran a photo essay on the meaning attached to different sports apparel. Under a picture of a Black man wearing Celtics gear it said: 'This man is an Uncle Tom.' In the 1992 Public Enemy song 'Air Hoodlum,' Chuck D rapped about a basketball phenom who was 'so quick at 6-foot-6, down to be picked by anyone but the Celtics.'"[35] Major national stories of racism in Boston popped up intermittently: busing in 1974, the Charles Stuart murder case in 1989, and a more recent incident involving schoolchildren at the Museum of Fine Arts.[36] But there is at least a solid argument that the predominance of white stars in Celtics green was a matter of situation and not of design, bringing us again to the question of how legacies are created and reiterated, as well as the mass-media devices of associating place with particular narratives.

Attendance at Celtics games in the mid-1970s finally increased to over 11,000 per game on average, well eclipsing the 8,000 or so that had marked the last years of the Bill Russell era. But as our overarching narrative suggests, the market for spectator sports, and the population of the city, was in the process of changing too and would continue to change in the 1980s and 1990s. Still, the racist narrative that attached to the post–Bill Russell teams' successes at the box office does lend suspicion, if not credence, to the idea of the racist city. During the 1970s, the NBA was increasingly African American, and it was a period of relative retrenchment for the league. But success was around the corner, not just as a matter of changing social attitudes but also as a matter of the emergence of cable television sports and the reemergence of the city as a desirable locale for entertainment. Regardless, the NBA was marked as a "Black" league in a "Black" sport, and the consumerist white fanbase remained at least skeptical of the product, leaving open the boxing-based narrative of the search for the Great White Hope.

When Larry Bird and Magic Johnson entered the league in the fall of 1979, the NBA was not a thriving organization. Many blamed this failure on the disconnection between white fans and Black players, as attendance languished and TV rights stagnated. The leading scorers and reigning stars—Bob McAdoo, George Gervin, Kareem Abdul-Jabbar, and Julius Erving—were overwhelmingly African American, with only a few white players—Dave Cowens, Rick Barry, Billy Cunningham, and Bill Walton—who could be counted among the league's best. The basketball journalist

Harvey Araton reported that in the early 1980s, several teams were in "dire financial straits."[37]

The search for this "great white hope" occurred in a context shaped by the issue of drug use in the league and, visibly, among African American players. In the 1980s, Lewis Lloyd, Michael Ray Richardson, and Mitchell Wiggins were all permanently banned from the league for cocaine use—though all were eventually reinstated. John Drew, Duane Washington, and Chris Washburn were also banned but never reinstated, as were Richard Dumas and William Bedford in the early 1990s. In addition, many players went through the league's drug treatment program, contributing further to the public relations woes of the sport.[38] The Celtics' number one draft pick of 1986, Maryland forward Len Bias, was set to become the heir to Larry Bird, and perhaps the first African American superstar to play for the Celtics since Bill Russell, when he died of a cocaine overdose in the spring of 1986, soon after the draft.

This all came on the heels of the most devastating on-court fight in the history of pro sports in 1977, when African American forward Kermit Washington punched white forward Rudy Tomjanovich as Tomjanovich raced toward Washington, ostensibly to break up an altercation. The result was a major head injury, as Tomjanovich went down in a pool of blood and spinal fluid. This violent incident was only one of a number of physical altercations between white and Black players but certainly the most serious. Washington's career was never the same after his six-month suspension and $10,000 fine.[39]

When David Stern became the league's executive vice president in 1980 and its commissioner in 1984, there was much work to be done in promoting the sport. Larry Bird was an important part of that redemption job. Bird, through no desire or fault of his own, became the poster boy for white basketball players and found himself immersed in racial controversy almost from the time he entered the league. The fact that Bird was a lifelong Celtic who played in a highly visible era was a matter of happenstance. The team went on to win sixty-one games during Bird's rookie season, thirty-two more than they had the year before. Although the 1980s were clearly dominated by the Lakers, led by Magic Johnson, James Worthy, and Kareem Abdul-Jabbar, the Celtics were the second-best team of the era, winning championships in 1981, 1984, and 1986; indeed, this rivalry had a racial resonance that contributed to the embedded Boston story. Whether the extraordinary whiteness of this successful team was by design or not is hard to say. But that fact played into the narrative of place that increasingly took on the baggage of team.

Larry Bird was not only white; he was a small-town guy from southern Indiana with a noticeable regional twang. His skin was pasty, he was not particularly fleet afoot, nor could he jump high. He was resolutely unsophisticated and most comfortable in jeans and a cap. He was also, at his peak, a great basketball player, possessing soft hands, a skilled shooting touch, and a genius-level court sense. But given his presentation, as well as the state of the game when he entered the league in 1979, and his subsequent success, it is hard not to see Bird's success as a boon for attendance, particularly among white fans. And that such success came in Boston just added further grist to the vision of place already entrenched when he arrived. Writes Alex Criblez, "Discussions about Bird inevitably centered on the color of his skin. For legions of white fans, Bird was an everyman—someone with whom they could identify because of his race and because of his perceived physical shortcomings."[40] Indeed, when Bird sat down with Isiah Thomas to address the controversy regarding Thomas's and Rodman's comments about Bird's inflated status within the game as a matter of his whiteness, Bird smirked and noted that the game required a great deal of effort for him, to compensate for his lack of speed and inability to jump.

The association of the Celtics with the racist legacy of the city became increasingly irrelevant with the end of the Larry Bird era. The Celtics languished throughout the 1990s, as the hangover of the death of Len Bias gave way to the sad story of Reggie Lewis, who was drafted by the Celtics in 1987 and began to emerge as a star for the team in 1988, only to be diagnosed with a heart ailment in the spring of 1993 during the NBA playoffs. Lewis died in the preseason in the late summer of that year. His death was not without controversy, as the team doctor had told Lewis that his condition was potentially life-threatening. Lewis, wishing to continue his career, went in search of a second opinion that would allow him to play. But his death developed a racial dimension when the issue of drug abuse came into the picture and people learned that the Celtics had chosen not to test him, fearing a public-relations issue. The details of the team's behavior, which in hindsight seems mostly honorable, got lost in the controversy that surrounded Lewis's death and became another means of associating the Celtics with racism.

The question of Lewis's drug use was a charged topic because of what were then perceived as the impediments to the NBA breaking through as a national and international sport. Questions about the commercial trajectory of the predominantly African American sport remained, and the association of NBA players with extant narratives of urban criminality, notably defined by drug use, made the league a difficult sell to its white audience. Three major antidrug bills passed during the Reagan/Bush era, in 1984, 1986, and 1988, all of which, among other foci, targeted drug use and distribution, and all of which disproportionately impacted African Americans. The 1986 bill was notable for making significant sentencing distinctions between the use and possession of powdered cocaine (more costly) and that of crack cocaine (less expensive). The former, partially due to the cost difference, was generally associated with white users and the latter with users of color. These bills, along with the comprehensive crime bill of 1994, seemed to affirm a racist trope of Black criminality and provided the means to mass incarceration. Indeed, these bills can be seen as cultural markers that well fit with an era in which Charles Stuart blamed a Black assailant for the death of his wife and Willie Horton became a major force in the 1988 presidential campaign.[41] Again, such assertions were magnified by the existence of cable television. But as the sport changed and the media landscape also burgeoned, little national attention was directed toward the Celtics, given their mediocrity. Still, when they reemerged in this brave new world of media-saturated commodities, including sports, the half-life of their historical narratives of team and place would intermittently appear.

The Digital Celtics

Gradually, the NBA made headway as a commercial entity and prospered in the still-new era of cable television. As of 1981, only seven of the NBA's twenty-three franchises made a profit. As Steven J. Jackson and David L. Andrews wrote,

> By the mid-1980's through the early 1990's the NBA redefined itself to such an extent that it could justifiably sell itself as a basic American pastime, as much a part of mainstream culture as baseball. This was evidenced by the rapid rate of growth in the league's gross revenue derived from ticket sales, television contracts, corporate sponsorship, and the

retailing of licensed merchandise. In quantitative terms the NBA's gross revenue leapt from $110 million at the start of the 1980s, to over $1 billion by the end of the 1993-94 season. Yet, for very pragmatic reasons the NBA was forced to embrace a world and market outside of America.[42]

The NBA, like the Red Sox, benefited exponentially from the rise of cable television in the late 1970s and 1980s. The NBA had been a limited presence on national television during the 1970s and 1980s, but as cable television reached more and more subscribers, it became increasingly ubiquitous in the nation's homes. In addition to the transmission of what were essentially regional transmissions over far-flung cable networks, as of the 1984 season TBS began broadcasting a national slate of NBA games. This exponential growth in visibility came in the midst of the Larry Bird/Magic Johnson era and segued into the period of Michael Jordan's dominance. Jordan became the signature product of the league, one powered by the transcendent branding of Nike. He was a figure of both a type and a moment that allowed him to emerge as a major media presence. As others have pointed out, perhaps beginning with William Julius Wilson in his 1978 book *The Declining Significance of Race*, African American society in the post–civil rights era had become largely bifurcated, with a distinctive class, but not a majority, reaping the benefits of greater access to education and advanced employment, and an underclass locked into marginality, including unemployment, underemployment, and limited housing. Such a clear distinction in opportunity and access followed the increasing bifurcation of U.S. society as a whole in the wake of neoliberal politics and economics emerging in the 1970s and accelerating in the 1980s.[43]

Players such as Jordan and, to a lesser degree, David Robinson, Charles Barkley, Reggie Miller, and Grant Hill were important figures in the marketing of the league. All possessed, to varying degrees, the same qualities as Jordan in their offering a kind of Blackness that could be marketed to a multiracial—but still predominantly white—audience. This shift in marketing had implications for all teams, including the Celtics. David L. Andrews and Ron L. Mower explain, "Originated in the early 1980s, Jordan's national popular persona was hewn out of a solidifying neoliberal political conjuncture, which his commercially imaged identity helped to normalize. Jordan was manufactured as an idealized raced neoliberal subject, whose carefully managed identity resonated with neoliberalism's colour-blind ethos that neutered racial difference as a political, if not an aesthetic, category."[44] Such star power, as well as the savvy leadership of David Stern, made the NBA a truly major sport, as well as an international one, and a major presence in a neoliberal age in which the rhetoric of multiculturalism was an important commercial discourse. The league's use of contemporary marketing devices and its effective branding led it into the 2000s as a rival to baseball and football domestically, as well as made it a sport with far more international reach than those mainly American games.

All of these changes had significant implications for the Celtics as they, like many NBA properties, ceased to be merely a regional brand and instead were, at least eventually, largely situated in the mass imagination as part of a much larger and visible entity, the NBA. For individual franchises, this meant that visibility and marketing—brand definition and management—took on a dimension that allowed for exponential projection that could lead to geometric growth. For a league like the NBA, and for a team like the Boston Celtics, those fans live all around the world. Explains the team's president in a podcast: "'Social media has really opened our eyes to exactly how big our fan-base is' says Rich Gotham, President of the Boston Celtics, on the *Outside In* podcast. 'We have more social media followers in the Philippines than we do in the greater Boston area. The same is true for China and Australia,' he says of the team's more than 12 million global fans and followers."[45] But in order for a team to succeed as an international brand, it must have some competitive relevance and a resonant marketing strategy. Until 2007, the Celtics had the latter but only a little of the former.

The Celtics remained a valuable property but were only moderately successful on the court in the 1990s and early 2000s. They still maintained a dimension of their historical legacy, but such matters were not much considered as the sport became increasingly international and digital. The reigning stars on the early 2000s teams were Paul Pierce and Antoine Walker, both African American, both estimable talents but neither quite talented enough to make the team a title contender, though they did make it to the conference finals in 2002. The fortunes and visibility of the team changed dramatically with the acquisition of Ray Allen and Kevin Garnett in 2007. For the first time in the team's history, the three most visible players—Allen, Garnett, and Pierce—were all African American and were also coached by an African American, Doc Rivers. Clearly, with the glistening TD North Garden as their home, and a city that was largely remade physically since the Larry Bird era, the post-2007 Celtics were a *new* Celtics for the *new Boston*—or at least mostly.

The team was fully successful commercially and competitively and went on to win the NBA championship in 2008. That team stayed together for three years, though often beset by injuries to its aging central players, and played in the NBA finals again in 2009, losing to the Lakers. But the legacy of the team and the city remained. Initially, Kevin Garnett resisted coming to Boston. The given reason was his reluctance to leave Minnesota, where he had played since joining the league, but it is hard not to see at least part of his reluctance as coming from the city's reputation as a racial snake pit. As an accident of propinquity, I found myself sitting next to Garnett at a Red Sox game on August 1, 2007, after he had thrown out the ceremonial first pitch. We talked briefly about the enthusiasm of the Red Sox fans and of the Boston sports scene more generally. He was obviously not a baseball fan and likely could not help but notice the whiteness of the crowd. Still, as the nation during the Obama era apparently entered the "post-racial" era, so the Celtics *apparently* put the regional legacy of racism and the negations of the Bill Russell era behind them. Indeed, Russell, at the age of seventy-four, had become a visible figure in Boston, attended games from time to time, and developed a close friendship with Garnett.

As mentioned earlier, the Celtics, despite their on-the-court success, were the poor stepchild of Boston sports in the 1950s and 1960s. Their owner, Walter Brown, was a man of relatively limited means. When he died in 1964, the team was passed to his wife, who sold them the next year. The team would pass around to various owners for the next almost four decades. In 2003, a group led by the finance entrepreneurs Wyc Grousbeck, Steve Pagliucca, Robert Epstein, and H. Irving Grousbeck—Wyc Grousbeck's father—bought the team. In addition to his other entrepreneurial activities, H. Irving Grousbeck was the founder of Continental Cablevision. This merging of those with finance backgrounds and those with media experience was a logical one given the place of sports in both the media and investment landscapes, a range of expertise that also marked the post-2002 ownership of the Red Sox. The relative success of the Celtics speaks well of the efficacy of those conjoined foci and reiterates the place of professional sports in the symbolic urban economy of the 2000s. That is, in the post-industrial era, where information industries are definitional for the prosperity of a given place, to advertise that success and brand a place strategically creates multiplier effects. This remaking of the team as a digital powerhouse with savvy media professionals at the helm marked a team that was built for contemporary success and one that, through savvy marketing, could extract the bad from the good in building its brand on embedded narratives of "tradition" and "authenticity," without racial stereotypes and racist legacies. Indeed, the reemergence of Bill Russell provided a perfect example of this trajectory.

The Celtics' success on the court in the 2000s was mirrored by their success as a financial entity. The cable revolution in television sports was soon followed by the digital age. The online website NBA.com launched in 1999, and the media site became NBATV in early 2003. The Celtics began their movement away from over-the-airwaves transmission in the early 1980s when PRISM began broadcasting a number of games. After various shifts in the digital/cable carrier, the team's rights reverted to NBCSports-Boston, with whom the Celtics have a highly lucrative relationship. With the shift in the technical dimensions of the medium came a commensurate alteration of its range of dissemination. Celtics broadcasts are available digitally anywhere in the world. Indeed, on many days, I discuss the prior night's game with a friend and former colleague who is now living in Warsaw, Poland. With its favorable fiduciary relationship with its network, the Celtics are currently the fourth most valuable franchise in the NBA, a ranking disproportionate to the relative size of the region's population.

The recent exponential increase in team value is related to the ways in which the team is embedded in the post-industrial economy. NBCSports-Boston is available to a national audience, both by direct subscription and through the purchase of an NBA League Pass. It is also a testament to the ways in which mass media and financial services magnates cross over to the world of professional sports and imbricate their teams—as sports properties—in a broader economic strategy. This process becomes clearer when we look at the shifting teams of owners and their specific ownership strategies.

But part of that success is not simply access; it is both marketing and branding, or in this case rebranding. And that focus, especially since the team reemerged as a competitive success after 2007, has been to maintain the terms of "tradition" and remove from that signifier the embedded aspect of racism. This has involved walking a fine line. Explains one marketing and branding expert: "The Celtics have had the most consistent on-court look of any NBA team, having made only minor adjustments to the wordmark on their jersey. The basic template has remained unaltered for nearly 70 years. The 'Celtics' nickname is appropriate for a city renowned for its large Irish-American population. In fact, Boston has the largest population of Irish-Americans of any city in the United States. The use of green as the team's main color perfectly matches the team's Irish theme, as Ireland is popularly associated with that color."[46] The Celtics maintain the same logo, with some modifications, and team colors that they have used over almost the entire life of their franchise—a logo devised by Red Auerbach's brother, Zang, in the early 1950s. That image features a leprechaun in a Kelly green circle, balancing a basketball on his finger. In order to strip such consistent and white symbols of their nefarious and racist past, it is important that the team actively work to excise that history and substitute a new one.

And while there are a number of factors that make these teams and their fortunes particular to Boston, in many ways their success and connection to their city's name is emblematic of the transformation of both the material dimensions of "the urban" in the late twentieth and early twenty-first centuries and the conceptual parameters of that term. Spectator sports did not magically grow as the national economy entered its post-industrial phase; rather, their cultural roles and revenues grew exponentially as a result of their involvement with and response to the era of globalized trade and gentrified cities, and the related burgeoning of the devices and reach of mass communication. If we think of professional sports as aspects of the information age and the neoliberal, nonproductive economy, then their explosion in the 1980s and 1990s makes perfect sense. The current ownership, and particularly managing partner Wyc Grousbeck, has effectively sought to make the team one that embodies antiracist values. On Twitter, Grousbeck tweeted about his, and the league's, antiracism:

> In the aftermath of George Floyd's death by police, he said in a team statement that: "Sometimes things just need to be said out loud. A statement needs to be made. Black lives matter. It's time for us all to get together and get rid of racism once and for all. . . ." Grousbeck said that it's on him and the rest of his ownership group to carry on the Celtics' legacy in fighting for what's right. "The Celtics have always been leaders in civil rights," Grousbeck said. "We've read a lot about Bill Russell in recent days, but it goes all the way back. The Celtics had the first Black player, the first all-Black starting 5 and the first Black head coach. So, we don't stand second to anybody and I'm trying to carry on in my lame way,

because I'm not one of those greats that built this team, but I'm trying to help with my partners to carry it on."[47]

The team has been centrally involved in the NBA's efforts to support current antiracist activism, and the team's young star Jaylen Brown has been at the center of the league's efforts, with the full support of the team. This is part of an effort to manage the narrative of team and place vigilantly. But even such Boston boosters as Paul Pierce and Kevin Garnett acknowledge that, as Pierce said recently, "Boston is not a place where people consider to play.... It has never been a huge free agent destination.... You can go back to the players who got traded there and never thought they would be there and talk to them. And they will say [positively], 'I didn't know Boston was like this.' The reputation is it's a racist town. But as a sports figure, you don't see it."[48]

Nonetheless, there remain variables that cannot be controlled. With lingering narratives of the racist past always extant, incidents like former Celtic Marcus Smart being addressed with a racial epithet after leaving the Garden disrupt the team image of the *here* and *now* with the *there* and *then*, as Marc J. Spears notes:

> The perception of the city, which had a population that was 53% white and 25% Black in the 2010 census, was not helped by recent events involving Black athletes and Boston sports fans. In 2014, P. K. Subban, who played for the Montreal Canadiens at the time, received racist tweets after a game-winning goal against the Boston Bruins. In 2017, then-Baltimore Orioles outfielder Adam Jones was berated by taunts of "N-word" at Fenway Park while a fan threw a bag of peanuts at him. In 2019, a Celtics fan called then-Golden State Warriors center DeMarcus Cousins a racial slur and was banned from TD Garden for two years.[49]

That same slur was directed at Golden State Warriors player Draymond Green during the 2022 NBA finals.[50] Clearly racist elements persist within the city even as the sports franchises try to minimize them and act immediately when they are in evidence at their arenas. But are these types of occurrences more likely to occur in Boston than in, say, Philadelphia? What does it mean to call a city racist? Does the common culture allow these types of expressions? The legacy of racism, and particularly the association of the city with racism and sports, seems unbreakable, even in an age when images are virtual, infinitely plastic, and ubiquitous.

SECTION III
Boston on Location
Filming the City

FOLLOWING THE ways in which sports have become complicit in furthering extant narratives of place, in the chapters in section 3 I turn to feature-length films, which share with professional sports high visibility in the entertainment marketplace. I consider the place of these films in the production of "Boston" through their strategic use of images of place, as well as the ways in which their narratives reproduce and extend recurring tropes of the city

In chapter 5, I begin by looking at the representations of the city of Boston in a group of films shot mostly on location in the moments that began to define the post-industrial terms of that city, in the 1970s to the early 1980s: *The Friends of Eddie Coyle* (1973), *The Brinks Job* (1978), and *The Verdict* (1982). These films moved toward the moment when the contours of a far more cosmopolitan and prosperous place would become visible in the late 1990s, yet that urban entity would still appear parochial and insular even as the city in fact would become decidedly multicultural and international in its flows of people, capital, and commerce by the turn of the century.[1]

I follow my consideration of those three films with a discussion of a transitional film, *Good Will Hunting* (1997), which was a cultural marker that changed the presence of Boston in film and ushered in a period of far more extensive production. That film accelerated the careers of Matt Damon and Ben Affleck not only as actors but also as producers, writers, and directors, and they have been highly significant to this post-2000 era of production and to the dominant image or representations of Boston in film. As in other chapters, I am vitally interested in the ways in which representations that are embedded in material factors are mitigated by residual relationships to historically received tropes. As a matter of such relationships, assumptions of place are oddly intransigent, creating a dissonance between text (film) and material context (city).

After 1997, film production in Boston burgeoned. Most of the films that featured Boston in focal ways offered a vision of place that was connected to existing tropes of the city with re-elaborations of Boston noir occurring in any number of films, including *Mystic River* (2003), *The Departed* (2006), *Gone Baby Gone* (2007), and *Black Mass* (2015). This list of Boston noirs ignores many other notable films: *The Town* (2010), *The Boondock Saints* (1999), *Monument Ave* (1998), *What Doesn't Kill You* (2008), and others. That such films became the relative norm for location shoots suggests the ways in which the city became a placeholder that meant white, ethnic working-class culture with a strong tie to a vision of the past that remains insistently present. The films provide a vision of a place where the winds of change are actively resisted.

The first part of chapter 6 focuses on the three representative examples: *Mystic River*, *The Departed*, and *Gone Baby Gone*. All three consider the complicated ways in which the past weighs on the present. I consider these films primarily for their intriguing use of location as an element of their thematic focus, a use of place that enhances the resonance of their narratives. They are meditations on the power of history to shape circumstances even as conditions are in the process of changing. This emphasis furthers important tropes of place, exploring ideas of tradition and authenticity by engaging related matters of ethnic solidarity and racial privilege.

In the second section of chapter 6, I look at two films that iterate related matters, *Spotlight* (2015) and *Black Mass*, though these two films add the condition of "based on a true story." Both are cases considered with respect to a journalistic pre-text discussed in chapter 3. This second section considers how journalism serves as the raw material for more involved narratives that assert their status as fact-based, but it also shows how such films morph into representations of a city that emphasizes a received history and affirms its preconceived social characteristics. These productions are akin to literary nonfiction, but as films they become a form of docudrama. An emphasis on place in visual media typically creates a realist effect, much as that realist effect creates recurring narratives of place.

CHAPTER FIVE

The *New* Boston and the Grip of Tradition

This chapter focuses initially on a group of films set—and at least partially shot—in Boston between 1973 and 1982: *The Friends of Eddie Coyle* (1973), *The Brinks Job* (1978), and *The Verdict* (1982). It notes the general ways they portray the city and their lack of a strong or resonant vision of the material city in its particulars. It then focuses on *Good Will Hunting* (1997) as a transitional text, ushering in a period when productions would employ the city and its locations as a featured piece of both the narrative and the visual text. This shift ushered in a new age of the mediated city, coming as it did at the beginnings of the digital age, a period of significant change for all manner of media productions but particularly so for feature-length motion pictures, which would become all the more available as the age of the VCR morphed into that of the DVD, and then of streaming platforms. Indeed, all of these films essentially achieved another life as they were reissued in new and higher-resolution electronic formats, as their analog images became digital.

Boston prior to the 1990s was the site for relatively few feature films so its presence as a media projection was limited. The few films that did employ the city as a location were major public events—*The Thomas Crown Affair* (1968), *The Out of Towners* (1970), and *The Paper Chase* (1973). But the latter two provided only fleeting images of the city—*The Out of Towners* employs the city as a starting point for a trip to New York City, marking the departure city as provincial relative to arrival in the "Big Apple," while *The Paper Chase* employs Harvard Law School as something of an island unto itself. *The Thomas Crown Affair* did shoot more widely in the city and employs notions of class and caste traditionally connected to Boston, but the film is deficient in a developed conception of place, lacking landmarks and neighborhoods and falling into its generic status as a caper film. All three films use their locations ornamentally rather than integrally. More generally in the industry, the concentration of urban films notably concerned with place as location occurred after the 1960s, when location shooting burgeoned. But for most cities, including Boston, such productions only occurred in significant number after the late 1990s.[1] Some examples of even earlier Boston films include *Mystery Street*, a relatively low-budget police procedural (dir. John Sturges, 1950) that did shoot on location, employing Harvard Medical School as a site for its action, as well as Beacon Hill and Cape Cod. Similarly, an anticommunist procedural based on a story by J. Edgar Hoover, *Walk East on Beacon* (dir. Alfred L. Werker, 1952) employed Boston locations, including Beacon Hill and Scollay Square. But the most Boston-centric of features, the previously noted adaptation of Edwin O'Connor's bestselling 1956 novel *The Last Hurrah* (based broadly on the life of former Boston mayor and congressman James Michael Curley) was made into a film shot entirely on soundstages, directed by John Ford and starring Spencer Tracy in 1958. *The Last Hurrah*, in both forms, serves as a reminder of an earlier narrative of place, a story that highlights the ongoing power structure between an entrenched white Anglo-Saxon Protestant aristocracy and an Irish American political class.

There are many technical and economic explanations for this shift to location shooting. In the 1960s and 1970s, while studios could save on the construction of sets by going to a location, they also increased other costs by employing this strategy, including travel expenses. Further, location shooting was unpredictable, subject to fluctuations in weather and other local factors. But by the early 1970s, as film stock became more sensitive and cameras and processing equipment smaller, the prospect of defining a kind of physical realism through the capturing of images of actual places became increasingly attractive. The macro-economic state of the film industry also created the environment for shooting outside of Hollywood. With the gradual demise of the studio system in the 1960s, an economic event that mirrored broader changes in the U.S. economy that ushered in the post-industrial age, Hollywood had largely abandoned its production-line method of making films. This movement away from the studio system was, to some degree, initiated by the Supreme Court's *Paramount* decision of 1948, which required that the studios divest themselves of their theaters, thus ending the vertical integration of production and exhibition, and furthered by changes in the audience for theatrical presentations.[2] By the 1960s, studios were shedding the contracts of their film workers and moving toward a model of independent production. Such a model enhanced the allure of small-scale location shoots. As Lawrence Webb explains, "For an independently produced film, even with guaranteed distribution from a major company, location shooting was likely to be the cheaper option."[3] Further, the "New Hollywood" filmmakers were often the products of film schools that emphasized location shooting. That new generation of directors included autodidactic film buffs as well as those who had emerged from documentary or industrial films. In all cases these backgrounds brought a value and experience to filming outside of studios. The predominant aesthetic of the New Hollywood moment (1967–80) emphasized a kind of neorealism that valued the presumed authenticity of place. With the inducement in many states of filming tax credits and the creation of production facilities after 2000, location shooting became a more viable option for producers. In the earlier 1970s, states and cities often even lacked a film office to help coordinate the logistics of production.

The films that form the focus of the first part of this chapter—*The Friends of Eddie Coyle*, *The Brinks Job*, and *The Verdict*—are intriguing for their representations of a city on the cusp between relative dissolution—in the 1950s and 1960s—and substantial demographic change and economic success (as a center for finance capital) in the 1990s and 2000s. While these films offer few signature landmarks, they do, at times and unevenly, provide textures of the city: its class structure, its ethnic groups, the local patois. They also show it as physically modest, and at times down at the heels. Boston was a site of production for narrative reasons, but it is invoked in ways that are broadly atmospheric. Clearly it is decidedly less glamorous or resonant than New York or Los Angeles, and lacks the counterculture imprimatur of filmic San Francisco, or even the noir legacy.[4]

In the sense that cities that succeed in the digital age are concerned with their image and brand, which are synergistically combined with more palpable factors, these films, and especially *The Friends of Eddie Coyle*, provided a template that would serve later filmmakers, who in turn would further distill and refine it. This gradually emerging definition of the city of Boston suggests a vision of the urban that is all but in direct contradiction of Kevin Lynch's definition of "success."[5] That is, cities gain value for their conceptual navigability and not for their geographic articulation for their residents. These films are all geographically problematic, with *The Friends of Eddie Coyle* being the most articulate in its representation of proximate spaces. The others imagine the city in a range of relatively distinct venues, offering a place that is expressively available but largely unmappable as a coherent entity.

Boston before Branding

It is a broad depiction of place that occurs in these three films.[6] They define a Boston that is not the bifurcated city of rich and poor that we see in more contemporary productions; rather, the city is more clearly caught in the maw of its history and the residual class resentments of that past, populated by ethnic groups that were highly visible in the earlier twentieth century but that would be a relatively smaller proportion of the late twentieth- and twenty-first-century metropolis. Such visions of class and ethnicity play well with the tropes we have been locating in other forms of communication. In these films, we can see their more nuanced expression. In *The Friends of Eddie Coyle*, we see only fleeting images of a more prosperous city and largely remain amid the less affluent, with Boston looking much like the news footage broadcast during the busing crisis of the next year, though we do at points spy an upper-middle-class, suburban home. *The Verdict* shows the lavish, urban neighborhoods of well-compensated doctors and the regal residence of the princes of the Catholic church, anticipating the many views of Cardinal Bernard Law's estate that appeared in news reports after the story of sexual abuse in the church broke.

But largely in these films, Boston is a city stuck within the tightly circumscribed bounds of its history, in which a glimmer of a changing world can be glimpsed, but it is not a world that is even clearly changing. These earlier films define their working-class communities as socially articulate and geographically so, separated from the core of Boston by a significant expanse, both physical and aspirational. All three films engage in a kind of temporal vision that is either nostalgic or static. Of the three films, *The Verdict* is the most centripetal in its organization, and almost claustrophobically so, as it is centered around Beacon Hill and the Statehouse, and its wealth is urban rather than suburban—though the place-specific articulation of that centripetal organization is very broad, since it features a substantial number of exteriors that are tagged as "Boston" but that are actually of New York City. The city we see in all three films is one anchored in the past with little in the way of momentum to push it toward a future horizon. This vision, then, imagines the relative non-place of Boston in the moment just before it became a more usual virtual presence. In these films "Boston" becomes a kind of placeholder for the post-industrial, pre-global city of the northeastern United States. We find the city of the busing crisis, the Charles Stuart murder case, the story of Whitey Bulger, and the priest abuse stories. These films, as narratives of a broader geography, delve into places outside of South Boston and downtown Boston, into nooks and crannies that nevertheless still retain a clear connection to those more iconic places.

Boston Noir and the Bonds of Tradition

The Friends of Eddie Coyle, directed by Peter Yates and based on the Boston noir novel by George V. Higgins, is the most site specific of these three films: its exteriors are all shot on location in the city's immediate region. It is very much a Boston movie, defining a narrative of place that would continue to serve as a kind of model for future narratives. The city is a bit rundown, with the exception of the recurring presence of the city's gleaming new City Hall Plaza, which is a paean to a kind of top-down urban planning that marks the era, that sees the goal of new architecture as divorcing sites from their broader and decayed, urban context. The film's central character, Eddie Coyle (played by Robert Mitchum), is an ex-convict, a low-ranking member of an Irish American crime network, who is cooperating with the FBI in order to have his sentence for gun selling reduced. Also cooperating, unbeknownst to Coyle, is one of the gang's key figures, Dillon (Peter Boyle). In the climax of the film, Dillon arranges for Coyle's assassination at the behest of the crime boss. Only after Coyle's death do we learn that Coyle's death was ordered for an act of betrayal by Dillon, not Coyle, with the FBI. That Dillon and FBI agent Foley (Richard Jordan) meet twice at City Hall Plaza contextualizes that place as one decidedly unwelcoming to the residual populations of the city's ethnic enclaves, and indeed Dillon seems smaller and particularly out of place photographed there.

Coyle himself is spatially and socially isolated in the urban sprawl, but this isolation defines his natural context and relative comfort zone. It is a sprawl that encompasses a region that has access to public transportation, and which stands as a projection of neighborhoods connected to a nearby inner city. But it also takes in the city's further sprawl, its exurban regions that include gravel pits and distant construction trailers as far away as New Hampshire, about sixty miles north of Boston, and its suburban train station with service to New York. It is a textured narrative. The film operates within the crime genre with many of the noir trappings that were often employed within the era—shadows, terse dialogue, hard-luck characters, and generally urban and gritty textures.

Opening up the narrative just slightly, we can see beyond its geographic and social insularity. It is intriguing to think of the film's central Irish American characters (Coyle, Dillon, Foley) as part of the ongoing Boston-Dublin traffic, a movement that had been going on for over a century at the point of film production, a movement of humans that, while diasporic, is largely conceived as outside of the conventional definitions of cosmopolitanism.[7] Indeed, Coyle's wife is an Irish immigrant, emphasizing the historic and ongoing movement of Irish nationals to the city where they have historically and culturally been a defining presence. But this immigrant group would be less proportionately significant in the 2000s, when Boston had more immigrants than it did in 1950, but fewer proportionately than the city had in 1910.[8] And while Irish ancestry would remain significant in the city and in the region, later immigrants would be from a range of nations. Per a mayoral demographic report, "As of 2000, more than 25% of Boston's population is foreign-born. The fastest growing communities are Latino and Asian. The top 10 countries of origin of these new Bostonians are Haiti, Dominican Republic, China, Vietnam, El Salvador, Cape Verde, Jamaica, Ireland, Colombia, and Brazil."[9]

Spatially, *The Friends of Eddie Coyle* is very much a Boston film of the 1970s. It offers no images of distinctive urban streetscapes, nor does it envision urban charm. In one scene where the gun seller provides arms to would-be revolutionaries near Harvard on Memorial Drive, we do see the Boston skyline (such as it was), including the Prudential Tower, in the distance. But there is no lingering over that image nor is there a strategic framing. It operates as a visual fact in the background. Similarly, although Harvard and MIT are close to the filming location, they are off screen. That the film does not fetishize signature locales and structures speaks to Boston's generic status as a *type* of place, rather than as a locale to be embraced and celebrated.

The Friends of Eddie Coyle looks to the sprawl that was a feature of the decentered city of the 1950s and early 1960s, a city that was conceived as a business center but was deemed by urban planners as unfit for middle-class residency. Unlike the subway-defined city of *Good Will Hunting*, which takes place along the Red Line of the Metropolitan Boston Transit

Authority (MBTA), *The Friends of Eddie Coyle* is mostly a world of cars and highways, with the exception of the non-driving character Dillon, who uses mass transit to traverse from Quincy Center to Government Center in downtown Boston. But again, unlike in *Good Will Hunting*, that trip is implied and never shown, giving the viewer no opportunity to take in and fawn over the sights they may encounter along the way. And when Dillon encounters his FBI handler, he is mocked for not having driven.

Coyle lives outside of the city, in the Wollaston section of Quincy, about two miles north of where Dillon catches his train. Unlike Dillon, Coyle has a home we see, including a wife and kids. Quincy was then a predominantly working-class, Irish American enclave, and largely functioned as an extension of the Boston neighborhood of South Dorchester, both demographically and architecturally. The film also largely takes place in the modest southern suburbs of the city, showing scenes shot in Dedham and Canton and then entering the city on the edge of Dorchester. It features a pivotal scene in the old Boston Garden at a Bruins game, and two scenes at the then newly constructed Boston City Hall in the Government Center district of the city, a region completely rebuilt in the early 1960s.

The Brinks Job is a quasi-historical drama based on one of the largest armored car robberies in history, the holdup of the Brinks cash depot in Boston's North End in 1950. Yet the film does little with the locales and textures of the city, nor does the film invoke Boston's urban history. There are a few identifiable shots in the city's North End, a fleeting glimpse of the Custom House Tower, and in the North End scenes there are shots of the Old North Church, most famous as the place where the lanterns were hung in a signal to Paul Revere. But much as Peter Yates effaced his photographing of the Prudential Tower and the internationally known universities in Cambridge, so did William Friedkin refuse to linger on these sites or to frame them to emphasize their significance. They are merely incidental parts of his landscape. *The Brinks Job* becomes a kind of touchstone for later films, perhaps as a matter of its scale of production and its emphasis on a significant local tale. This heist was later used by Ben Affleck as a model for a robbery in *The Town* (2010). Friedkin does reconstruct a facsimile of Boston in the late 1930s, 1940s, and early 1950s, and in doing so develops a film that is spatially constrained, even as it suggests the existence of contiguous regions that are easily accessed by cars, and which have a disproportionate role in the film considering its setting and chronology.

The film begins in an alley built for the shoot, in the entertainment district of the city as it existed in the late 1970s. The title tells us it is "Boston 1938," and because of the cobblestone streets and theatrical marquis in the background, this seems broadly possible, though the scene lacks the textures seen in *The Friends of Eddie Coyle*. Viewers can spy the Pilgrim Theater, an old burlesque house and then a movie theater—and finally a porno theater in its last days—in the background, defining the so-called Combat Zone on lower Washington Street. The scene is very stylized, with musicians playing in straw hats amid the back alleys, with a painted sign on the building advertising burlesque. It is also a set that broadly evokes place but is not discernably of Boston, suggesting that Friedkin was more interested in nostalgia than in history.

The Boston depicted in *The Verdict* is less poetically nostalgic and more gritty and realist. The film is a courtroom drama in which Paul Newman plays a struggling attorney pitted against the Protestant legal establishment and the Catholic church over a wrongful death case that took place at one of the archdiocese's hospitals. Yet, almost none of the film is actually shot in the city, offering many New York locations as stand-ins for those of Boston. Nonetheless, the film does offer shots of Back Bay Station, the Suffolk County Court House, and the Massachusetts Statehouse, as well as a few fairly nondescript parts of South Boston. But even with its taking place in a locale that seems spatially urban, the locales are neither geographically coherent nor do they invoke Boston in particular.

All three films trade on Boston's embedded sociocultural narratives of place, but each is limited in its depiction of the material spaces it thematizes. Each film approaches the city slightly differently. In *The Friends of Eddie Coyle*, we encounter the world articulated in George V. Higgins's Boston noir novels, with their air of authenticity and emphasis on honor—or the absence and lack of it—among thieves. It is the film that pays the most attention to accents and vernacular among the three. Even Robert Mitchum affects something of a Boston accent, an unusual gesture for this actor and a concession he rarely made throughout his long career. In *The Brinks Job*, there is a gesture toward a kind of historical documentation but through a lens that places that world at a distance. It retains elements of the crime world in *The Friends of Eddie Coyle* but removes the dimension of authenticity by infusing the narrative with a kind of ironic distance. This occurs through the at-times ironic dialogue, the distancing of character and event that is a matter of its visual strategy, and its use of midcentury popular jazz in its soundtrack. Such a postmodern gloss also finds its way into films like Ben Affleck's largely unsuccessful *Live by Night* (2015) and even Sean Duffy's much more successful *Boondock Saints* (1999). But in *The Brinks Job*, the presence of such elements, techniques that are the antithesis of those Friedkin used in his earlier *The French Connection* (1971), are a bit jarring.

The Verdict's emphasis is on class and ethnicity, a focus that becomes part of the shorthand of many Boston-based features of the post-2000 era, including a film like *Spotlight* (2015). But this trope is one that preexisted the 1980s, serving as an earlier version of a predominantly regional narrative, and featured in the novel and film *The Last Hurrah* (1958), among other films. *The Verdict*, though, employs the downwardly mobile Irish Catholic lawyer Frank Galvin (Paul Newman) as the protagonist, and thus shifts how viewers encounter the Protestant-Catholic divide.

The New Old Boston and the Old New Boston

The paucity of films shot on location in Boston in this period illustrates that the city as a place was not prominent in the mass consciousness of the nation. Unlike New York City, for example, which became a recurring site of production during the New Hollywood era, no film producers were taking multiple trips to Boston to scout for locations.[10] *Altered States* (1979) and *Starting Over* (1979) employed Boston in passing. In *Field of Dreams* (1988), Fenway Park has an important cameo. *Good Will Hunting* was released in the same year (1997) as the Boston-specific *Monument Ave.* and the less Boston-specific *A Civil Action*. *Good Will Hunting* is also notable as a transitional film made at a moment that was already on the way to a more significant Boston "brand" televisually: the two successful television series *Cheers* (1982–93) and *St. Elsewhere* (1982–88) were ostensibly set in the city, as was the later series *Ally McBeal* (1997–2002). The appearance of an ersatz Boston that primarily existed on Hollywood soundstages is an interesting complement to these three films of roughly the same period, which are both place-specific and yet also not so specific.

While the "new" Boston was slow to emerge, the "old" Boston is ever present. This view of the city as possessing residual historical significance, one that easily provokes nostalgia and intransigence in its popular rendering, conveniently finds its way into these films. Boston in these films is white, ethnic, and built during earlier eras. *The Friends of Eddie Coyle* is a film of the older, working-class suburbs of the inner ring, a film that basks in the long-established criminality of Irish American and Italian American gangs, their internal doings, and their slippery codes of ethics. The same mix is available in *The Brinks Job* and also to some degree in *The Verdict*. Boston is white, graying around the edges, and beset with historical resentments and rivalries. These definitions are so much a given that these films offer nothing physically new, and instead provide a Boston that, while not quite a place in itself, is a compendium of images that prominently trade in residual definitions of the city.

The Brinks Job, in effect, creates its own city, with sets that are built on city streets but are only specific to the film, functioning as a kind of *essence* of the city. That is, rather than featuring the city that was there in the time of this film's production and focusing on the elements that would recall the city as it existed during the chronology of the narrative, this film devises an ersatz city that attempts to distill "place" and represent it through period construction. It finds not a city that informs the narrative but a series of urban sites that assert a kind of theatrical artifice. This type of location shooting recalls the Hollywood practice of the 1950s and early 1960s when films like *On the Waterfront* (1954) and *West Side Story* (1961) essentially employed city locales as soundstages. In the most filmed street scenes, we have a market set up in the region near the Boston Common, but the fronts are far more Hollywood than Boston. The Egleston Diner where Tony, the film's protagonist (Peter Falk), works, and which seems to be contiguous to that street, is in East Boston, quite a way from that location in real life, and the renamed Egleston Square is in Roxbury, a place that is miles away and has nothing to do with East Boston. The most coherent geographic strategy employed is that which locates the Brinks Depot in the North End, and which actually films in the contiguous streets, the same streets that Ben Affleck used in *The Town*. But again, the viewer is provided with little sense of place or space. In 1950, the North End of Boston was a teeming, substantially Italian American neighborhood where one was as likely to encounter a North End–specific, accented Italian as a Boston-accented English. The film does little with such precise historical details.

The Verdict is even less exacting regarding place. While it does offer some appropriate Boston locations, many of its scenes were shot in New York. Its most recurring location is a bar where the failing lawyer Frank Galvin parks himself for many of his waking hours. His preferred perch is at a pinball machine by a window that overlooks a corner of a park, but the park is neither the Boston Common nor the Public Garden. Indeed, the latter location seems to be the one evoked, a place also employed in *Good Will Hunting* to mark and define the context of the narrative. But in this very claustrophobic rendering of a sort-of-particular place, we are given a view of a bar on Avenue B in the Lower East Side of New York, and the park is a corner of Tompkins Square. Similarly, we see street shots of Brooklyn Heights, the Otto Kahn mansion at East 91st Street, and the Tweed Courthouse in Lower Manhattan.

As we encounter these three films, "Boston" seems to be an amalgam of fairly particular vocal inflections—though this is less true in *The Brinks Job*, where New York–reared actors like Paul Sorvino and Peter Falk make minimal efforts to capture the local sound. But certainly in the other two films, the Boston accent is an important marker. The other defining characteristic seems to be a residual racism, one that defines both the parochialism and the class resentments of place, though historically, that world was starting to ebb, or at least it was by 1980. This demographic shift suggests that at the point when these films were released, the city was at or near its lowest in population and significance, a fact highlighted in these representations, which lack bustling, teeming crowds; central gathering places; and in the case of *The Friends of Eddie Coyle*, much of the city itself.

In mass cultural terms, then, the representational irony of these films, and virtually all subsequent ones, is that the Boston shown as a residual bastion of working-class life is a city in which the working-class increasingly ceased to exist as we move from the 1970s to the 2010s. Such an emphasis is reiterative of the notions of place that were so central to my analysis in earlier chapters. And although these films portray Boston as a locale defined by its working-class population, they seem to present little evidence of the locales of work. To be of the working class is more a matter of limited wealth and taste than it is of the work one does. The films show modest living conditions, limited aspirations, and, above all, a kind of white tribalism.

This backdrop of the city where racial, ethnic, and class antipathies abound, a vital dimension of the city's national profile and one that still obtains—but to a lesser degree—forms the broad image of the represented Boston, and there are certainly many continuities between these earlier films and the later ones. Within the apparently place-specific narratives of these three films, the meaning of the city includes both a deep parochialism and a residual racism that finds itself in the texts at certain key moments. The fact and persistence of such sentiments and related allusions to that narrowness of vision and experience by class, race, and ethnicity becomes more apparent.

The narrowness and class distinctions of Boston are all over these films. *The Friends of Eddie Coyle* is immersed in the world of small-time gangsters and gun-runners; in *The Brinks Job*, it is safe crackers and bank robbers (see *City on a Hill*, 2019–22 and *The Town*); and in *The Verdict*, it is the regional, class divide from a different perch, dwelling in the world of the fallen elite and the elite itself, while in this cloistered world of lawyers, cardinals, monsignors, and doctors, the working-class hero is a female Irish immigrant and the victims are all, while Boston-born, of similarly modest means. More generally, we catch glimpses of economic activity that would employ a group of midlevel workers, such as the gravel pit where guns are transacted in *The Friends of Eddie Coyle*, a site on the urban periphery and which is in keeping with the larger geographic orientation of the film. In *The Brinks Job*, the thieves rob a gumball factory and a chicken abattoir. These are all small, regional enterprises, also away from the city center, and indicative of a vision of pre–World War II sprawl, an era that prefigured the rise of interstate highways in the 1950s. Also notable is the fact that these places are not in operation when we encounter them, so viewers never see actual work being done. In *The Verdict*, the focus is moving toward the emergent orientation of the city—it is focused on the urban core and it is a matter of professionals. The courtroom drama focuses on the paralysis of a working-class woman who aspirates into her mask as she is being sedated. The woman's advocates are her sister and brother-in-law, who are marked as working-class by their dress, speech, and aspirations, yet, we are never provided even a clue as to the work they do.

This last film points to the fact that the city and the region by the early 1980s already possessed the academic and intellectual infrastructure to begin moving toward its ultimate success in the coming post-industrial information age in the elaboration of the technological sector that was housed largely beyond the city limits, to the southwest. By 1990, the regional workforce had morphed into one that was geared toward technology.[11] After the 1950s, the region's spatial orientation was decidedly away from the urban core, which is evident in *The Friends of Eddie Coyle* and, to some degree, *The Brinks Job*. Each of these films develops a vision of the city that is substantially centrifugal and sprawling outward, a world of roads and cars. Such an "urban" vision (and then its undoing in *The Verdict*) suggests how these films represented the changing spatial emphases of cities as they rehearsed the emergent post-industrial development of the movement of elite populations *back* to the city core. Such change is the driving force of gentrification, as inner cities increasingly house the genteel and educated classes, while the residue of the working class is in suburban locales. This is certainly the case with Boston and the relative absence of a more contemporary sense of space and place that dates these first two films.

Race and Ethnicity in Boston

Boston as of 1972 was a spatially segregated city with its African American population overwhelmingly residing in the neighborhoods to the south of downtown, primarily Roxbury and Mattapan. It also was a city with only a very small percentage of nonwhite residents, 18 percent, most of whom were African American. Philadelphia, for example was over 33 percent African American in 1970.[12] But even though that was a fairly small number, and distinctly small for a city of that time in the Northeast Corridor of the United States, that population had doubled over the past ten years, since 1960. Each of these films has a recessed racial commentary that is nevertheless significant and effectively can be brought to the fore and employed as a key interpretive element. Indeed, these films—by picturing the spatial logic that both reifies and reproduces the fact of segregation, the key demographic rationale for court-ordered busing—show us a city with virtually no Black or Brown faces.

As my discussion has indicated, class *and* race are easily placed at the center of these films. This emphasis is further justified by the fact that the busing crisis serves as their general temporal context. Each of the films has at least a moment where considerations of race become pronounced, if not exactly emphasized, and through a noting of those moments, we may come to see the embedded conception of place that animates these 1970s and 1980s explications of Boston.

The Friends of Eddie Coyle starts with a kidnapping that is the beginning of a bank robbery. But rather than occurring in an ornate, downtown depository, this robbery takes place in a nondescript branch, one that is in the inner-ring suburb of Dedham. This introductory scene is a reasonable entree into the decidedly downbeat world. But beyond our plot, spatially the film rehearses the moment just before gentrification became an important regional shift, a later time when industrial suburbs like Quincy served as a fulcrum between the gentrified zones of the inner city and the wealth of certain bedroom suburbs. Both Dillon and Coyle are vestiges of another time, a moment when cities and their immediate environs were the zones of those left behind. But even as we see those spaces, we are provided with a vision of a kind of urban renewal, such as shown with the new City Hall Plaza, which opened in 1968. This unappealing landmark suggests the failures of urban renewal as a governmental enterprise. Indeed, it may have the impact of elevating the significance of the preserved and redeveloped past, of the comity of spaces like Quincy Market and Faneuil Hall. The plaza stands as a replacement for former public spaces that far more effectively provided a welcoming space for the public. It signifies the demise of that sphere and, in effect, heralds the coming of the neoliberal regime. As of late 2022, the plaza reopened in a renovated form, offering a more inviting and commodious space.[13]

Ultimately, we see Eddie's demise set up in the parking lot of the Quincy mass transit station, a modern domain of heartlessness akin to the ugly City Hall Plaza, a place of no honor among thieves, and the prelude to the execution takes place in the old Boston Garden. The scene reeks of authenticity, showing the grimy arena and its working-class patrons from a second balcony perch, complete with spilled beer. Yates employs the grimy, claustrophobic, and crumbling facility as part of his vision of place. The all-white crowd loves its team in an unquestioning way and is quick to respond to the blood on the ice. In an ironic aside, the beer-addled Coyle stands up and affirms his appreciation for Hall of Fame player Bobby Orr, commenting on both his talent and his great future—as of 1972, Orr was only twenty-four years old; however, due to repeated knee injuries, he was already hobbled and would play his last full season in 1974–75. Yates captures the unthinking, vaguely inhuman aspect of the generic crowd and of this crowd in particular, and his depiction is knowingly space-specific. The shooting occurs in the parking lot of Boston Bowl, a bowling alley in Dorchester.

When Eddie Coyle and Dillon are out and about in Boston, Quincy, or Dedham, the faces we see are only white. This is both historically accurate and elaborative of the terms of spatial segregation in the city. When the

FIGURE 13. Eddie Coyle and Dillon watch the Bruins. —Courtesy Screen Shot.

various banks are robbed in the film, neither a Black patron nor a Black worker appears at any of those institutions, though the distance from Mattapan, an increasingly African American neighborhood as of the early 1970s, to Dedham is only about five miles. It is notable that Coyle's Quincy would be substantially Vietnamese and Cambodian by the 2000s.

In a key scene in the film, Eddie Coyle, in conversation with his partner in crime and ultimate betrayer, Dillon, confides that he needs one last payday before he goes off to prison, so that his "wife will not have to go on welfare, like a n****r." This racial and racist language is uttered in passing without embellishment and elicits no comment. This is a world where African Americans are broadly reduced and where assumptions of behavior track clearly with such racism. In ways, this moment, along with the absence of Brown and Black faces from public spaces, opens out into a world defined by the racial antipathies displayed in the busing crisis. In this manner, then, the accents so carefully elaborated by the various actors, which provide the sound of authenticity to the film, are easily employed in the service of racist utterances.

The Brinks Job largely depicts the interethnic alliances and conflicts between Irish and Italian criminals, including somewhat more established and successful Irish criminals and including some who are—apparently by their accents—recent émigrés to the United States. And just as *The Friends of Eddie Coyle* has its moment of racial elaboration, one with broader implications in the world depicted, so does *The Brinks Job*. About four-fifths of the way through the film, after some of the robbers have been apprehended for profligately spending their ill-got gains, the next scene depicts the main characters, Jazz and Tony—both Italian American—discussing what has happened to their compatriots and how to stay out of jail. This conversation takes place as they walk through the elevated railway Dudley Station, in the heart of Roxbury, the center of the city's African American community, then and now. Apparently, this scene was shot in Roxbury because the old station was abandoned and condemned for demolition. This historical fact was a matter of racial demographics, and the proposed building of the inner-belt highway through Roxbury was also a matter of racial demographics, although that road was never built.

The larger effect of this scene in this location on the narrative is intriguing. By 1950, the African American population of this district had roughly doubled in the previous decade from 5,700 to 11,000. Our historical sense of the district is further enhanced by the memoir of Malcolm X, who called Roxbury home during the 1940s, and wrote, "I didn't know the world contained as many Negroes as I saw thronging downtown Roxbury at night, especially on Saturdays. Neon lights, nightclubs, pool halls, bars, the cars they drove! Restaurants made the streets smell—rich, greasy, down-home Black cooking! Jukeboxes blared Erskine Hawkins, Duke Ellington, Cootie Williams, dozens of others."[14] Yet, the Dudley Station Tony and Jazz walk through is all white. Similarly, when they walk off the station platform, there is no sense of an African American presence, although the film is very aware of period details, such as campaign signs, local products, and period clothing. This erasure becomes a matter of the film's vision of place and what constitutes a nostalgic look back at it. The fact that Dudley Station maintains its period "look" appears to be the motivation for this location, but its use also tracks with a broader vision of time and place.

In the last of these films, *The Verdict*, we have perhaps the most powerful expression of casual racism in any of the three. In this courtroom drama, the case against the archdiocese brought by the Irish lawyer, Frank Galvin, of Boston College Law School, depends on the expert testimony of a doctor, who vanishes just as he is about to take the stand. This leaves Galvin scrambling for another expert witness, and he finally gets a Doctor Thompson to take the train from New York. When Thompson arrives, Galvin lets him walk past, not recognizing him until Thompson introduces himself.

The fact that he is African American, something Galvin did not previously know, clearly causes a great deal of consternation. The camera dwells briefly on Galvin's shocked expression. Galvin never recovers his equanimity, and the court also treats Thompson with minimal respect. Galvin's upset may be a matter of his own racial orientation and prejudices, but the broader treatment of Thompson suggests a more systemic form of institutional and urban racism.

The Verdict also emphasizes the connection between the Roman Catholic church and other centers of power in the city—all of them monolithically white—in effect making it a political organization more substantially concerned with its own authority and wealth than with any abiding sense of justice. Similarly, the judiciary is represented as deeply involved with the city's centers of power and less with its role as a neutral device for the exacting of justice. In this moral positioning, *The Verdict* engages the broadly liberal political dimension of the early 1980s in order to focus on the residue of retrograde, reactionary dimensions of the city tagged as "Boston." Such a view is a vital aspect of the film's narrative and one that plays off of broad mass-cultural associations of the city with racism and reaction.

Good Will Hunting and Mediated Boston

In the fifteen years from 1982 to 1997, this image of Boston became further distilled by events such as the Stuart case and the gradual emergence of the Whitey/Billy Bulger story, among other mass-media expressions. *Good Will Hunting*, written by and starring former Cambridge residents Matt Damon and Ben Affleck, is in fact a celebration of particular images of Boston. Some of these appeared in the earlier films and would become codified over the next two decades in any number of additional films and television shows, but now with a gallery of images that had already become chronotopes of place and time. Where these earlier films *assume* class distinctions, *Good Will Hunting* and its successors *explore* class distinctions, suggesting the resentments and dislocations of the neoliberal era while simultaneously eliding them, employing Boston for its residual associations with working-class ethnicity—particularly Irish. In an outtake from the film, this intention, which pervades the film as a whole, is highlighted by a loving and languid treatment of South Boston's St. Patrick's Day Parade. And while it is clear why this clip failed to make the final cut of the film—it adds nothing to the narrative and is merely reiterative of a kind of local color—it is a further affirming aspect of the film and a foreshadowing of very similar set-piece that concludes *Mystic River* (2003).[15] Its very presence defines the broad intentions of the director and writers. This film is the beginning of a series that celebrate South Boston and the ensconcing of these Boston place-specific chronotopes: the three-decker house as an emblem of the city, working-class white ethnicity, and other images shown in the coverage of the busing crisis, the sexual abuse by priests crisis, and the Bulger brothers. While references to those iconic images appear in at least two of the earlier films—*The Friends of Eddie Coyle* and *The Verdict*—it is only in this film that such images become definitional, the symbols that define place through their emplacement in the narrative, through their recurrence, and in the ways the camera lovingly dwells on them.

The very fact of the film's production speaks to the state of moving pictures in the late twentieth century and the way that condition relates both to the post-industrial economy and its representations. As explained previously, Hollywood's industrial era had largely ended by the late 1960s. At that point, studios became more focused on distribution than production, and productions were largely left to independent entrepreneurs, thus decentralizing the industry and making film work a type of labor that occurred largely on demand. There were far fewer set builders and lighting crews under contract to major studios, and no more contract screenwriters. The absence of such contract workers was a factor in promoting location shoots, since the industry's workforce labored on demand rather than by an ongoing contractual relationship with a studio. By the 1990s, this mode of production was already well articulated, and the fact that outsiders like Damon and Affleck could be so important in the development of a film was indicative of the new system. Damon originally wrote the screenplay when he was still a college student, and then further developed it in consultation with Affleck throughout the 1990s. Both actors are from Cambridge, a city of many classes and ethnicities. Both are children of divorced parents, and both had amassed social capital (if less financial capital) by the time they were pitching this film. *Good Will Hunting* astutely employs Boston's geography as a means of articulating questions regarding the relationship between wealth and talent, dramatically illustrating how opportunity is relatively unavailable to those of great gifts but a certain class. This film articulates the issue of social mobility by defining it as one of geographic mobility.

That these two then-young emerging actors attempted to control the fate of their written work recalls the case of the young Sylvester Stallone in the mid-1970s as he shopped his screenplay for *Rocky*. Like Damon and Affleck, Stallone was a struggling actor who had written a marketable screenplay. In return for the sale of the screenplay, the film's producers assured him that he would star as the film's title character. The film was shot economically on location in Philadelphia, providing iconic scenes of that city. In this emphasis, *Good Will Hunting* also evokes *Rocky*. That film grossed over $225 million worldwide on a production budget of just under a million dollars. Stallone received award nominations for his screenplay and for his acting in a lead role. Stallone's ability to maintain his centrality in the project reveals the ways in which the film industry of that period was relatively open to newcomers and how major producers, in this case Irwin Winkler and Robert Chartoff— perhaps best known as the producers for a number of Martin Scorsese's films, including *New York, New York* (1977), *Raging Bull* (1980), and *Goodfellas* (1990)—were open to relatively risky enterprises. Winkler and Chartoff were emblematic of the independent producers of the period, and *Rocky* had the markings of many of their projects—quirky, driven by an individual, and lacking a bankable star. In *Good Will Hunting*, as in *Rocky*, the money-saving strategy of shooting on location only enhanced the resonance of the film's narrative by making it about an urban place (Boston, Philadelphia) riven by issues of race and class in a decidedly post-industrial context.

Good Will Hunting also evokes *Rocky* in its paradigmatic use of urban space, which translates post-industrial urban decay into gritty authenticity. This vision of life in the underclass recurs in *Good Will Hunting*. In addition, the narrative arc of *Rocky* is, to a great degree, reiterated in *Good Will Hunting*, but rather than mobility emerging from the brute force of boxing, as in *Rocky*, *Good Will Hunting* gives us the power of a savant-intellect, an appropriate post-industrialist and financial-capitalist substitution given the rise of the neoliberal economy, marked particularly by the ascent of finance capitalism in Boston among other cities. That intellect produces opportunity is affirmed by the transformation of Will's geography of home from South Boston to Palo Alto. This transition recalls that of "The Italian Stallion" (Rocky). Explains Lawrence Webb of Rocky's famous jog up the steps of the Philadelphia Museum of Art, "Through his paradigmatic movement from the old neighborhood to the monumental space of American democracy, Rocky's 'urban voyage' becomes a figure for upward social mobility and the revitalization and renewal of the city more generally. Through this celebratory, highly influential rise-to-success montage sequence, Hollywood film can be seen as having regained its 'action image,' which is here aligned with individual enterprise and entrepreneur."[16] Will's meanderings back and forth from South Boston to Harvard Square trace a journey with a similarly individualistic motivation, suggesting the ways in which earlier visions of the urban inform the representation of neoliberal cities.

Good Will Hunting similarly puts both actors, Matt Damon and Ben Affleck, on the map, advancing their careers significantly and forever associating them with the place of their youth. The film was also shot on a tight but adequate budget and directed by a gifted and experienced Hollywood figure, Gus Van Sant, who had had some limited box office and critical successes by this point with *Drugstore Cowboy* (1989) and *My Own Private Idaho* (1991). That the producers were willing to invest in this property suggests the increased power and confidence that independent producers had amassed over the two decades since *Rocky*. Miramax produced the film. Bob and Harvey Weinstein founded this well-connected Hollywood production company in 1979. The brothers and business partners started out as rock concert promoters in Buffalo and then by 1978 began producing concert films.[17] In 1996 and 1997, for example, its releases included Kevin Smith's *Chasing Amy*, featuring Affleck, with *Swingers*, *Copland*, and *Jackie Brown* among its successful properties. By the time *Good Will Hunting* went into production, both Damon and Affleck were emerging, as was the female lead, Minnie Driver. The film grossed over $225 million (on a budget of $10 million) and was nominated for nine Academy Awards, winning for best screenplay and best supporting actor (Robin Williams). Among its nominations were best picture and best actor for Damon.

Van Sant, in fact, had gone to the Rhode Island School of Design in Providence, about fifty miles from downtown Boston, and had spent significant time in Boston, so he brought his own sense of place to the film. But its screenwriters truly made the film such a signature narrative of place. That is, it elaborated extant if recessed mass cultural narratives of place with a kind of astuteness that seized on all manner of iconic images. It took prior aspects of place branding to new levels of prominence as it made such images central to its narrative. Production designer Missy Stewart affirmed, "We would talk about what would make it more 'Boston.'"[18] Indeed, the film as a whole is driven by a culturally lodged vision of authenticity, one that derives from earlier films that had employed location shoots to make a particular and resonant geography an important, even *signature*, part of the film. The New Hollywood period of U.S. filmmaking emphasized, among other things, the resonance of place as a textual emphasis. *Good Will Hunting* built on this earlier emphasis: "As Hollywood's new production practices and developments in urban public policy catalyzed a new engagement with urban space, New Hollywood cinema established what Thomas Elsaesser has referred to as 'a new iconography of place along-side a new emotional topography.'"[19] That emotional topography would become definitional for many films of the urban into the late twentieth and early twenty-first centuries, including almost the entire Spike Lee New York oeuvre of the 1980s and 1990s, films such as *Eight Mile* (Detroit, dir. Curtis Hanson, 2002) and *American Gangster* (Harlem, dir. Ridley Scott, 2007), among many.

The association of Will Hunting with his home district, South Boston, is an anchor of this tale. It is his place of comfort, his place of associations, and the lair from which he encounters the world. That this is a more general geographic belonging than a specific one makes both narrative sense and affective sense. The narrative tells us that Will is an orphan and has lived in any number of foster homes. So it is neither a house nor a family to which he returns when he goes "home." His apartment in South Boston is decidedly downscale and a place we barely enter, but one that blends into the images shown in the busing coverage and in the stories of the church sexual abuse scandal and that of Whitey Bulger.

That Will's home is a neighborhood—not a house—and none too commodious suggests an attachment to place that is a matter of assumed history and authenticity. He revels in the life that place suggests and in the place that his life suggests. But the vision of permanence and solidity that defines South Boston as an authentic homeland for a particular type of people was eroding as the film was being made, and has further eroded since. Intriguingly, South Boston increasingly has become the identifying place for the broader city, serving as shorthand for Boston. In the earlier chapters, we saw how this tendency was affirmed by the post-industrial landscape. As districts such as South Boston became unaffordable for its less prosperous inhabitants, place enlarged in importance and emotional significance, and those who in other contexts might have seemed mired in a place now become the "authentic" spirit of a particular region and derive their identities from that form of belonging. Tim Cresswell writes of branding and marketing that make new housing areas seem authentic and appear to have historical depth, asserting that marketers attempt to imbue these new developments with a narrative that provides them with an aura of depth and historical significance.[20] In a world that is increasing defined by images, such affirmations take on emotional and cultural significance. In cities that are succeeding economically like Boston, those places that had emotional associations can easily disappear under the pressures of development, a fact that has the power both to enlarge the significance of place as well as make its preservation even more urgent.

South Boston as defined by a working-class, Irish American population and ubiquitous three-decker houses stands in for the lost ideals of community, neighborhood, and continuity. Will's status as an orphan is addressed by the qualities of place and by the affirmation of his need to remain there, that is, to belong. For audiences, in a world of increased transience of all types, Will's longing (and desire for belonging) is also their own. As Cresswell tells us, these qualities are the terms employed by marketers of new developments, seeking to make their sterile environments less alienating for their target consumers: "A good place to live [the definition of "home"] is constructed through the promotion of a particular exclusive history [and] a selective romantic history."[21] Will's South Boston is precisely a selective and romantic place buttressed by a history, both general and personal, that is, a matter of longing that reduces the material facts of place and people to aspects of that romance. It becomes a good place to live as a matter of the associations it creates, the (lost) family it evokes, and not because it is necessarily commodious or pleasant.

In 1997, as *Good Will Hunting* was being shot, those paying attention were being apprised by newspaper journalism and televisual and digital media—such as they were—of the continuing saga of Whitey Bulger. As of 1995, Bulger, realizing that his deal with the local FBI agent was unraveling and that he was about to be apprehended, disappeared. In 1997, newspapers reported that his FBI handlers, and particularly John Connolly, were also facing indictment.[22] But in the coverage of this tale of corruption, Bulger emerged as a kind of Robin Hood, a mythic hero or antihero, and his South Boston "village" a quaint place where *omerta* rules. This persona, of course, has nothing to do with the reality of this vicious sociopath who terrorized his home city with a notable and savage brutality. But this mythic dimension of Bulger (as a media figure) further added to the images of this "quaint" place in Van Sant's film, and such images also recalled those seen during the journalistic coverage of the busing crisis in Boston in 1974 and the lurid, horrific accounts of sexual abuse of children in the Boston archdiocese story.

Good Will Hunting has a sharp eye for resonant details of the landscape and for how narrative film can glean precise elements from that locale to amass an entity with the apparent features of a particular and significant place. We see this repeatedly in its use of locations, even when those aspects of the landscape make little sense within Will's movements. For example, in the sweep to Cambridge (in the film's opening scene), as he is being driven by Chuck (Affleck), there is no geographic necessity for the Longfellow Bridge or Harvard Yard to appear in the montage, especially since Harvard is to the west of MIT, so that Will would be unlikely to pass there on his travels from home. Similarly, when Will returns to South Boston after solving Professor Gerald Lambeau's equation, we view a lighted Fenway Park from his train: but no transit line goes by Fenway Park above ground, and Will's rail line would not go anywhere near there, since his train would pass under the city's commercial and financial district (just east of Boston Common). Both of these incidents highlight the director's awareness of the terms of city branding that the film emphasizes. The idea of "authenticity" emerges not only from location shoots but also from a branded notion of a real place, and this shorthand becomes the means by which the post-industrial city emerges through recurring images. The strategy animating this film is also one seen in many other post-2000 Boston-based films. It is a strategy that is antithetical to that of the three earlier films in its emphasis on a defined and increasingly resonant vision of place featured in lingering and centered shots. Such distinctions say a lot about how visions of the urban have changed over the past twenty-five years.

Will's gift is his savantism, a photographic memory attached to a capacity for higher mathematics. This potentially redemptive quality could provide deliverance from his life as a construction laborer, a marginal worker in a sector of the economy that does not provide stable employment. His innate gifts come neither from the nurturing of a mentor nor from a family member, nor from assiduous and motivated hard work, and his savantism is what most distinguishes him from his larger community. The fact of his intellectual constitution provides us with a means of questioning the truism of meritocracy, since his gift does not necessarily result in social mobility in and of itself. In an embedded critique of meritocracy, it is only a number of fortuitous coincidences that redeem Will: his assignment to janitorial duties at MIT; his brush with Lambeau, an esteemed MIT professor who becomes Will's sponsor; his chance meeting at Harvard of a woman, a student, who becomes his romantic love interest; and his almost random connection with a psychologist who shares his class background. Such is, admittedly, the feel-good stuff of film narrative, but as a map of inevitability, it illustrates how talent does not necessarily denote achievement.

Will is both of and not of South Boston. The character's vacillation between the class-bound confines of his home neighborhood and that of the elite universities of Cambridge is employed—spatially and socially—as a means of distinguishing among classes and questioning the devices that affirm those distinctions. In this film, which elevates the "information economy" as the key to wisdom, wealth, and mobility, the settings alternate between South Boston and Cambridge, the home of Harvard and MIT. The film ignores universities such as Boston College, Boston University, and Northeastern University, although each is a notable part of the city's educational landscape. Further, Will barely traverses the city's downtown, and when he does, it is represented by shots of Toronto (where, for financial reasons, part of the film was shot), leaving it as part of the unbranded, or placeless, aspects of the film. It is this bipartite division of space that distinguishes this film from earlier treatments of class in the city, since the educational elites are really not *of* the city, nor are they provided their status as a matter of their distinctive and place-bound lineage *in* the city. They are part of a putative meritocracy, although Will's unusual intellectual gifts begin to erode away that assumption regarding earned stature.

Part of Will's journey to the realization of his innate potential is his relationship with his therapist, Sean, a fellow native of South Boston (Robin Williams). Sean is a figure whose roots and relative accomplishments allow him to see a world where mobility is a choice, which becomes a means of inserting Will's savantism into a narrative of meritocracy. Will has the tools to achieve but does he have the will to succeed? In a key scene, Sean takes his patient from his office at Bunker Hill Community College to the Boston Public Gardens for a heart-to-heart that goes beyond a doctor-patient discussion. As the film depicts it, it is an immediate geographic transition. We are out the door and then at the park, averting the two or so miles that separate the two places. This is not to say that all movement must be represented

The New Boston and the Grip of Tradition   191

FIGURE 14. Will Hunting and Sean take their session to the Boston Public Gardens.
—Courtesy Screen Shot.

literally; rather, it is only to say that such a compression of space has the impact of squeezing the city's geography into its emphasis on education and tradition. This is vital, since the needs of such an economy are mostly filled from without the city and not from within its urban bounds. At the Public Gardens, Will and Sean sit intimately on a park bench, initially shot from the back overlooking a pond, and then to a closeup of Sean in a monologue, until the camera moves out to gradually locate Will on the edge of the frame. In this speech, Sean makes an impassioned distinction between Will's sheer intellect and his undeveloped emotional life, his relative depth of experience and compassion. This scene is pivotal in its eventual power to inform Will's movement from the social and economic periphery of neoliberal, urban life to mixing it up in its center. That this takes place in a setting that cloaks such a transition in the verdant and central spaces of Boston's most famous and historic urban respite moves him significantly in his journey out of a vision of authenticity that begins and ends in South Boston. Yet, this midground of the city of business is barely treated in passing, never appearing again in the film's narrative, and Will seems to avoid it altogether when he passes from Cambridge to his home. This fact suggests its resonance is such that it requires no further comment or identification.

The recurring physical movement of the film depicts Will's repeated traversals from South Boston to Cambridge. These trips are filmed as a series of images of modest backyards and passing green spaces. Of course, this is not at all the route Will would have traversed, since much of this trip takes place underground, and if it were above ground it would have passed through the eastern extreme of Boston Common, very close in fact to the Massachusetts Statehouse—and so would have featured large buildings and urban congestion. In the opening scene of the film, just after we locate Will at his South Boston home, the means of traverse is a sweeping zoom over the city, moving from the low-rise South Boston of 1997 to a broad view of downtown and then to a closeup of Harvard and finally to a signature building at MIT. These various views that cut out Boston's downtown suggest a neoliberal vision of the city in that it simply divides the city not only into haves and have-nots but also into an educational elite and those with little or no access to education, and so with no place in the post-industrial economy. In the few scenes with verbal references to work, it is mentions of high-tech government and private think tanks. It is as if productive enterprise has all but ceased to exist. Rather, those who are ensconced in Cambridge are cosmopolitans, members not of traditional Boston but of the neoliberal city born from the wreckage of the post-industrial economy, which is largely of the service sector, both informational and financial.

The fact of this film's loving embrace of a nostalgic vision of Boston and its various iconic images begins a cycle of films—discussed in the next chapter—that celebrate the city, even as they primarily brand it for its apparent residual working-class population. Such images contribute to what Myria Georgiou defines as the "symbolic power of cities." By this phrase, she means the ways in which the contemporary global city feeds on its images, the way in which it is branded and imagined in the post-industrial economy precisely in order to produce and reproduce itself symbolically and economically. Georgiou argues for the distinctiveness of the neoliberal/digital moment, basing her view on the "digitalization and the expansion of the media in all elements of urban life; the intensification of urbanization and migrations; and the neoliberal advance in the urban world. In this context, the relationship between the city and media is one of interdependence."[23] Indeed, Boston is a site of a varied and highly variable range of apparently conflicting images, cast as both a place dominated by the terms of the neoliberal economy, even as it (apparently) contains a defining enclave of working-class culture. That Will's home is of that enclave allows a viewer to identify through the character with that particular region. Moreover, the elevation of that district attaches to other recurring images in other media, as well as further develops the concept of the city as a place of working-class, white ethnic, even Irish American authenticity.

Good Will Hunting, despite its reification of a vision of the white, ethnic working class, is best viewed as a kind of meta-commentary around the produced, represented, and digitally circulating concepts of "Boston." Will's plight is that of a younger Eddie Coyle and one taken up repeatedly in *Monument Ave, Mystic River, Gone Baby Gone*, and *The Town*, among others. In these films, Boston is employed as a fairly fixed social entity around which a certain few, like Will, are employed as human experiments in social mobility and broader social change. In such models, as in *Good Will Hunting*, the gentrifying district of South Boston—and sometimes the more gentrified Charlestown—is both romanticized and viewed as slightly unstable, but only slightly. Mostly they serve as fixed poles of working-class life, solid and ever resistant to change. Will's reluctance to leave is both a psychological condition and a failure of his imagination. But it is a failure that his friends also seem to share. That Sean, his therapist, who despite having completed a PhD and an undergraduate degree from MIT, also still lives there further affirms the power of that place to retain its offspring. As Will contemplates leaving to go to Stanford University with his girlfriend, his best friend applauds his prospective departure. But such a transition for the character does not substantially change our city or its meanings, ones that romanticize a place that is increasingly no place and a body of conditions that celebrate the very insularity and relative paucity of opportunity that most of us lament. For most who remain in this particular place, the *new* Boston, in effect, becomes the *old* Boston, a city where little changes and where comfort is defined, as Chuck says, by watching the Patriots game with a friend whose father watched the Patriots games with your father. But this is far from the *fact* of the city. The gentrification of the inner city and the gradual fact of geographic mobility, if not economic mobility, *is* the *new* Boston. After 2000, even South Boston began to change: from 2000 to 2010, Asian and Asian American, African American, and Latinx populations within the neighborhood grew by over 40 percent for each ethnic group. The neighborhood's population swelled to 35,200 by 2010, up nearly 12 percent from 2000, according to U.S. Census data and the Boston Redevelopment Authority. That reversed a trend seen between 1950 and 1970, when the population shrank by nearly a third according to a city report. Yet, such facts are at least recessed if not elided in these narratives of place.[24]

By the later 1990s and early 2000s, film production in Boston would pick up—to some degree thanks to the career successes of both Matt Damon and Ben Affleck and to the impact of *Good Will Hunting*. This increase in visibility continued, and in *Mystic River*, a success by any measure, views of the fictional East Buckingham section of Boston, included as a compendium of the working-class districts of Chelsea, South Boston, and Charlestown, also including the iconic Mystic River Bridge (now known as the Maurice Tobin Bridge, from which Charles Stuart jumped), loomed over the action. In a later scene, Celeste Boyle, the wife of one of the film's principles, considers revealing her husband as a murderer as she looks across the bay to the shadow of the Prudential Tower. In films such as *The Departed* (2006), *Gone Baby Gone* (2007), and *The Town*, among others, we see an identifiable city, one that we associate with its presence in other films, television series, news stories, and shots from blimps and cranes accompanying the many nationally televised Red Sox, Patriots, or Celtics games—but particularly those of the Red Sox, who play in the most resonant and place-specific brand of those three. But all of these images—and the narratives they support—retain elements of the "Boston" we find in these three earlier films. In effect, the *new* Boston retains residual elements of the older one. And while the presence of South Boston as an anchor in the portrayal of the city was not monolithic, it was and is disproportionate. Although not all films based in Boston are crime films, the number that works in that genre is quite substantial. Arguably, Boston became branded as a city of parochialism, closed Catholic cultures, and crime as a matter of the appearance of a particular region, just as that region was and is still being transformed into just another high-priced sector of the city, one with new buildings, affluent real-estate owners, and finance capital, and the consumer- and service-based economies that subsist and inhere within post-industrial, information, digital, and finance capitalism.

CHAPTER SIX

History, Fact, and Nostalgia

Feature films of Boston in the early twenty-first century differ from pre-1997 examples in that they revel in images that identify and celebrate place, images that are geographically specific but apparently temporally fixed. That is, we are provided with images that seem to define a city that is spatially and architecturally inert even as time clearly passes by. Such a vision of place tracks with the notion of mediated images (of the city) and distilled narratives (about urban space) that persist over time, as Boston becomes a recurring presence in mass communication which increasingly stands for social and material stasis, that is, a meme or chronotope, even as the city changes. This sense of the city as socially and materially unchanging follows the narrative emphasis of *Good Will Hunting*, which served as a major influence. Like *Good Will Hunting*, the films of this chapter confidently and affirmatively explore place, proceeding from the idea of Boston as a given and employing it as a textual feature that can bear the weight of considered narrative explorations. That South Boston occurs centrally in three of these five films, and does so less focally—but still appears—in the other two, is significant for the media presence of the city, its mediated image, and the intransigence of a certain distilled or sedimented narrative of place. That references to busing, priest abuse, Whitey Bulger, and the Red Sox abound suggests that the signposts set up in other forms of public narrative—journalism of all types, sports coverage, fiction—remain operative if not central, as their resonant possibilities are developed in a fluid, cultural terrain that pays homage to a conception of "Boston." Although Boston as a place does not nearly have the prominence of some other locales, as digital media became more and more culturally central, it emerged as a presence with a defined significance. In the cinematic Boston of the 2000s and beyond, films invoke the *new* Boston, but the terms of that place are affixed to a body of landmarks and narrative conventions that privilege images which affirm a vision of authenticity and tradition, and that summon a mix of history and nostalgia: the brand of the city is a narrative feature, a virtual "given."

Mystic River (2003) and the Legacy of Place

The first of these films chronologically is based on a noir novel by Dorchester-born crime novelist Dennis Lehane and directed by Clint Eastwood. It is the story of a murder in a neighborhood called The Flats and the misidentification of the murderer, resulting in a misplaced crime of vengeance. As the film proceeds, it tells the tale of three men who had been boyhood friends, and how the life-changing abduction of one, Dave, played by Tim Robbins, by two pederasts altered his life and ultimately all three of their lives. The other two are, respectively, Sean, a cop, played by Kevin Boyle, and Jimmy Marcum, an ex-con and gangster/convenience store owner in the neighborhood, played by Sean Penn. Through Eastwood's use of working-class space, he affirms the intransigence of time. No one "moves on" either metaphorically or literally, although Sean's efforts are the most notable, even if limited in result.

The location is an amalgam of various working-class neighborhoods that abut the city's central business district, but on the whole The Flats surely references South Boston, though it is "placed" primarily in East Boston for reasons of metaphor, which are central to the overall resonance of the film's narrative. Locating this neighborhood in East Boston allows the Tobin Bridge, formerly the Mystic River Bridge, to loom over the action, and the Chelsea Bridge as well. Like in Hart Crane's *The Bridge*, these edifices become a means of demarking space and showing the bridges' connection to and estrangement from those regions that border them, revealing them as a device of transition between meaningful places. In this case, we never see the current residents of The Flats leave that neighborhood or pass over the bridges. The character of Sean does seem able to move more freely—as well as to perch on the Tobin Bridge—but as the film proceeds, he becomes more and more mired in the legacy of the past and therefore in the space of The Flats.

The shots that do not feature the bridge come from Charlestown, South Boston, Mattapan, or Jamaica Plain, but none is explicitly identified. In general, East Boston is a stand-in for South Boston. Although East Boston had a large Irish American population at the turn of the twentieth

FIGURE 15. Opening shot of The Flats in *Mystic River*, with the bridge in the background. —Courtesy Screen Shot.

century—Joseph P. Kennedy was born there and lived there as a youth—by the later 1900s, it was predominantly Italian American, and by 2000, roughly the setting of the film, it was about 45 percent Hispanic and 42 percent foreign-born.[1] Jimmy Marcum's store is in South Boston, the bar where his boyhood friend Dave encounters his daughter on the night of her murder is in Jamaica Plain, and the park where Sean recovers the body is on the border of Roxbury and Mattapan. The absence of African American and Latinx characters is atypical of any of these areas, except for South Boston, though we learn that Jimmy's deceased wife was Latina, as is his daughter. Lehane and Eastwood build on the lore of place that was so much a part of the first section of this study, though fiction allows them to move locales into more convenient geographies and to imbue those geographies with particular significance.

The film begins in 1975, with references to the Red Sox team of that summer, and thus engages in a kind of nostalgia that soon becomes the associative stuff of nightmares. We know it is 1975 because the Red Sox hat, with the red crown and the blue brim that Dave wears, was used only during that season. These references to team as a marker of place further confirm the role of the Red Sox in defining local culture and notions of authenticity. But the chronology referenced in passing throughout the film makes numerical sense. In this opening scene, a motif is established that plays throughout the film. This scene defines the social and physical limits of this area and the ways in which crimes of the past can never be quite forgiven or tolerated. While the busing crisis exploded in 1974, Eastwood keeps references to those historical events from the film. The novel does employ busing as a cause of sorts, employing it as an explanation of the limited social mobility of certain characters, including Jimmy, but also the figure of Val Savage, one of Jimmy's henchmen. The novel is far more concerned with the class distinctions among the three boys, articulating Sean's relative advantages in relation to the other two boys, as it clearly differentiates between neighborhoods, defining the lower-middle-class Flats and the less rundown Point, each on a side of fictional Buckingham Avenue. As Nicolette Rowe explains in her insightful treatment of the film and novel:

> While the film articulates some aspects of Boston's racial/spatial order, the movements of the characters, perceptions of class, personality, and the nature of social interactions are further implicated in the novel. Most importantly, the genre of the novel allows a racial history of Boston to be told and connected with the storyline in ways that the film only begins to accomplish. For example, in the novel, a short description of how the "desegregation busing" of the 1970s affected Boston's urban landscape informs our understanding of the tensions between those who "belong" to the neighborhood and those outside of it. Jimmy and Val are two characters that grew up in a relatively poor area, the Flats, and were troublemakers in their school. Their punishment of sorts was to get bused halfway across the city to a mostly Black school, Carver.[2]

That the film leaves embedded, and not explicit, this historical framing is a choice to emphasize space over time, and to leave class a broader category than in the novel, as well as to make causation emanate from the recurrence of The Flats and not as a matter of the environment of The Flats versus The Point. In this telling, then, the distinction between the working lower middle class and the erratically working or nonworking even lower middle class collapses.

The film begins with a crane shot showing us the elevated structure of the bridge with a group of three-decker wood-frame houses in the foreground. The chatter of seagulls affirms the nautical setting. The camera tilts slightly down and pans to the right as we see two men sitting on the rear porch of one of these houses, on the second level. The first words we hear, though still at a relative distance: "Did you say who's pitching tonight?" As the men go on to talk about baseball, the scene briefly shifts to a boy of around eleven years old with his hockey stick, apparently the young Sean, and as the scene shifts back, we remain eavesdroppers to the men's conversation, looking at them through the slats of the porch railing, as the Red Sox pregame show plays in the background. The pregame show features the voice of Quincy native Ken Coleman, though he did not broadcast for the Red Sox in 1975. Coleman's regional accent further adds to our sense of local color and authenticity. Given the light and the apparent temperature, this temporal reference seems to be to June 26, 1975, an early summer night, just around when school would have been dismissed for the summer, and one of the two games that Luis Tiant started against the Yankees that season. While fixing this date as an anchor for the narrative is not absolutely necessary, that it can be determined speaks to the ways in which time is employed in the service of the film's narrative. That the Red Sox are the anchor for the larger tale affirms the place of the team as a marker of narrative space.

The film then cuts to three boys playing street hockey in front of the very same house where we saw the men on the back porch. The signature three-decker frame makes reference to the city as presented in the films of chapter 5, as well as discussed in section 1. The Flats are cut off from the rest of the city and apparently fixed in their system of social relations. The images tend to emphasize either the restricted space of the street (as shot from east to west), or the way in which the bridge borders the neighborhood. After Dave, by mistake, projects the ball into a sewage drain, the now aimless boys look for other activities. The intimacy of the locale and the relationship among the three boys is elaborated in a series of closeups and midrange shots. The narrowness of the street and the fact that the camera shots are generally toward the bridge, which serves as a limit on the space of The Flats, positions this world as a closed environment that could be traversed but only with difficulty, and perhaps only by devising a way to scale the height of the bridge and then cross it. But we never see a ramp.

After Jimmy proposes stealing a car and taking it "around the block," which the other boys clearly reject, they come across a recently replaced sidewalk square with wet concrete. Again, the scene is shot in a series of closeups emphasizing each boy, at times offering one of their points of view, and then the etching of his name in the concrete. As Sean marks the sidewalk, Jimmy says, in a closeup, "See. Now it will be there forever." Dave then takes his turn, and as he finishes the DA portion of his name, an older man pulls up in a car that looks like an unmarked police car, a Ford Fairlane 500. He walks around the front of his car with force and purpose, flashing his badge: "Let me ask you something." He berates the boys, asks where they live, and, determining that Dave is perhaps the weakest of the three and also the only one whose house is not on the street, he orders him into the car so that he can tell his mother "what her punk kid's been up to." The car Dave enters is filthy, with another even older man sitting in the passenger seat. As Dave is literally thrown into the car, that man turns around and smiles, showing his gold ring with a raised cross, suggesting his Catholic affiliation and the likelihood that he is a priest. Of course, such a "tell" in 2003 would be an obvious link to the *Boston Globe* Spotlight stories of 2002 and the ongoing scandals surrounding the sexual abuse of minors by priests. Dave looks through the back window of the car with sadness and resignation as the car pulls slowly away. He is taken to a suburban basement where he is repeatedly raped, until he finds a way to escape after four days. We see him return to The Flats, wounded, with a crowd of neighbors looking on, and hear Sean's father say, "Looks like damaged goods to me." The shot cuts to Jimmy and Sean looking up at Dave in the window, then to the temporal present, some twenty-five years later, making it the year 2000 and the three boys now thirty-six-year-old men.

The film asserts that the present can never be satisfactorily extricated from the past, and that the past casts a deforming shadow on the present. Such views of time and place easily derive from notions of "Boston" that have circulated over the last three decades. In this case, the link that firmly tethers the past to the present is the recurrence of space. Certainly, Dave's trauma is cataclysmic. But its looming presence becomes most notable in the spaces where the event initially occurred. Indeed, as Dave walks his son, Michael, home from a baseball game after school, now wearing a "classic"—seemingly timeless—Red Sox cap with a blue crown and brim, Dave reminds his son that he is an heir to a legacy of athletic success: "Dave Boyle, star shortstop, Trinity High School, 1978 to 1982." A tight two-shot affirms the closeness of Dave and Michael. Such continuities are definitional for the film and assert the power of legacies, which are assumptively desirable. More generally, such continuities suggest a kind of determined existence for those who cannot extricate themselves from their physical context. The past weighs heavily on the present and particularly so if one remains in the geography that was formative, and perhaps was even formative for previous generations.

As Dave and Michael walk, the houses they pass seem to constrain their world. Dave briefly and fondly reminisces about playing in the street as they pass by what had been Sean's house. But when he comes upon the markings in the concrete that he had helped to create some twenty-five years before, the other two boys' names and his own truncated name—DA—he grows visibly disconcerted. The camera shows us his eyes becoming distant and his face and body language revealing extreme discomfort. A point-of-view shot focuses on the concrete square, and viewers find him literally reliving the moment when the faux police officer told him to get into the car. This assumption of legacy, affirmed by Chuckie in *Good Will Hunting*, as watching the Patriots with a guy whose father watched the Patriots with your father, continues the trope of place that has prevailed and accelerated over some thirty years, as the city moved out of the industrial age and into the information economy. As images of place abound through a burgeoning media world, meanings of space not only become calcified but the need to solidify particularly resonant geographies is amplified, acting as a hedge against the ephemerality of place as a digital projection. Dave *needs* to stay in place since this *is* his home, his anchor in the world, but by remaining in The Flats, he remains subject to his truncated name etched in concrete.

The ostensible center of the film is the search for the murderer of Jimmy's daughter, Katie. But the entrenched tangle of relations and the physical recurrence of places that were central in that tale's preamble steers the film's emphases, making it more broadly about the power of the past. Even as Katie's murder is uncovered, we find Jimmy at the police station to identify his daughter's body and to "answer some questions," telling Sean, one of the investigating officers, how if *he* had gotten into the car that day, the day of Dave's abduction, then he would have been too wounded to have approached Katie's mother, and then Katie would never have been born. But of course, he did not get into the car and very likely would not have, and he did approach Katie's mother, and Katie was born. Such counterfactual propositions only further reveal the power of the past for these men who are so connected by place. What might have been, then, constitutes a virtual impossibility.

The key figures of this narrative are clearly Jimmy and Dave, who, as a matter of the insularity of their existence, find themselves married to cousins. Sean, on the other hand, has been to college, no longer lives in The Flats, and is a state trooper. But his relationship to the other two central characters of this narrative recalls the connection between John Connolly and Whitey Bulger in the way that boyhood affiliations create ongoing bonds between investigators and suspects in places where such bonds of affiliation and continuity maintain themselves in extraordinary ways. These connections may not result in the best or most honest police work. Indeed, Sean is attempting to extricate himself from the neighborhood and his prior associations as we encounter him for the first time. The scene dissolves from Katie driving off with her boyfriend, Brendan Harris, in her car from Jimmy's store to a high shot that lifts from the street level, accompanied by the whirling of helicopter blades. We are lifted onto the bridge platform with an aerial shot of cars backed up at tollbooths. Although we have a sense of Sean's connections to past and place, we first encounter him performing his police duties on the Tobin/Mystic River Bridge as a case of road rage by a middle-aged white man in a BMW brings him and his African American partner, Whitey, played by Laurence Fishburne, to the scene. Whitey's role is significant in that he remains an outsider by virtue of his race *and* his not being from The Flats. That he becomes the means to define belonging and *not* belonging marks the film's racial commentary as both tribal and starkly ontological. As the crime is addressed in the background, we find Sean providing a rare view from the bridge, defining a moment where the bridge is a perch and not a gate restricting movement. Sean gazes over Boston Harbor to the east and slightly to the north, as Whitey asks him what he is looking at, to which Sean replies, "the old neighborhood," as a point-of-view shot shows us East Boston in the distance. This shot associates, at least propositionally, Sean's view with a panoptic one. But he has neither the distance nor the persistent height nor the conceptual discipline to gaze in this way. While he is ostensibly associated with the encroaching powers of bureaucratic and administrative forces, an example of Henri Lefebvre's vision of representational space, Sean is too much in the mix, too much a matter of his personal history in that space of The Flats to view it through the devices of surveillance or to offer a disembodied, panoptic vision actualized by the high shot and the sound of helicopters.

Yet, as The Flats develops its own system of narrative and justice based on the past, the film questions that system's ethos and enabling power, as it concurrently offers a means of questioning whether space can ever be experienced without subjectivity. This disjunction becomes materially dramatized in the next scene as Sean returns to The Flats to look for Katie's body at the same time that Jimmy sends the Savage brothers as his personal envoys to do the same. The disconnect between the two investigations, as well as their overlap, becomes an important means of distinguishing between the power of Jimmy and that of the state, as well as a system that operates in The Flats and that which is connected to the administrative state. The officers of law literally hold both Jimmy and his envoys at bay as they investigate the crime scene, with Jimmy expressing his extreme pain and grief as he is kept from the body. Sean remains less moved but can sympathize sufficiently with his boyhood friend to note the pain he would be in and to register sincere grief as he looks at the young woman's remains. Sean, in his investigation, is literally on the same level as Jimmy, and so he has relinquished his elevated perspective as he enters the crime scene and what is in effect Jimmy's world. The direction emphasizes how Sean's view is not godlike by cutting from his reaction shot to Jimmy's extreme grief to a disembodied crane shot where Jimmy is seen thrashing from straight above, growing smaller as the camera moves further upward.

Jimmy, on the other hand, may be the king of The Flats. From his position as a proprietor of a centrally located convenience store, he has the knowledge and relationships that distinguish him within this social system. Part of his status stems from his prior role as a central member of a criminal enterprise, much like that of Whitey Bulger's. But as Jimmy moves outside of his domain early in the film (after his daughter has been murdered) to the police building, he is a subjected figure and so reduced by the power of the administrative state. The scene transition from the park to the police building is accomplished by a cut from the panoptic perspective to that of a camera tilting upward, showing a glimpse of the sky and then landing in a sterile building. As he identifies his daughter's body, we see how the sterility of that space impinges on him, and how he is subject to the administrative gaze, as the scene is shot both from within the morgue room and through the venetian blinds that mark its windows—in a film noir reference—as Whitey establishes an external point of view, again elaborating a position of relative disinterest and externality.

We next see Jimmy and his wife, Annabeth, played by Laura Linney, sit knee to knee in a small, Formica-topped booth, across from Sean and then across from Sean and Whitey, who never joins the three in the booth.

While Sean and Jimmy explore their common past, when Whitey returns the conversation becomes a more conventional police interview, including the revelation of Jimmy's criminal record. Again, in this context, Jimmy and Annabeth must answer the questions and not ask them, as Jimmy can in The Flats. Whitey looms over the couple, never meeting them on their level or yielding his authority, which in this case is related to his role as an outsider.

One of the striking things about this film is the way in which the working-class enclave remains remote from other environs, and as a result, the past is never the past. As space constrains character and the arc of achievement, so it keeps time from moving on. This Boston and the Boston beyond the water are very different places, and the meaning of those spatial distinctions become elaborative for understanding the relative temporality that informs each: one is of the changing present, and one is of the unyielding past. This point is brought home when Dave's wife, Celeste, looks longingly out at the Prudential Building and downtown in the rain as she contemplates that her very disturbed husband may have killed Jimmy's daughter, and, more generally, a life other than the one she lives. In effect, she looks for a relief from her spatial constraints in order to break out of the perpetuity of the moment of Dave's abduction. But that relief is no place. Dave is lost in the nightmare of the past, and knowledge of Dave's trauma is so central to his community that the past is always present. Dave, like the concrete block on the sidewalk, is the material testament to the fact of his abduction.

As we move on in our whodunnit movie, the two theories of the crime come into conflict, and each is associated with a particular network of investigators. The truth of the present doesn't win out. The illusion of the truth of the past does. Dave is so deeply lost in the maze of his memories that he is unable to see what is past and what is present. Indeed, the fact that he is telling the truth about having killed a pederast in Buckingham Park is increasingly treated as a rationalization that attempts to hide his murder of Katie. When the Savage brothers come for him, largely as a matter of suspicions confirmed by his wife, but erroneously so, he is vulnerable as a matter of his place in the social structure of the community as well as by his geographical place, which has remained largely unchanged over some twenty-five years. He cannot say no. The scene of the four men, eventually including Jimmy, crowded into the booth recalls that of the booth in the police station, but now it is Jimmy's investigation that is operative, and the drink is Irish whiskey and not coffee. Jimmy's face remains in shadow as he looks at Dave across the table. The two-shot closeups shift back and forth from Dave and Nick Savage to Jimmy and Val Savage. Since Dave is on the inside of the booth, there is no means of escape.

As Jimmy clinks glasses with Dave, the scene jump-cuts to the house of Brendan Harris, Katie's boyfriend, again a three-decker with a grimy and dark kitchen. Brendan walks purposefully through the space and finds a stool to stand on so that he can reach the attic crawl space, where he feels for a gun that has been there for more than a decade. When he finds that the gun is no longer there, a knowing and angry expression comes to his face. We then crosscut back to the bar where Val, in a midrange shot, says, "Remember when we took Ray Harris here that time?" Ray is Brendan and his brother Ray Jr.'s father, a former crime associate of Jimmy's who Jimmy killed some thirteen years before in the same place. We then cut back to the kitchen, where young Ray and his friend enter. The scene moves back and forth between the Harris house and the exterior of the bar, with Brendan and Jimmy concurrently seeking a confession from Katie's killer. The scenes are intimate, shot in a succession of closeups and punctuated by emotionally wrought dialogue. Jimmy executes Dave, in error, since Dave did not kill his daughter, as Sean and Whitey come to the Harris kitchen where Ray Jr.'s friend, John O'Shea, is holding Brendan at gunpoint. Both of these situations are references to the power of the past when space remains constant and restrictive. The key to uncovering the murder of Katie is returning to the liquor store where Ray had once worked and then held up, and recovering a bullet that had been in the wall all of these years, a bullet traced to the same gun that killed Katie. The liquor store owner is played by Eli Wallach, who many years earlier had played the character Tuco alongside Clint Eastwood's No Name in *The Good, the Bad, and the Ugly*.

The ongoing role of "Just" Ray Harris Sr. in all of this is pivotal. He is the person that Jimmy previously killed on the same site on which he later kills Dave, also as a matter of "justice." Since Ray's testimony was responsible for Jimmy's arrest and conviction, he had to be punished. In the Harris kitchen, where Ray once lived, it is his gun that fires the shot that kills Katie, the trigger pulled by his son, whom he never knew, since Jimmy executed him just after Ray Jr.'s birth. In an aside, Jimmy, as a matter of guilt, has been sending the Harris family $500 a month since Ray "disappeared." The death of the elder Ray Harris was for his "crime" of snitching, a renunciation of the local law of *omerta*, a credo that is consonant with the image of honor attached to Whitey Bulger, who affirmed at his trial, "I'm not [a] f***ing informant," even as John Connolly's testimony affirmed that he was.[3] And that Jimmy has already killed for crimes against the community credo in this very place allows for his subsequent execution of Dave, for the crime of remaining in the community as a wounded remnant of his former self and as a reminder of the vulnerability of all. Indeed, it is Dave's denial of his own vulnerability that creates the need for his lie regarding his murder of the pederast; to admit that his scar is that deep and that present is beyond his ability to accept who he is and what he has done. Instead, he admits what he has *not* done and is executed for it.

Mystic River is about a web of relationships that only get deeper and more complex over time because no one can ever physically move on. As Dave gets drunker and drunker on Irish whiskey, Jimmy eventually through coercion exacts a false confession before he stabs Dave to death and throws him in the river. Jimmy utterly controls the scene, and his vision of justice is fully operative. Upon hearing that Dave's version of events was true, and that Katie had been killed by Ray Jr. and John O'Shea, Sean asks Jimmy in a closeup, "What did you do, Jimmy? When was the last time you saw Dave Boyle?" Jimmy replies, since they are standing in the same spot where Dave was abducted, "The last time I saw Dave Boyle, he was in the back of a car." As Sean understands what has happened, a two-shot shows him saying to Jimmy, "Sometimes I think all three of us got in that car. . . . In reality, we're still eleven-year-old boys locked in that cellar."

Eastwood knew great material when he saw it, and the director recognized the quality of Lehane's noir novel: "The whole book moved me. I loved all the characters and I loved the kind of gritty feeling of it."[4] But the visual realization of the screenplay is a powerfully resonant depiction of the city that doesn't miss any opportunity to inscribe place on narrative and narrative on place. "Boston" becomes the place you can never leave, the place where the web of the past is inscribed so powerfully because that web always encloses the same geography. The Flats never changes; it remains the place where Whitey Bulger lived, the place where busing remains a present insult, the place where crime families are, like the building trades, since they are an intergenerational enterprise. The film ends with a quasi–St. Patrick's Day parade (called the Buckingham Day Parade in the film). The parade signifies perpetuity, endurance, and ritual as Jimmy and Sean acknowledge each other knowingly, as if to recognize that the events that have transpired

History, Fact, and Nostalgia 207

FIGURE 16. The final shot of *Mystic River*: the three boys' names written forever in concrete.
—Courtesy Screen Shot.

were overdetermined. Sean cocks his thumb as if to shoot a gun, as Jimmy shrugs his shoulders in resignation. The final shot again shows us the concrete block where the two full names and the one partial name were etched twenty-five years ago, an inscription of legacy and perpetuity—if one remains proximate to the locale.

The Departed and the Ruptures of Time

Some three years later, Martin Scorsese directed a film even more steeped in noir conventions, *The Departed* (2006), starring Jack Nicholson and written by Boston-born William Monahan. The film, besides adding various Irish American and Anglo-Irish actors, also featured two of the three reigning Boston-born actors working at the time, Matt Damon and Mark Wahlberg. The Nicholson character has a strong scent of Whitey Bulger, one acknowledged by Monahan, and the criminal/cop connection again brings easily to mind the John Connolly/Whitey Bulger relationship.[5]

The film is based on a Hong Kong production, *Infernal Affairs* (2002), from which it heavily adapts its plot of deception, duplicity, and betrayal. But as *Infernal Affairs* offers a similar plot, its fast-paced, pyrotechnical shooting style all but erases context while the U.S. version enhances it. Writes Li Wanlin, "American reviewers sometimes take the Americanness of their films for granted, but localization or Americanization can be a driving creative force in cases of transcultural adaptation such as *The Departed*. The fact that Monahan located the film in his native city, of which he has an intimate knowledge, partly demonstrates the filmmakers' determination to transplant the Asian story into an indigenous American setting."[6] Indeed, for the purposes of most viewers who are not film scholars, its connection to films like *Good Will Hunting* and to *Mystic River* as a matter of place, and focalized place within place at that, is far more notable. Again, the Boston to which it perpetually refers is centered in the apparently static neighborhood of South Boston, and although it is not necessarily as focused on the presence of the past as *Mystic River*, its complicated plot, about betrayal and misidentification, derives heavily from definitions of place and from the elaborations of the power of place to maintain the core, definitional elements of the past, offering a nihilistic vision of individuals who are both defined by place and the past, as well as by their desires to employ those connections strategically as a matter of resolving them and moving on. That is, the more that South Boston recedes as a place of material presence, the more our central characters drift into a morass of amorality.

Scorsese, of course, became famous as a director for his ability to portray New York life vividly, often focusing on Italian Americans engaged in criminal enterprises, in films such as *Mean Streets* (1973), *Taxi Driver* (1976), *Raging Bull* (1980), and *Goodfellas* (1990), among many others. But this foray into Boston provided him with an alternative site for his vision of the bonds among criminals, one that allowed him to make a film connected to those earlier films but distinct in certain ways. In addition to Scorsese's facility with gangster films, *The Departed* also employed the skills of William Monahan. His vision of place is a vital force in the emphases of the film, one that is akin to that of the better-known Dennis Lehane in *Mystic River*. Monahan won an Academy Award for best-adapted screenplay for his work on the film.

The film begins with a voiceover by the Jack Nicholson character, Frank Costello, as we watch the very same TV news footage of school busing from 1974 referenced in chapter 2. The violence and insularity are not only a device to set the film in time and place; they are also a means of elaborating continuity and discontinuity, as Costello introduces his philosophy, that one need not be made by the circumstances of the world, to be "a product of your environment." Rather, the goal is to create circumstances, that is, "My environment will be a product of me." Such a sentiment is a kind of recognition of the situation encountered in *Mystic River*, a narrative that shows the inexorable influence of place over time. But in this case the impulse is to resist such determined notions of circumstance and to remake the world through wile and will. Costello goes on to offer a view from what seems to be the Tobin (Mystic River) Bridge similar to that given through Sean's eyes early in *Mystic River*, but in this case it is murky newsreel footage, images that appear as chronologically consonant with the busing crisis and thus evocative of the past city as a network of interethnic battles and affiliations. He invokes the Catholic fraternal organization, the Knights of Columbus, as he looks over East Boston. He then makes that group a gang-like force of ethnic violence, "real head bangers," and laments the fallacy of the civil rights movement, that African Americans will believe "they will have things handed to them." Such a vision of race and power defines Costello's world as that of ethnic continuity and discontinuity, of a kind of tribalism that elevates place, even as place is less focalized than it was in *Mystic River* and therefore subject to revisions of meaning and strategic relocations by former denizens.

As noted in chapter 2, the core of the Whitey Bulger informant tale is a legalistic distinction made by federal law enforcement officials between Irish gangs and Italian American organized crime—the mob or the mafia. Bulger was recruited to inform on the Providence-based Patriarca family, which was in direct competition with his Somerville–South Boston–based Winter Hill gang. This bit of local history finds its way into the film, as we see William Costigan, played by Leonardo DiCaprio, take offense at the shaking down of a South Asian convenience store owner in Southie by two Providence-based thugs, who are clearly infringing on Irish territory, and beats them senseless. Costello then aids Costigan in fending off retribution, which results in the death of two Italian hit men. Again, this interethnic violence reinforces a kind of tribalism connected to place, and the place of South Boston in particular. Also of interest is the fact that the store owner is neither white nor Irish, a fact in direct contrast with the opening scene of the film, which finds the young Colin Sullivan (Matt Damon) in a South Boston convenience store, Irish-owned and -operated, as Costello comes in for his payoff. The change of proprietorship and the terms of the shakedown suggest a changing world, but one that occurs without comment.

Choosing to name the Whitey Bulger–like figure Frank Costello is a stroke of narrative genius by Monahan and Scorsese. Frank Costello was the name of a reputed New York City crime boss who led the Luciano family for more than two decades from 1937 to around 1960. Costello's birth name was Francesco Castiglia. Costello, despite its ending in a vowel, is actually an Anglicized form of a Gaelic name, but given Frank Costello's notoriety and the sound of the name, it suggests an ambiguity as an ethnic identifier. By making this Irish character a Costello who is at war with the Providence gangs, whom he refers to in terms that denigrate their ethnicity, the character throws just a bit of doubt into the viewer regarding his origins and depth of affiliation. Such doubts make a film about deception and duplicity all the more confounding.

Rather than the fictional Flats of *Mystic River*, *The Departed* is more generally oriented to South Boston, which is referred to far more than it is actually pictured; in fact, the screenplay makes some twenty references, but often in the setting of scene, so that we are supposed to view some of the action as taking place in South Boston, and even when it is not the locale, South Boston provides a meaningful point of orientation. It is an anchor that defines the film's three key characters, Costigan, Sullivan, and Costello. But as Sullivan becomes wealthier as a matter of his skullduggery with Costello, he moves on to downtown Boston with a view of the Statehouse. As Costello basks in his criminal enterprise, he chooses a waterfront condo in Charlestown, one befitting a hedge-fund manager or a real-estate mogul. It is hard to say where Costigan lives, but he intermittently pops up in his aunt's three-decker house ostensibly in South Boston but according to the production credits is actually in Dorchester.

The film's preamble is extensive, situating each character in his past prior to entering the "contemporary" action of the film some eighteen minutes in. By that point we know that Sullivan's father has died and that he was brought up by his grandmother; that Costello has defined himself as akin to the devil and has invoked James Joyce's *The Portrait of the Artist as a Young Man* with his affirmation and advice to Sullivan, *non serviam*; and that Costello reiterates his philosophy of making the world according to his will—not God's, not the Providence mob's—as he is shot in shadow and silhouette. As Costello tells the young Sullivan in a succession of closeups, "When I was your age, they would say you could become cops or criminals. What I'm saying is what's the difference." As the young Sullivan's smiling face dissolves into the twenty-something Colin at the police academy, we can see the guiding hand of Costello forming the moral universe of the younger man. As Sullivan graduates from the State Police Academy, Costello and his sidekick, a Mr. French, played by the British actor Ray Winstone, celebrate him as his parents might have—except they are celebrating his use and usefulness to them as a plant in the state police.

Sullivan's counterpart is William Costigan, who resembles him remarkably in his coloring and stature but not at all in his demeanor. Where Sullivan is glib and ingratiating in a salesman's way, Costigan is angry and brooding. He comes from a South Boston family on his father's side and the North Shore suburbs on his mother's; he is a divided character by both class and place, suggesting how his social definition is a matter of training and of situation. In his initial interview with Sergeant Dignam (Mark Wahlberg) and Captain Queenan (Martin Sheen), we learn these details, as Dignam berates Costigan for his middle-/upper-class associations—Deerfield Academy, a code-switching accent, his links to a decidedly pedestrian aspect of South Boston criminal life through his father and "Uncle Jackie." The fact that Costigan has two different accents is a source of irritation to Dignam, who seems genuinely of one place. In a media world where the regional accent is a vital measure of authenticity, this fact brings the film to the ways in which place is defined in a mediated world. We never "see" Costigan's backstory, as we do Sullivan's, but as the film proceeds, it becomes evident.

It is in this scene that Monahan uses a version of Nathaniel Hawthorne's line from *The House of the Seven Gables*, set in nearby Salem, affirming "families are always rising and falling in America," with Queenan recognizing the quote. But his recognition is a misrecognition, since it is a paraphrase of the observation by the nineteenth-century novelist: "The truth is, that once in every half-century, at least, a family should be merged into the great, obscure mass of humanity, and forget about its ancestors." And though this is a distillation of a vision of America as the new land, it is distinctly at odds with the social landscape we find, one that abounds with figures who are tied to their past and legacies in one way or another, even as identity is ever shifting and thus difficult, if not impossible, to ascertain. In that landscape, however, the realization of Hawthorne's social world may be more deleterious than the world of continuity he disavows.

Costigan is employed as a plant in Costello's gang thanks to his ability to code-switch and to perform certain social behaviors as though they were part of his integral self. But such abilities suggest not that one's behavior shapes one's environment but that one's environment shapes one's behavior: the opposite of Costello's credo. In this case, South Boston becomes the ubiquitous space, even as our principals are either not quite from there or extricating themselves from it as a home environment. In effect, place has evolved into a kind of credo and symbolic locale, but all the while its definitional powers remain—much as the brand of Boston becomes a thematic orientation linked to a prior definition of place.

The power of *omerta*, the depth of affiliation, and the erosion of both ultimately becomes the foci of the film. This rewriting of the gangster ethos, and of the ethos of "Boston," defines a postmodern approach to identity in a generic context where identity and ethics had been a recurring definitional marker. This is now a world of chaos and deception where assumptions of identity, and the trust and certainty that rely on such assumptions, cease to operate. In the film's final scenes, we find that Costello himself has been, unbeknownst to Sullivan, an FBI informant. Such a breach so disturbs Sullivan that during the confrontation between the two, as the state police bust a drug transfer, he shoots his mentor in order to protect his "identity." But what is that identity? Is it that of a mole for organized crime? Or is it as an undercover policeman?

As Sullivan takes Costello's phone from his bloody, inert hand, he answers the call coming in, from Costello's girlfriend Gwen, and tells her, "We lost Frank." Moments later, he announces to his fellow police officers, "I got him." The scene is composed with intermittent high angle shots, showing that Frank is "objectively dead," even as the meaning of his death remains a matter of competing assertions. The problem of identity and its meaning are further compounded by the erasure of Costigan from the state police system, once Sullivan realizes that he has been the man inside Costello's operation and thus could conceivably out him. That Costigan's digital trail, a vital part of who he is, can be eradicated in one keystroke points to the crisis of ontological definition in a postmodern regime, a world in which our identities are a matter of their bureaucratic representation in easily eradicated digital form. Costigan responds by providing his love interest and therapist Madolyn (Vera Farmiga), who is also Sullivan's love interest— more duplicity!!—with a compact disc of Sullivan colluding with Costello, thus affirming both his own identity as an undercover agent and Sullivan's as a mole. But even these affirmations of "true" identity are not, as we see in the next scene, unassailable, nor are they inviolable, as the disc can be easily destroyed. In the end, Costigan's identity cannot be affirmed in a timely and effective way. As he meets and attempts to apprehend Sullivan, he is told, "I am a Boston State Police Sergeant, and you're nobody." Sullivan's fellow officers attempt to apprehend the "criminal" who is holding the "cop" hostage, when finally another cop kills Costigan and then kills another member of Sullivan's team. We find that this cop, Barrigan, is also a Costello plant, so he has a related identity and interest to that of Sullivan.

As the plot of the film is resolved, we remain largely outside of South Boston, suggesting that the removal of the anchor of place has allowed these figures to float in an ambiguous moral universe. These killings occur either at Sullivan's apartment, at a rooftop on Washington Street in the central, historical commercial district of downtown Boston, a place that was once the home to two major department stores, Filene's and Jordan Marsh, but which is actually on Farnsworth Street, a locale in the newly developed district that abuts the World Trade Center and Commonwealth Pier, a gleaming, high-priced symbol of the *new* Boston. The fusing of these two locales is an interesting emphasis within the film.

The remnants of the past operate only on the surface, but the present suggests the perils of being unrooted. As Madolyn uncovers Sullivan's role in Costigan's departure, she does so through a letter from Costigan, sent from 13 Conant Street, Boston, to 20 Pickering Street, Boston. Neither address is plausible. Conant Street is in Revere, and Pickering Street is in predominantly African American Roxbury, nowhere near the Statehouse and somewhat ironic in a world in which there are very few African Americans. It is as though this film, which began resolutely in the deep structure of South Boston affiliation and local ethnic crime, has devolved into a kind of gentrified placelessness, leaving individuals to fend for themselves and to make their own way as free economic agents. In this cynical vision, then, place becomes the thing that has been erased, and without fixed and recurring space, so too does identity distend and vanish. Boston, and South Boston in particular, remain ghosts of a prior regime, a regime of sequence and continuity, even of authenticity. This "Boston" becomes not the city of Costigan's aunt's house but the backdrop for the murder of Queenan and Costigan, a building under construction in downtown Boston, which is set against a backdrop that would seem totally alien to Eddie Coyle. We view one after another shiny new skyscrapers, in a district that abuts South Boston but that is actually part of the redeveloped Seaport district. The actual building is now the home of a software developer. This view is not that of the stated address, 344 Washington, in the heart of the business district, and thus would not have offered such a clear view of the *new* Boston. That such environs can breed this treachery points to the disenchantment of the new city, offering a kind of nostalgia for the old that is very much a part of the city's brand. The death of Sullivan at the hands of Sergeant Dignam, the very man who questioned Costigan's authenticity, constitutes a kind of justice, and poetic justice at that, one deeply connected to notions of place that we have seen circulating for some thirty years.

Gone Baby Gone and the Multiethnic City

Gone Baby Gone (2007) is once again based on a Dennis Lehane novel, directed by Ben Affleck, who along with Aaron Stockard cowrote the screenplay, and stars Ben's brother Casey Affleck. It builds on prior visions of place and authenticity but provides an intriguing vision of a more contemporary Boston, though it also slides into more familiar Irish, Polish, French, and Italian versions of the city. The film, like the others, begins with a preamble, but in this case a far briefer and more modest one. In the film's opening car-based tracking shots, we traverse one of the most ethnically diverse neighborhoods of early twenty-first-century Boston, that of North Dorchester, perched between Roxbury and Mattapan, and the predominantly white and Irish neighborhoods of South Dorchester.

The distinctions between the novel and the film are notable and of a kind. Ben Affleck seeks to make Boston more of what it actually was in the early 2000s: a diverse community with a number of Black and Brown immigrants. As a matter of this emphasis, Affleck changes the location a bit, moving from the edges of white North Dorchester further north and west toward Mattapan and Roxbury, which changes the ethnic mix of the characters on the edge of the action. But he also changes the ethnicity and origins of some of the characters closer to the center of the action. For example, the character of Captain Doyle, a good, Boston, Irish name, is played by the Black actor Morgan Freeman, which makes him more clearly an outsider in the Boston police force. The characters of Devin, a fairly minor role, and Cheese, a more important character, are also cast as African Americans in the film. And while Affleck in a DVD interview affirmed that this was "color-blind" casting, it so fits with the broader changes from the novel that one can only conclude that showing a more diverse Boston and Boston police force was a consideration for the adaptation. In choosing to set the film in North Dorchester, Affleck allowed viewers a slice of Boston that is more diverse and so more in line with the contemporary city than the Boston seen in earlier films, recognizing the ways in which the city has changed demographically since the early 1970s. North Dorchester in the early 2000s had a population that was 35 percent white and around 20 percent Cape Verdean and Vietnamese.[7]

In the opening credits, a montage, viewers are provided with a strategic tour of the neighborhood and its broader environs. The narrator, Patrick Kenzie, played by Casey Affleck, talks of the souls of these urban dwellers and how it is "the things you don't choose who make you who you are. Your city, your neighborhood, your family. People here take pride in those things, like it was something they'd accomplished." By offering such a view, we see the montage of working-class residents in this downtrodden part of the city as possessing a certain pride and dignity, one that need not reflect on their possibilities of social mobility. Kenzie goes on to tell of his vocation of searching for lost people, and knowing that to find them, "it is better to know, where they began."

These are indeed mean streets. Still, Ben Affleck goes to lengths not to romanticize them but rather to accept them as a matter of life's circumstances and to see their impact on their residents.[8] The film fans out to predominantly Black and Hispanic Uphams Corner, then to Dudley Station in Roxbury, which is also overwhelmingly Black and Hispanic—over 95 percent, in fact. As the movie goes on, we repair to the gritty streets of Chelsea, an abutting suburb immediately over the Tobin Bridge, which is predominantly Latino (67%), and then to Everett, which is also a majority Black and Brown, as well as 43 percent foreign-born, post-industrial suburb. And while the environs that Kenzie and his partner, Angie Gennar (Michelle Monoghan), traverse are decidedly mixed-race, the protagonists of the film are mostly, but not monolithically, white.

Although the film begins with a statement of deterministic belief in environmental causation, in direct contrast to that voiced by Frank Costello at the beginning of *The Departed*, it does not reify place in the manner of the previous two films. The world that Affleck portrays in *Gone Baby Gone* is a Boston akin to that in *Eddie Coyle*, but now in the core of the city and outside of its gentrified districts, rather than those inner-ring, southern suburbs. South Boston is absent from this film and never referenced. Nor is there an attempt to romanticize Kenzie's Irishness or the (unremarked upon) post-busing landscape of Boston's schools, as Kenzie has clearly mixed with a variety of people, including Haitians, Cape Verdeans, and Southeast Asians.

Still, place and continuity are inscribed in the film's representation of the city. That Kenzie is the point-of-view character in the film allows for the narrative to further the project of representing "Boston" in a manner that refers extensively to prior representations. While North Dorchester isn't romanticized, we do know that Kenzie has lived his entire life there. His knowledge of place adds to his local knowledge of the world, asserting that he can interview people who won't talk to the police, in a way creating an unofficial investigation that is akin to that effected by the Savage brothers in *Mystic River* but without the violence and coercion.

Networks of association play an extraordinary role in *Mystic River* and *The Departed*, and those networks are a logical outgrowth of the recurring geography of South Boston or The Flats. In *Gone Baby Gone*, though, while they are important, they are less so than in the earlier two films and not necessarily the factor that defines Patrick's and Angie's characters and their worlds. As the McCreadys—Lionel and Bea (Titus Welliver and Amy Madigan)—hire these detectives, they are contacted not through prior association but because of their proximity, which suggests the power of geography. Yet, as we see the detectives in their dark and cramped first-floor apartment, located in a three-decker house, they seem to have little commerce with either friends or neighbors, offering the possibility of associations but few of more involved relationships. We meet associated characters of the neighborhood petty crime world—Steve Penteroudakis, Slaine, Cheese, and Devin—as a matter of past associations, mostly from school, and while they provide some vital information, there is little sense of a deeper connection or even one that is a matter of depth from having roots in a particular place. We find information that leads somewhere but not necessarily to the unraveling of the kidnapping plot.

The use of "outsiders" here, police officers Remy Bressant and Captain Doyle, as key elements in the plot makes the binding of social networks by deep social structure both inclusive and exclusive. Both Doyle and Bressant are from Louisiana and came to Boston together to work on the police force. This is distinct from the novel, and even Bressant's name is changed—from Broussard (without a clear rationale)—as well as his backstory. In the novel, he came to South Boston as a young boy so is very much a product of the streets that he polices. In the film, he arrived in Boston as an adult. Bressant's outsider status in the film, then, is enhanced, even as he easily melds into the French-Canadian element of Boston and New England life. Nonetheless, he utters the line, "I'm not from here, but I've been here longer than you've been alive" to Kenzie. Similarly, the fact that Doyle, who is made an outsider in the film, is captive not of his initial environment but of life's circumstances—the death of a child—suggests how an arc of experience can change one's character and impact one's choices.

But all of this occurs within a place, Boston, where narratives of constancy and ethnic definition and association are always at play, although Affleck apparently seeks to complicate such easy notions of place. As we look at a world that includes so many recent immigrants, we can see the radical impact of world historical events on, say, the Haitian character Cheese or his Laotian girlfriend. But our focal characters, who are from this neighborhood, in the end are definitional for the film. Like *The Departed*, this is a film about misrecognition and misrepresentation, as we actually see two discrete mysteries at work: the mystery that is apparently resolved by the death of the kidnapped child, Amanda, and the mystery of the staged death of Amanda and Cheese that ends with the real solution to Amanda's kidnapping, as well as the ethical choice by Bressant and Doyle to take the little girl from her unfit mother and raise her as Doyle's and his wife's. We ultimately end where we began—in a three-decker house in North Dorchester where an unfit, drug-addled mother neglects her little girl.

Kenzie's point of view controls the narrative despite the shadow of a different city that touches him. The film's resolution is a kind of irresolution, one deigned by his rigid system of ethics, a system connected explicitly to his Catholicism, an orientation that defined the film's preamble, quoting from Matthew 10:16: "You are sheep among wolves; be wise as serpents, yet innocent as doves." Now, after the execution of the pederasts in Everett, a shootout in which the police officer Poole—Bressant's partner—is shot, Kenzie returns to his Catholic teachings as a matter of dealing with his guilt: "My priest says shame is God telling you what you did was wrong." Indeed, this inflexible sense of right and wrong is what keeps him from accepting Amanda's abduction by Doyle as positive and informs his inability to forgive Bressant for his role in spiriting the child to a family that will clearly allow her a better childhood and a better life. In the scene prior to Lionel's confession of his role in this subterfuge, the viewer sees him at home amid the many pictures of Amanda, and then the camera pans to show his extensive statuary and pictures of saints, images of innocence and holiness that both speak to Lionel and torment him as he comes to terms with his transgressions. Lionel, like Kenzie, is a man of this world of continuities and cannot evade his guilt at having done wrong even in order to ultimately produce a clearly better outcome for the girl.

As in the other two films, Affleck's version of *Gone Baby, Gone* presents place as an anchor that tethers to a kind of morality, one that affirms the resonant teachings of a lifetime. In the film's final scene, as Kenzie agrees to look after Amanda and as her mother heads out for a date, she tells the detective, "You're a godsend, Patrick." This use of language is no accident. Patrick Kenzie is a product of place, and as a matter or result of his intense identification with that locale and his vision of its continuities, a static moral thinking informs his concept of his soul. Such a worldview keeps him in place even as it ensures that Amanda will be reared by her mother and grow up to be just like her; in effect, she will inherit her place.

Narratives of Time and Place in Docudramas: *Spotlight* and *Black Mass*

"Boston" develops as a location that is related to the city-in-fact, and that cinematic presence connects to its recurrence in other media. It is only fitting, then, that some of the more prominent news stories featuring the city would find their way into films as source material. "Based on a true story" as a claim is, among other things, an assertion of a kind of narrative constraint on the story being told. Unlike in the previous three films discussed in this chapter, the dramatic arc of these two filmic stories, or docudramas, is somewhat reduced by purporting to just tell the facts as they happened—more or less. Neither *Spotlight* nor *Black Mass* (both 2015) explores the meaning of place with the power of *Mystic River* or either of the other earlier films. Nevertheless, they do develop an articulate vision that shows the historical and spatial continuities that result in a kind of inevitability of circumstances, although *Spotlight*—much like the earlier films, and particularly like *The Departed*—does imagine an end to this sequence of predictable outcomes. Unlike *The Departed*, however, *Spotlight* optimistically asserts the power of those from outside the system, a group that was virtually nonexistent in the earlier films, to present countervailing insights and institutional heft.

In the Academy Award–winning *Spotlight*, we move from the prevalent drama-defining place, the crime or noir narrative, and shift to the not entirely unrelated journalism film, or docudrama. This type of film has a long arc, from *The Front Page* (1931) to *The Post* (2018). And while such films may or may not have nonfictional antecedents, the tendency in more recent times has been to base them on preexisting journalistic narratives, with *All the President's Men* (1976) serving as something of a paradigm for many of the subsequent films.[9] Like *All The President's Men*, *Spotlight* also asserts in a pre-credit title that it is "based on actual events." Of course, most viewers already know this before the film begins, since the story of sexual abuse by Boston priests was a powerful narrative of the early 2000s and one that continued to resonate as subsequent instances of abuse were uncovered.

The next title, "Boston, 1976," sets the beginning date for the film's chronology as well as broadly establishes place. This date is striking since it apparently has nothing to do with the case. There was no legal complaint against John Geoghan in 1976, though he was assigned to a parish in Jamaica Plain at that time, so this event is plausible but not in line with the documentation of the wider sex abuse case. Geoghan did assert, incredibly, that his attraction to young boys began in 1976. The date does, however, bring us back toward both the school busing issues of the previous years (in 1974 and 1975), as well as to the bicentennial, so it focuses on a time when the city was increasingly in a national view. The scene takes place in a District 11 police station, a locale actually filmed in Toronto. District 11 in Boston is in Dorchester, not far from the setting of *Gone Baby Gone*, so within the area that later in the film we see canvassed by the various *Globe* reporters. But this locale has nothing to do with the visuals of this opening scene. The further elaboration of place occurs by accent and situation—the known locale of this narrative, as well as the ways in which Boston is inscribed by its Catholic population and attendant institutions. When we hear the older sergeant affirm that there will be no arraignment and that they will be complicit in keeping the complaint from the public, we are immediately apprised of the power of the church and the ways in which it conspires with the various elements of law enforcement to protect those who transgress the law and ethics. The scene ends as the priest and lawyer are driven off in a massive Lincoln Town Car as the officer, smoking a cigarette outside of the station, watches the perpetrator and his defender leave, recalling the opening scene of *Mystic River* in which Dave is driven away by his abductors, suggesting that justice is a diminishing spot in a rearview mirror.

This scene effectively conveys the institutional problem that the film portrays: the power and desire of the Roman Catholic church to protect those priests who are sexual predators from the scrutiny and judgment of both the public and the legal system. This pre-credit scene triggers the viewer's outrage almost immediately. The film then cuts to the *Boston Globe* newsroom in 2001, as one of the *Globe* staff, named Stewart, retires. The bonhomie of the staff provides a context for introducing the paper's new editor, Marty Baron, played by Liev Schreiber, who has just moved to the *Globe* from the *Miami Herald*. The introduction of the new editor—a non-Bostonian and a Jew—becomes a cornerstone of the film, though the Baron character is not on screen very much as the investigation develops. Baron's outsider status is the catalyst for the investigation at the center of the film, which point to the city that we have so fully encountered in other films. Repeatedly, Baron is shown as apart from crowds and even estranged from his staff, rarely appearing other than in his office and behind his desk. Indeed, *Spotlight* ignores the criminality (murder, gambling, loan sharking, etc.) that is definitional for the city of the Boston noir, and instead explores the cultural associations that connect the city with insularity and silence, focusing on the role and power of the Catholic church.

The Boston we see here is distinct from that of the previous films in that the focus here is corporate and institutional—although the church is certainly present in the other three films. But, unlike there, here Catholicism, its institutional muscle, and its wide range of affiliations is explicitly central. Fittingly, then, unlike in the visual coverage of the actual sex abuse cases, the film's institutional focus is more on the church and less on its leader, Bernard Law. Law appears intermittently and is seen as powerful in his advocacy, but the looming presence of spires and the awesome power of the church to forestall testimony is far more a matter of emphasis than in the news coverage. The film uses the term "Lake Street" multiple times as shorthand for the cardinal's institutional power. Lake Street was the street address of the cardinal's regal residence, a site that was also an important locale in *The Verdict*. It abuts St. John's Seminary, where many of the rogue priests, including

John Geoghan, were trained, in Brighton, just across the street from Boston College.

The continuities that define place are affirmed visually. The *Globe* is depicted not simply as an information source but as part of the city's social fabric; it remains, though, a bit outside of the center of the city. Its reporters, readers, and editors all seem to come from the same place, the same schools, and the same religion; our most visible characters are Sacha Pfeiffer, who avers that she does not come from Boston but who seems to live with her grandmother in South Boston, and Michael Rezendes, who is a bit of an outsider, being Portuguese and coming from East Boston. But his "outsider" status suggests how insular this place is. Walter Robinson is very much the Catholic insider, a golf-playing native with extensive ties to the church and its lay supporters, as well as a graduate of the reigning Jesuit secondary school in the city, which happens to be geographically right across Morrissey Boulevard from the *Globe*, at least at that time. (The newspaper has since moved its offices downtown.)[10] It also draws on the conventions of male bonding, including a strong interest in the Red Sox, an anchor of place defined in chapter 4 but here affirmed by discussion of the ties the team creates, which become essentially a kind of civic religion. When we first meet Baron, he is reading *The Legend of the Curse of the Bambino* written by longtime *Globe* baseball writer and then columnist Dan Shaughnessy. In an early scene, four reporters, including Ben Bradlee Jr., Rezendes, Matt Carroll, and Steve Kurkjian, attend a Red Sox game, providing the requisite Fenway Park shot from the stands and advancing the story through discussion of the case during this mostly male ritual, which is so much, as Baron's reading matter affirmed, a matter of place. Indeed, one of the first things Robinson tells Baron is that the *Globe* has Red Sox season tickets. Again, in its portrayal of place, the film elaborates key aspects of definition and affiliation. Indeed, as Rezendes and Bradlee (shot in an intimate two-shot) discuss the emergent investigation, Kurkjian affirms his closed lips by taking a vow of *omerta*, one of our key terms to connect religion and criminality.

The emphasis here is the insularity of place as defined by discrete space. The church and the *Globe* are set up as colluding institutions, and now with Baron's hiring, as institutions at odds. Spatially, and true to the journalistic narrative/genre, much of the film's action takes place in the *Globe* building, which is located appropriately in Dorchester for its exterior shots (interiors were shot in Toronto). But as the story proceeds into the investigative mode, the city we encounter is precisely the one we see in previous films—working-class neighborhoods defined by their insularity and featuring three-decker homes, clearly referring to Dorchester and South Boston, so also presumably white. Interestingly, these parts of the film are shot in either Roxbury or in the less white parts of Dorchester. But, unlike in *Gone Baby Gone*, these regions are whitened for the sake of the narrative, which is exclusively filled with white faces—again, this fact remains true to the story being told, since the victims and priests were overwhelmingly, if not solely, white. But since we are out and about in the city in the 2000s, we might presumably see some Brown or Black faces.

The spaces of Boston, then, are a kind of petri dish for priests to assert their coercive powers and for the church to flex its muscles. Visually, rather than neighborhoods being zones of entrapment, the looming power of the church, which is affirmed by the spires of Catholicism, is what towers over the action. At least eight times in the film, as other action occupies the foreground, a church steeple emerges in the depth of field. Thus, rather than the constraints of space we saw in other films, there is a redefinition of place by the persistence and power of the church. This institution defines Boston, but as Baron becomes a prominent voice, he becomes a device that characterizes a kind of intrusion. As Jim Sullivan tells Robinson as the two men bond over a game of golf, "So the new editor of the *Boston Globe* is an unmarried man of the Jewish faith who hates baseball?" Sullivan gives voice to the unvoiced and unconsidered (and at times considered) antisemitism that pervades upper-class Catholic circles.[11] Baron is also suspect for his lack of interest in the rituals of masculinity, suggesting how, in a patriarchal environment, these rites are used to maintain social control.

The Boston we predominantly see is very much that which we recognize from previous texts. But there are certain exceptions: we encounter neighborhoods of single-family dwellings, both comfortable and more than comfortable, even luxurious. In each case, the church reaches into these places and dwellings. In a rare shot of a largely suburban area still within the city limits, set in West Roxbury (the site of historic Brook Farm), Matt Carroll reacts with alarm when he learns that a group-home for priests who are accused of sexual misconduct is in his immediate neighborhood. These scenes employ Carroll's point of view and maintain his street-level perspective. They were actually shot in the neighborhood depicted and show us a world dominated by Catholicism and the amorality of its leaders. Such a vision imposes insularity, even as it offers a distinctive view of place. Similarly, when Robinson goes to his friend Sullivan's house to verify the names of the eighty-six priests the *Spotlight* team has uncovered, he finds himself in a more lavish locale of even larger single-family homes. Although this scene was shot in Toronto, the house and neighborhood look a lot like the abutting Boston suburb of Brookline, which includes streetscapes of similar design and vintage, as well as lavish homes that are essentially a part of a far more urban, densely populated region. Since Sullivan is a high-priced attorney who has worked for the diocese, we can see his privilege as connected to the power of the church. Indeed, although Sullivan confirms Robinson's list, he does so with regret and anger, articulating the divide between morality and subservience to the institution. In more general terms, the Boston of this film is far more expansive than that which we saw in the various crime films in that it encompasses far more of the business district and seems to venture at least toward the suburbs. Still, the core of place remains constant, as do its institutions and mores. Despite the post-2000 setting, the Boston depicted remains a figment of the past, mired in social continuities that remain central. As the film ends with a wave of phone calls coming in to the Spotlight offices in response to the *Globe* exposé, it is difficult to affirm change, even as the response suggests a wide awareness of the exposé.

Black Mass is far more conventional in its depictions of place and a less resonant narrative in general than *Spotlight*. It is based on the book of the same name written by Dick Lehr and Gerard O'Neill, which stemmed from their investigative reporting for the same Spotlight team (though with different reporters) at the *Globe* that had earlier investigated the church's coverup of priestly sex crimes. It was a large-budget shoot, directed by Scott Cooper, mostly shot in Boston, and starring Johnny Depp—who plays Whitey Bulger and who is made up to look alarmingly like Whitey Bulger—and featuring Joel Edgerton and Benedict Cumberbatch as John Connolly and William Bulger, respectively. Unlike *Spotlight*, *Black Mass* was neither a critical nor a box-office success, though it did make a modest profit of about $40 million on a budget of just over $60 million. Unlike *Spotlight*, which employs the generic markers of a newspaper/detective film, *Black Mass* largely, but not totally, does away with the conventions of "how I got the story," employing it as an afterthought and with little consistency, and instead becomes a more conventional noir/crime film. Nonetheless, it does nod to its journalistic basis at times by employing interviews to define scene transitions and titles that mark time and place. But we don't see our reporters, Lehr and O'Neill, until about seven-eighths of the way through the film, as the camera records a meeting at a dark booth between them and John Morris, who was head of the organized crime unit for the FBI's taskforce working out of the Boston field office. But this is far from our first glimmer of Morris, since he plays a subordinate role in the drama that precedes this meeting. *Black Mass* instead loosely involves the conventions of a crime film, employing the interview with suspects as a device for wading into the Bulger story and asserting the reliability of the narrative. The primary figure for this technique is that of Kevin Weeks (Jesse Plemons) who "Boston's up," so to speak, for this role—gaining weight, building muscle mass, and acquiring a quite convincing South Boston accent. Weeks tells us of the descent of Bulger from sociopath to *true* sociopath. His testimony follows the emphasis that we have already seen in *The Departed* and that affirms the lack of honor among criminals, despite their own affirmations of a "code."

This is a film of dark interiors and subjective camera filming, a claustrophobic crawl both through the city and through the violent mind of James Bulger. And while the film does not employ the journalists as central characters, it does draw extensively from the details of Lehr and O'Neill's book, including the use of the death of Bulger's son, Douglas, whom he fathered with his girlfriend Lindsay Cyr in 1973, as a turning point in Bulger's increasingly violent life. But beyond the basic details, the film is about conventions of criminality and what are by now conventions of place. Like the earlier films discussed in this chapter, the bonds between the Bulger brothers—Jimmy and Billy—and the FBI agent John Connolly are a matter of their common place of origin, South Boston, a locale that is definitional for the film. As former associate Weeks provides testimony to the FBI, his voiceover narrates a montage that defines affiliation and loyalty as a matter of place. As it comes out that Bulger has been working with Connolly as an informant, Bulger asserts that this was a lie, fostered by those with no "loyalty or honor," assertions we can see by this point in the film as patently false and hypocritical, but which Whitey conveniently employs to affirm the code of *omerta* among his compatriots. No sin of testimony or disloyalty can be forgiven. All are punishable by death—presumably. All of this apparently stems from Bulger's deep roots in South Boston, his role as a celebrity-like Robin Hood figure, a myth we have already seen as without basis. The film nods to this myth in an early scene, as Bulger, Weeks, and a less focal sidekick, Mickey Maloney, drive through South Boston (filmed in Charlestown), and as they encounter an older woman, Mrs. Cody, with her groceries on the street. As Weeks tells us how "a lot of people in Southie loved Jimmy," the camera looks on at the three criminals fondly cavorting with the older woman, employing Bulger's crime lieutenant Steve "the Rifleman" Flemmi as our eyes as he looks out from the driver's seat. It is in this sequence and through Weeks's narration, a very noirish convention, that we learn of Connolly's connections to the Bulgers, having grown up near them in the Old Harbor—now the Mary Ellen McCormack Housing project in South Boston, a housing area also shown in *The Departed*—and who was "in awe of Jimmy." While actually shot in Charlestown, the scene still invokes the insularity of South Boston, a place of unrelieved whiteness and Irishness in this telling. This version of "South Boston" is picturesque and cohesive. But it remains so as a result of its erasure of Bulger's violent role in the busing crisis, a matter that does find its way into the Lehr and O'Neill source material. Apparently, scenes were shot of Bulger and his younger brother Billy, who enhanced his political standing in his district through his support for those who resisted the court order during the 1975 busing crisis, but they did not make it into the film's final cut.[12]

This introduction to Connolly sets up a view of the FBI agent leaving his South Boston apartment (which was shot in East Boston), and then shows him in a meeting at FBI headquarters in Boston, where the focus on the investigation and prosecution of the Italian Mafia is announced. Just prior to introducing newly reassigned agent Connolly in 1973, we see a map of Boston and Massachusetts Bay in the background, suggesting the ways in which administrative space will be imposed on the untamed districts of the city. As Connolly goes to meet William Bulger, then a relatively new Massachusetts state senator, Weeks's voiceover tells us that it is South Boston, as a particular place, that creates the indistinct lines between cops and criminals. Weeks narrates as Connolly meets with William Bulger at a lavish club (filmed at the Harvard Club on Commonwealth Avenue in the Back Bay), "just like on the playground, you couldn't always tell who was who." That William is the focus of the scene with Connolly suggests a deep well of political corruption also, although this is not really part of the film's story. It is also notable that we see Bulger and Connolly talking about the Red Sox, establishing another cornerstone of place and male bonding. Interestingly, they briefly discuss the greatness of soon-to-be Montreal Expos catcher Gary Carter. But, as of 1973, Carter was an unknown minor leaguer, and the Red Sox had future hall of famer Carlton Fisk playing that position: so much for chronology. There are other errors of chronology here too, so that sequence and accuracy seem far less significant than the reiteration of the evocative powers of place. For example, the film conflates the dates of Whitey's disappearance and Connolly's apprehension, which were actually some four years apart.

Primarily, this film offers a less embellished version of the emphases found in *The Departed*. Its setting for the FBI headquarters is the same as in that film. It has the same structure of deception, and a similar pathology animates its central character. Like the earlier film, *Black Mass* celebrates and emphasizes loyalty, church, and *omerta*; silence, though, is more of a value than a practice. But it shows the recurring abrogation of such tenets: as Whitey informs, Connolly double deals, Billy lies, and the various gang members testify. This is a criminal business syndicate that is enforced with extreme violence. The claustrophobia and darkness of the film become representations of the souls of its central characters. Yet, throughout *Black Mass*, their bonds, which are fostered by a common place of origin, are unquestioned. And while the film is somewhat episodic and focused on the growing pathology of Bulger and his connection to the self-deceived Connolly, it does emphasize Boston as a petri dish for the growth of such individuals. The film ends with an episode from long after the book was published, with the arrest of Bulger in California in 2011. As I argued in chapter 3, Bulger is cast as a distinctive product of a vision of the city, a highly mediated digital city, and also a city as commodity, which by 2015 had solidified into a vital narrative of place, even a chronotope. Filmmaker Scott Cooper has spoken of his desire to make film that is of a time and not looking back at a time.[13] But this is antithetical to his use of the device of testimony—confession—as well as his lack of context and deeper analysis of his characters in the 1970s, 1980s, and 1990s. In his review of *Black Mass* in *The New Yorker*, the critic Richard Brody writes, "Some critics have expressed Boston-fatigue, taking the accent as a generic signifier for white ethnicity and urban grit. But it's something more: Boston is the leading cinematic signifier of whiteness, of white ethnicity and ethnic solidarity outside the South and without the taint of white Southern revanchism."[14] Indeed, the allure of such behavior is more than a guilty pleasure for filmgoers. Rather, it is far more caustic than that. In this chapter, I have intentionally laid out and reiterated both its terms and its antecedents, showing how such affirmations are a matter of a reading of the past that has the power to project such realities into a present that is a very different set of circumstances, yet, the meaning of those circumstances, to a degree, depends on how critically we approach these renderings of the past.

Clearly in the earlier films, and particularly in *Gone Baby Gone*, the texts lay out some basis for a critical look at the way that Boston is employed as a symbol of stasis and excessive ethnic tribalism, even as they produce a city that looks exceedingly familiar in its geography and social attitudes. *Spotlight* provides a more overt critique, showing us a city where the pacts of complicity among major institutions have begun to expire, ending on a note where journalism ceases to protect civic institutions that are not serving the civic good. *Black Mass*, on the other hand, is bound by genre, an uncritical definition of place, and a reverence for its source material. Even as Whitey Bulger is ultimately apprehended, his status as a super-criminal is never textually compromised, nor can we remove his larger-than-life persona from the narrative. But even in the cases where we can mount a critique to recurrent and regressive ideas of place, these films are too easily apprehended in terms of the city's mythos, a myth that ignores its more recent history and demographics. As such, "Boston" remains a media projection that serves as a recurring chronotope of a world that no longer exists, a city defined by its immigration at the turn of the twentieth century and largely impervious to the changes of the late twentieth century and the twenty-first, a majority-minority urban center which recently elected its first woman mayor, and its first mayor who is not Anglo-, Irish, or Italian American. Yet, even those films that seek to shift the narrative of place still feature many of its mythic elements, further reducing place to typecasting.

CONCLUSION

Ray Donovan and the Essence of "Boston"

It is remarkable, but affirming, that the most "Boston" of all dramas is one that rarely pictures Boston. On June 30, 2013, some two years before the productions of *Spotlight* and *Black Mass*, Showtime debuted the television series *Ray Donovan*. The show centers around the doings of a South Boston–reared family that has moved to Los Angeles. The featured character, named in the title and played by Liev Schreiber, relocates after working on a Boston shoot of a film for producer Ezra Goodman, played by Eliott Gould. That film is titled *Black Mass*, though it was some two years before the production of that film and one year after the Dick Lehr/Gerard O'Neil book of 2012. The film noted in the series, as best we can surmise, has little to do with that book. That filming in the show's conceit seems to have taken place around 1998. During the location shoot, the film's star, Sean Walker, accidentally kills a woman. Subsequently, Ray helps frame his father, Mickey—played by John Voight—for the murder. Mickey is sentenced to twenty years in Walpole State Penitentiary, though he is released five years early. In Los Angeles, Ray serves as a fixer, primarily for Ezra and his partner Lee Drexler. It is a violent and insular world that Ray and his family inhabit, despite the suburban grandeur of their Calabasas home, their expensive clothes, and their access to the rich and famous. The series begins as Mickey Donovan is released from Walpole.

When the show debuted, it received ambivalent reviews. Wrote Emily Nussbaum in *The New Yorker*, for example, "From the poolside-pitch perspective, her [Ann Biderman, the showrunner's] new series sounds lively enough: it's 'Mystic River' plus 'The Fighter,' set in a noirish modern Los Angeles, then spiced with an Elmore Leonard-esque assortment of colorful losers. But the series exists within its own ugly system, mining the by now tired convention of the thoughtful thug." Similarly, Matt Zoller Seitz in *New York Magazine* opined, "The first show—about a family of tough South Boston Irish-Americans who relocate to Los Angeles, and start a boxing gym

FIGURE 17. Mickey Donovan as he leaves Walpole, driving by TD Garden on his way to kill a priest. —Courtesy Screen Shot.

and a combination private eye/protection service that caters to celebrities—is pretty good, if you're not burned out on the 'Tough White Dude Can't Control His Inner Demons but Has a Good Heart' genre."[1] Despite such initial equivocation, *Ray Donovan* ran for seven seasons. When the show ended in the fall of 2020, there was sufficient demand for a movie to act as the series finale that Showtime produced and aired that film in 2022.

As the show opens, Mickey walks out of the prison gates, enters a car, and drives to the north. We see the TD Garden pass on the right and a sign that announces the exit for Sullivan Square (Exit 28), a locale in the north portion of Charlestown, just across the Somerville city line. We see Mick exit the car, enter a church, and find a priest in the rectory. The camera, in close up, records Mick putting a gun barrel in the priest's mouth, calling him out for his sexual abuse, and then firing. The scene cuts to Doris Day singing "Hooray for Hollywood" accompanied by a panorama of that city shot from the air. The disjunction between the two places is both striking and surreal.

It is clear that we are initially in Boston and that anchoring the show in that locale is central to its narrative. In that first episode and subsequent ones we touch on all of the definitional elements of a mediated place. We pass by TD Garden, the home of the Celtics and Bruins; we see Mickey's first act as a matter of his release refers back to the legacy of priest abuse. In episode 2, when Mickey is shown in Los Angeles, we have references to his role in supporting the anti-busing movement in South Boston, noting not only his racism but also Ray's, as he refuses to acknowledge his African American half-brother. As the season goes on, the character of "Sully"

Sullivan, played by James Woods, appears initially in episode 6 and then in five more before he meets his demise in the season finale. Sully is our Whitey Bulger, who, with his girlfriend Katherine, has been missing for twenty years when Ray finds him in Boston. We also have some Red Sox cameos, with Ray's younger brother Bunchy burning his Red Sox pennant, a tie to his childhood, in one episode. When Ray returns to Boston to enlist Sully to kill his father, he gives a boyhood friend a wad of cash and tells him, "Take your kids to Fenway. Mine have never been."

The existence of this show and its emphases make it the most Boston-centric of all the fictional renderings of that city. *Ray Donovan* distills the essence of a vision of Boston, takes it to Los Angeles, and makes it definitional for its central characters; in effect, it shows us how "Boston" has become a star, a presence that is central to all surrounding action. One definition of stardom is its predictability: rather than the actor getting lost in the role, the role becomes subordinate to the recurring presence and qualities of the recognizable actor. As Gaylyn Studlar writes, "It is acknowledged that making your star unrecognizable is dangerous. This is because the value of stardom is most frequently measured in audience anticipation at seeing—and recognizing—their favorite box-office attraction."[2] "Boston," derived from its portrayal in a range of media and disciplines, becomes a dominant aspect of the series, yet that place is rarely employed as a location. After the opening scenes of the drama, we don't actually return to the city until season 6, though a Los Angeles church stands in for one in Boston—the nonexistent St. Josephine's—in episode 3, and when Sully is summoned to Los Angeles by Ray, we apparently return to his stomping grounds in South Boston and see a superimposition of the Boston skyline featuring the Prudential Tower through Ray's hotel window. Regardless, the scenes were all shot in Los Angeles. This image of a two-dimensional Boston defining both locale and persistent terms of behavior and interactions serves as a kind of synecdoche for the role of Boston throughout the series. Los Angeles becomes the perfect backdrop for seeing "Boston" in high contrast, allowing us to explore the Donovan family as fish out of water. In such a context, their Boston-ness becomes all the more visible and all the more defining.

One of the markers of the Donovan family's Bostonness, beyond its penchant for violence and racism, is its vocal mannerisms, its accents. The central characters take pains to perform a correct, working-class Boson accent, one that could accompany a South Boston upbringing. These vocal mannerisms become markers of both class and place, and therefore authenticity. Says one character about the speech of Ray's wife's, Abby, in season 1, episode 2, "I love her accent. It's so real." Indeed, the accent displaced to Los Angeles is all the more notable since there is no regional southern California patois to speak of. *Ray Donovan*'s "realism" flows from the Donovan's family accents, which become an index of their South Boston origins, an inescapable context in which they (mostly) revel. This connection of place to vocal expression defines how "Boston" becomes submerged in a reification of working-class behaviors. These vocal mannerisms include violent oaths, much profanity, and in Ray's case a disposition toward the laconic, which becomes an index of his working-class masculine ethos. And this ethos is not confined to Ray. All of the brothers have it, and later on Connor, Ray's only son, develops it. In episode 8, for example, when Mickey meets a woman named Linda (Roseanne Arquette) at a spa and takes her to one of the brother's house for a drink, their assignation ends badly. The scene ends with Mickey chasing her out the door, calling her a "tourist," in reference to her lack of gravity and authenticity, and asking pejoratively if he's too "authentic" for her. In season 2, as the Donovans seek to move from a McMansion in Calabasas to a modernist palace in Trousdale, Abby meets a prospective neighbor who comments on her accent, embarrassing her and making her self-conscious about her class origins. She attempts to change her speech by taking digital voice lessons but only ends up sounding stilted and inauthentic; she abandons her efforts. For all the Donovans of the older generations, authenticity connects to violent demeanor, speech, and lack of a filter.

As I have discussed, Boston as pictured in a variety of texts—though not much pictured in this series—is working class and strongly associated with the region of South Boston. This place becomes a marker of urban authenticity within a world where such apparent depths of interpersonal affiliations and geographical associations are eroding. To remove individuals so strongly connected to place and context from that world allows those markers of authenticity to become both caricature and bond. That the bonds are those of family and not community, as they might be were they not displaced, speaks to the ways such connection is necessary in order to produce "tradition."

In *Ray Donovan*, beyond speech, a marker of continuity and family is sexual trauma and its response—hypermasculine behavior. Beyond the repressive sexual structures of the Roman Catholic church there is the phenomenon of sexual abuse that marks all three brothers and Mickey. The response to that abuse includes acting out through hypersexuality, aggressive sex, and physical violence. The series allows us to see the events noted in chapters 1 and 2 as not only the retrograde protection of turf but also the protection of one's masculinity through a violent rejection of any apparent intrusion.

Ray Donovan serves as a kind of culmination of the use of the trope of "Boston" in the mass media, though it is not the last word by any means. In 2013, at the finish line of the Boston Marathon, two Chechen émigrés to Cambridge, the brothers Tsarnaev (who attended the same high school as Matt Damon and Ben Affleck) detonated a homemade bomb. This tragic event soon became the grist for a response that traded heavily in the prefabricated notions of place, including the elevation of the city as a site of resilience and authenticity, assertions that were broadly disseminated through digital media.[3] Said Red Sox star David Ortiz five days later, on April 20, 2013: "This is our f***** city, and nobody's gonna dictate our freedom. Stay strong."[4] That the primary suspect was apprehended in the modest suburb of Watertown meant that the images that circulated worldwide would show a city that easily fit preexisting narratives. And that the "other" here was a Muslim from central Asia, a figure who created a newer, post-9/11 version of racial exclusion, well maps onto the prior narratives of whiteness.

In 2016, Bostonian Mark Wahlberg produced and starred in the film *Patriots Day*, directed by frequent collaborator Peter Berg, recounting the marathon bombing story. Wahlberg, playing a fictional cop named Tommy Saunders, sports both the correct accent and the same working-class disregard for authority that marks our Boston everymen. This drama is formulaic, as Saunders's can-do practicality trumps the more refined approaches of his superiors and federal agents brought in from the outside. The culminating scene, in which Tamerlan Tsarnaev is shot, shows us a working-class suburb that could easily be Dorchester or South Boston, thus maintaining the look of "authentic" Boston. (The scenes were shot in Malden.) Again, the template that has been elaborated in so many other recent texts is easily referenced in shorthand and employed in this very broad drama.

The Boston legacy of productions that evoke a hardscrabble city dominated by ethnic Catholics continued with *City on a Hill*, on Showtime from 2019 to 2022, created by Charlie McClean and produced by Ben Affleck and Matt Damon, among others. The show follows a corrupt former FBI agent, Jackie Rohr (played by Kevin Bacon, accent and all), and his conflicts and alliances with a reformist African American district attorney, DeCourcy Ward (Aldis Hodge). The show allows for an image of a changing city and is set in the early 1990s. Still, the characters and settings of the city—Chinatown, the South End—evoke a world we encountered in earlier films. And its emphasis on police corruption not only evokes *The Departed* and *Gone Baby Gone* but also echoes the Whitey Bulger case and Charles Stuart murder. That the show provides a window into a city in transition, where "outsiders" enter the previously close social system, is apt and echoes Affleck's *Gone Baby Gone*, but the city we see is far from ready to change. It is not the city now governed by Mayor Micelle Wu, elected in 2021, a Harvard College and Harvard Law School graduate who moved to Cambridge from Chicago to attend college, the daughter of Taiwanese immigrants.

In 2023, Boston is a very different city than it was in 1980 or 2000. In 2020, it was 51 percent white and 43 percent Black and Hispanic. It includes more people who have graduated from college than not, and its median household income is over $80,000. That makes the city more educated than the norm—in 2021, about 38 percent of U.S. residents had college degrees—and wealthier, as the average U.S. household income was around $68,000 in 2021. In 2000, the city was 54.5 percent white, with only just over 35 percent having a college degree and a median, unadjusted income of just under $40,0000.[5] Yet, a certain sense of place persists, and despite that image gradually receding, recent films like *Spenser Confidential* (2020), starring Mark Wahlberg and directed by Peter Berg (the same team who did *Patriots Day*), and the remake of the *Boston Strangler* (dir. Matt Ruskin, 2023) picture the Boston found so often noted in the preceding chapters. Recently, novelist Dennis Lehane, who has been a recurring figure in this book as the writer of the source material for *Mystic River* and *Gone Baby Gone*, published his novel *Small Mercies*, set in the South Boston housing projects just as the order for mandatory busing went into effect. The novel evocatively recalls the moment and provides us with characters true to our prior sense of place.

***

My intention has been to elaborate how a place, in this case Boston, becomes typecast through a mass of featured roles: roles that emerge in nonfiction, sports journalism, and then in fictional films. The result of such continuity of textual and intertextual reference is a remarkable coherence and presence. The insularity and racism of the Boston defined in the busing coverage of 1974 and 1975 enabled the cautionary tale of Charles Stuart, whose initial story relied on the apparent credibility of racist tropes of place and region. That insularity and code of *omerta* became central in the stories of sexual abuse in the Catholic church and in the legend of Whitey Bulger; further, these powerful narratives allowed for overt racism to become recessed in stories of place but that sentiment never vanished. Indeed, exclusion and insularity become markers of place that readily allow for racial exclusion but under the guise of "community" coherence and working-class solidarity.

In section 2, we saw how sports are implicated in these notions of locale, as certain signature franchises become powerfully associated with place. This is a matter of not only their reflection of social norms and biases but also of their branding, a process that delves into the broad terms of symbol and identification. The Red Sox legacy of racist practices can be concretely connected to the years of ownership by Tom Yawkey, but subsequently, as the ownership has changed and the pallor of the team on the field has changed, the terms of association echo those of an earlier era, as well as the terms associated with place—tradition, authenticity, and the whiteness and racism of the fanbase. And as that signature baseball franchise maintains its identity, it reinforces both the extant terms of place and the terms of another sports franchise, the Boston Celtics, which are connected by matters of place and terms of identity. Both of these teams in their media prominence become important purveyors of Boston-ness, recurring symbols that appear many times a year for a population that far exceeds those who actually attend events.

Such a brand—a presence—then becomes the stuff of fictional texts, and all the more powerful for its role in both evoking a place and mythologizing that place. Films such as *The Departed* and *Mystic River*, well-crafted and powerful, pull together the strands of the nonfictional narratives in a manner that allows us to see Boston as a world of insular, working-class neighborhoods; petty intra- and interethnic grievances; and a profound racism. The Boston we see is powerfully dispersed through the ubiquity of contemporary mass media, which has an extraordinary power to disseminate and simplify a particular object, in this case a city. These simplifications find their way into the center of *Ray Donovan*. Such projections create and reinforce assumptions of place. In a digital world these depictions become a kind of feedback loop that supplants more nuanced and complex conceptions, though the persistence of such tropes make them far from inevitable. As we move toward the end of the first quarter of the twenty-first century, the factors that created the conception of "Boston" become more and more eclipsed and historically remote. Still, the resurgence of an ethnonationalism may make a place that apparently stands for a kind of whiteness an oddly attractive object for such ideologies. Such conceptions of place are rooted in the past and its mythology. And it is through the elucidation of such definitional contingencies that the broad and highly mediated notion of place may be viewed as other than a matter of fact.

Notes

Introduction

1. On December 10, 2017, the *Boston Globe* Spotlight Team began a seven-part series entitled "Boston. Racism. Image. Reality." See The *Spotlight* Team (Akilah Johnson, Todd Wallack, Nicole Dungca, Liz Kowalczyk, Andrew Ryan, Adrian Walker, and editor Patricia Wen), "Boston. Racism. Image. Reality," *Boston Globe*, December 10–16, 2017.
2. Akilah Johnson, "Boston. Racism. Image. Reality," *Boston Globe*, December 10, 2017.
3. Boston, Massachusetts, Population History, 1840–2021, Biggest U.S. Cities, January 4, 2024, https://www.biggestuscities.com; Edward L. Glaeser, "Reinventing Boston: 1630–2003," *Journal of Economic Geography* 5, no. 2 (April 2005): 119–53, 143 (quotation).
4. Lizabeth Cohen, *Saving America's Cities: Ed Logue and the Struggle to Renew Urban America in the Suburban Age* (New York: Farrar, Strauss, Giroux, 2019), 54–55; Thomas H. O'Connor, *Building a New Boston: Politics and Urban Renewal, 1950–1970* (Boston: Northeastern University Press, 1993).
5. John Agnew, "Space and Place," in *Handbook of Geographical Knowledge*, ed. J. Agnew and D. Livingstone (London: Sage, 2011), 316–30.
6. Eric Jay Dolin, *Fur, Fortune, and Empire: The Epic History of the Fur Trade in America* (New York: Norton, 2011), 145–60; Howard Bodenhorn, *A History of Banking in Antebellum America: Financial Markets and Economic Development in an Era of Nation-Building* (Cambridge: Cambridge University Press, 2000), 30–34.
7. Meaghan Dwyer-Ryan, "The Making of an Irish and a Jewish Boston, 1820–1900," *Historical Journal of Massachusetts* 44, no. 2 (June 2016): 40–85.
8. Mikhail M. Bakhtin, "Forms of Time and of the Chronotope in the Novel: Notes toward a Historical Poetics," in *The Dialogic Imagination: Four Essays by M. M. Bakhtin*, ed. Michael Holquist (Austin: University of Texas Press, 1981), 250–52.
9. See Cohen, *Saving America's Cities*, particularly part 2, "Boston in the 1960's," 145–251.
10. Cohen discusses this strategy in detail in her recounting of the West End Redevelopment Project; see Cohen, *Saving America's Cites*, 157–63.
11. See Barry Bluestone and Mary Huff Stevenson, *The Boston Renaissance: Race, Space, and Economic Change in an American Metropolis* (New York: Russell Sage, 2002), 91–99, 14–17.

12 Elihu Rubin, *Insuring the City: The Prudential Center and the Postwar Urban Landscape* (New Haven, CT: Yale University Press, 2012).
13 Sharon Zukin, "Changing Landscapes of Power: Opulence and the Urge for Authenticity," *International Journal of Urban and Regional Research* 33, no. 2 (June 2009): 543–53, 545, 548 (quotations).

Section 1

1 For discussions of their roles, see Avi Nelson, Moderator, "Boston Bussing through a Civil Rights Lens, Transcript of Left and Right: A Boston Bussing Debate," 1975, Salem State College Archive, Salem, MA, http://di.salemstate.edu, and Mark Frazier, "Spotlight: Avi Nelson," *Reason*, July 1977, https://reason.com. See also Steve Elman and Alan Tolz, *Burning Up the Air: Jerry Williams, Talk Radio, and the Life in Between* (Boston: Commonwealth Editions, 2008).
2 Richard Todd, "The Upstairs and Downstairs of Boston's Media," *Columbia Journalism Review* 29, no. 5 (January 1, 1991): 34.
3 Barry Bluestone and Mary Huff Stevenson, *The Boston Renaissance: Race, Space, and Economic Change in an American Metropolis* (New York: Russell Sage, 2002), 94–96.

Chapter One

1 Ronald Formisano, *Boston against Busing: Race, Class, and Ethnicity in the 1960s and 1970s* (Chapel Hill: University of North Carolina Press, 2004), 226–27.
2 The change has been swift: in 1970, the population of the 102-acre waterfront district was 943, up 72 percent in a decade. By fall of 1976, a state census put the number of residents at 3,400. John Kifner, "On Boston Waterfront, Instant Neighborhood Glitters," *New York Times*, October 23, 1976, https://www.nytimes.com; Morris Dixon, "New Life, Old Fabric," *Architect*, August 3, 2009, https://www.architectmagazine.com; Joseph Giovannini, "Boston Waterfront: At 25, a Model Urban Renewal," *New York Times*, September 21, 1986, https://www.nytimes.com.
3 *The Big Dig: Facts and Figures: Statistics from the Central Artery*, Project Highway Division, Massachusetts Department of Transportation, https://www.mass.gov.
4 See Henri Lefebvre, *The Production of Space*, trans. Donald Nicholson-Smith (Oxford: Blackwell, 1991), 73–77.
5 NBC Evening News, September 12, 1974, Vanderbilt Television News Archive, Nashville, TN (hereafter VTNA).
6 Matthew Delmont, *Why Busing Failed: Race, Media, and the National Resistance to School Desegregation* (Berkeley: University of California Press, 2016), 201; NBC Evening News, November 7, 1974, VTNA: "Police guard on hand as blacks enter Hyde Park area on buses. Greetings from neighborhood whites also concern Black students. Black students react to racial situation in Hyde Park schools."
7 "Historical Trends in Boston's Neighborhoods since 1950," Boston Planning and Development Agency Research Division, December 2017, 39–48, http://www.bostonplans.org.

8 Elijah Anderson, "The White Space," *Sociology of Race and Ethnicity* 1, no. 1 (2015): 10–21, 10 (quotation).
9 "Enrollment Profiles," Massachusetts Department of Public Elementary and Secondary Education School and District Profiles, https://profiles.doe.mass.edu.
10 Anderson, "The White Space," 17.
11 "From the Schools to the Streets," *Time*, October 21, 1974, https://content.time.com.
12 See Gerald Gramm, *Urban Exodus: Why the Jews Left Boston and the Catholics Stayed* (Cambridge, MA: Harvard University Press, 2001).
13 These disparities are well documented. See Tony Hill, "Ethnicity and Education: The Politics of Black Education, 1780–1980," *Boston Review*, October 1, 1981, https://www.bostonreview.net.
14 The proliferation of such images began with the opening of schools in September 1974. See John Kifner, "Violence Mars Busing in Boston," *New York Times*, September 13, 1974, https://www.nytimes.com, and the various network newscasts of that week, including NBC Evening News, September 11, 1974, VTNA. Later broadcasts continued in this vein; see NBC Evening News, October 7, 1974, and ABC Evening News, October 8, 1974, VTNA.
15 Matthew Delmont, *Why Busing Failed: Race, Media, and the National Resistance to School Desegregation* (Berkeley: University of California Press, 2016), 1–21. Delmont's book is an insightful and wide-ranging discussion of various instances of school busing, including pre-1974 resistance in New York and Chicago. There is some inevitable overlap. My study is about place and the ways in which segregated housing became naturalized in visual and verbal terms through the coverage of Boston in 1974 and 1975.
16 Delmont, *Why Busing Failed*, 197.
17 John Kifner, "Kennedy Jeered on Boston Busing," *New York Times*, September 10, 1974, http://www.nytimes.com.
18 A national panel on the busing crisis confirmed this: national television coverage of desegregation events in Boston, particularly incidents of violence during fall 1974, engendered a widespread feeling in that community that reporting had been sensationalized and thereby distorted. Deputy Mayor Robert Kiley testified, "It was important that the issue got covered. The press was very cooperative. And I have to applaud the press, the Boston press. The coverage they had was a very honest and balanced kind of coverage." U.S. Commission on Civil Rights, "Desegregating the Boston Public Schools: A Crisis in Civic Responsibility" (Washington, DC: U.S. Commission on Civil Rights, 1975), 200, 203.
19 "Backlash in Boston—and across the US," *Newsweek*, November 6, 1967, 29–34, and many articles in those two national papers spanning some two decades but most intensely from 1963 to 1976.
20 Andrew Ryan, "How the 1967 Mayoral Race Changed Boston," *Boston Globe*, October 21, 2017, https://www.bostonglobe.com. Hicks appeared in no less than 2,700 *Boston Globe* articles in the 1970s. *Boston Globe*, keyword search, https://bostonglobe.newspapers.com.
21 Eliot Weinbaum, "Looking for Leadership: Battles over Busing in Boston," *Penn GSE: Perspectives on Urban Education* 3, no. 1 (Fall 2004): 1–9.

22 The "new" city hall was conceived as an open and inviting space but, in practice, was anything but. Critics saw it as cold, oppressive, even antidemocratic. It was designed in 1962 and opened in 1967. See Nik DeCosta Klipa, "Why Is Boston City Hall the Way It Is?" Boston.com, July 25, 2018, https://www.boston.com.
23 Louis Masur, *The Soiling of Old Glory: The Story of a Photograph That Shocked America* (New York: Bloomsbury, 2009), 17–18.
24 Masur, *Soiling of Old Glory*, xi–xii.
25 Les Brown, "TV by Satellite: The First Decade," *New York Times*, June 28, 1975, https://www.nytimes.com.
26 J. Anthony Lukas, *Common Ground: A Turbulent Decade in the Lives of Three American Families* (New York: Vintage, 1986), 513.
27 Constance L. Hayes, "Husband of Slain Boston Woman Becomes a Suspect, Then a Suicide," *New York Times*, January 5, 1990, https://www.nytimes.com.
28 WNEV Broadcast: January 1990, WNEV News 7 Special Report—DiMaiti Press Conference/Stuart Case, Victoria Block—R. D. Sahl, https://www.youtube.com.
29 NBC Evening News, October 24, 1989; CBS Evening News, October 24, 1989, VTNA.
30 Marc Mauer, "Bill Clinton, 'Black Lives' and the Myths of the 1994 Crime Bill," Marshall Project, April 4, 2011, https://www.themarshallproject.org.
31 Fox Butterfield, "Massachusetts Says Police in Boston Illegally Stopped Black Youths," *New York Times*, December 12, 1990, https://www.nytimes.com.
32 P. J. Howe and Jack Thomas, "Reading Woman Dies after Shooting in Car, Husband, Baby Termed Critical," *Boston Globe*, October 25, 1989; S. Jacobs, "The Shattering of a Shining Life," *Boston Globe*, October 25, 1989; L. K. Tan, "Shooting Victim Aids Hunt for Wife's Killer," *Boston Herald*, October 26, 1989; L. K. Tan and G. Witherspoon, "Hub Set to Call Crime Emergency," *Boston Herald*, October 25, 1989; D. Weber, "A Terrible Night! Gunman Invades Car, Shoots Couple," *Boston Herald*, October 24, 1989; Roberto Scalese, "The Charles Stuart Murders and the Racist Branding Boston Just Can't Seem to Shake," *Boston Globe*, October 22, 2014, https://www.boston.com; Thomas W. Cooper, "Racism, Hoaxes, Epistemology, and News as a Form of Knowledge: The Stuart Case as Fraud or Norm?" *Howard Journal of Communications* 7, no. 1 (1996): 75–95.
33 Constance L. Hays, "Boston Agonizes over Street Violence," *New York Times*, October 28, 1989, http://www.nytimes.com.
34 "Presumed Innocent: Charles Stuart," *Time*, January 22, 1990, 20–24; "The Outrage in Boston: Murder and Deceit," *People*, January 22, 1990, 15–17; "The Boston Murder," *Newsweek*, January 22, 1990, 16–18; *Inside Edition*, September 27, 1991; Fox Butterfield with Constance L. Hays, "A Boston Tragedy: The Stuart Case—A Special Case: Motive Remains a Mystery in Deaths That Haunt a City," *New York Times*, January 15, 1990; Christopher B. Daly, "The Murder That Ravaged Boston: The Media Deceived and on the Defensive," *Washington Post*, January 7, 1990.
35 Boston's Stuart murder controversy: "Who's to Blame?" Donahue, ABC-TV, January 11, 1990, https://www.youtube.com; C-Span TV, "Media and the Charles Stuart Case," special broadcast co-sponsored by Boston Association of Black

Journalists and Harvard Law School Forum 1990, February 9, 1990, https://www.c-span.org; "The Boston Hoax: The Police, the Press, the Public. The Other Side of the News," WCVB-TV and PBS-TV, Columbia University Seminars, January 17, 1990, https://video.alexanderstreet.com.
36 Montgomery Brower, Dirk Mathison, and S. Avery Brown, "A Dark Night of the Soul in Boston," *People*, November 13, 1989, http://people.com.
37 Margaret Carlson, "Presumed Innocent," *Time*, June 24, 2001, http://content.time.com.
38 Fox Butterfield and Constance L. Hays, "A Boston Tragedy: The Stuart Case—A Special Case: Motive Remains a Mystery in Deaths That Haunt a City," *New York Times*, January 15, 1990, http://www.nytimes.com.
39 Charles P. Pierce, "Baltimore Burning: The Ghost of Willie Bennett," *Esquire*, April 30, 2015, http://www.esquire.com.
40 William Julius Wilson, *When Work Disappears: The World of the New Urban Poor* (New York: Vintage, 1997).
41 Alexander Hermann, David Luberoff, and Daniel McCue, "Mapping Over Two Decades of Neighborhood Change in the Boston Metropolitan Area," Joint Center for Housing Studies of Harvard University, January 2019, https://www.jchs.harvard.edu.
42 Henri Lefebvre, *Writings on Cities*, ed. Eleonore Kofman and Elizabeth Lebas (London: Wiley Blackwell, 1996), 147–59.
43 Anderson, "The White Space," 19.
44 Lukas, *Common Ground*, 553.
45 Lukas, *Common Ground*, 583.
46 David Harvey, *Spaces of Global Capitalism: A Theory of Uneven Geographical Development* (New York: Verso, 2006), 43.

Chapter Two

1 Shelley Murphy, "Bulger Linked to '70s Antibusing Attacks," *Boston Globe*, April 22, 2001, http://archive.boston.com; William M. Bulger, *While the Music Lasts: My Life in Politics* (Boston: Houghton-Mifflin, 1996).
2 See Mary Chayko, "Reality, Emotionality, and Intimacy in Digital Social Connecting: The Experience of Being Superconnected," *Sociologija* 61, no. 4 (2019): 513–20. Chayko writes of the ways in which digital connection fosters a kind of intimacy through its technological redefinition of both the personal and interpersonal.
3 Groups such as the Irish Dead Rabbits and Westies proliferated among the Irish; the Black Hand, which became the Mafia, grew among Italians during Prohibition. These groups also served as community organizations in ways and were associated with Jewish gangsters of the era. See "Irish Immigrants and Crime," https://macaulay.cuny.edu, and Justin Dombrowski, "The Curse of the Black Hand: The 1911 Unsolved Murder of Giovanni Baptiste Arecchi," Hagen History Center, October 21, 2022, https://www.eriehistory.org.
4 Robert D. McFadden, "Whitey Bulger Is Dead in Prison at 89; Long-Hunted Boston Mob Boss," *New York Times*, October 30, 2018.

5 NBC Evening News, January 12, 2002, Vanderbilt Television News Archive, Nashville, TN (hereafter VTNA).
6 ABC Special, March 14, 2002, VTNA.
7 CNN Evening News, February 11, 2002, VTNA.
8 Anthony Flint, "CityLab Design: Boston's Beloved Triple-Deckers Are Next-Level Affordable Housing," Bloomberg, May 17, 2023, https://www.bloomberg.com.
9 These are all popular websites that deal with law and crime: Robert Ambrogi, "Lawyer's Blog Tracks Trial of Whitey Bulger," LawSites, June 4, 2013, https://www.lawnext.com; John Cunningham and Dick Lehr, "Whitey Bulger: American Crime Boss," Encyclopedia Britannica, https://www.britannica.com; "Whitey Bulger," The Mob Museum, https://themobmuseum.org; Mark Holan's Irish American Blog, https://www.markholan.org.
10 There are countless renderings of this tale, as my elaboration of Whitey's ubiquity on the Internet suggests. Two thorough versions are Jeff Greenfield, "The Noir Life of a Fugitive Gangster," *Washington Post*, April 21, 2013, and Howie Carr, *The Brothers Bulger: How They Terrorized and Corrupted Boston for a Quarter Century* (New York: Grand Central, 2006).
11 Elizabeth Wolfe, Amy Simonson and Rob Frehse, "3 Men Indicted in the Beating Death of Gangster James 'Whitey' Bulger," CNN, August 20, 2022, https://www.cnn.com; Bill Hutchinson and Aaron Katersky, "Whitey Bulger, Notorious Boston Mob Boss, Killed in Prison," ABC News, October 30, 2018, https://abcnews.go.com.
12 *Whitey Bulger: The Making of a Monster*, dir. Ben Avishai and Daniel Mooney, Northern Light Productions, 2013; *Whitey: United States of America v. James J. Bulger*, dir. Joe Berlinger, Netflix, 2014; *My Name Is Bulger*, dir. Brendan J. Byrne, Discovery, 2021.
13 David Mizner, "Reporting an Explosive Truth: The Boston Globe and Sexual Abuse in the Catholic Church," Journalism School, Knight Case Studies Initiative, Columbia University, 2011, 1–22, http://ccnmtl.columbia.edu.
14 Walter Benjamin, "The Work of Art in the Age of Mechanical Reproduction," in *Illuminations*, ed. Hannah Arendt, trans Harry Zohn (New York: Schocken, 1969), 217–52.
15 Gillian Rose, "Rethinking the Geographies of Cultural 'Objects' through Digital Technologies: Interface, Network and Friction," *Progress in Human Geography* 40, no. 3 (2016): 334–51, 338 (quotation).
16 See the VTNA, which includes material from the three major television networks—NBC, CBS, and ABC—as well as CNN.
17 Jason Berry, *Lead Us Not into Temptation: Catholic Priests and the Sexual Abuse of Children* (New York: Doubleday, 1992).
18 ABC Evening News, September 22, 1992; CBS Evening News, September 23, 1992; NBC Evening News, December 6, 1993, VTNA.
19 ABC Evening News, September 22, 1992; CBS Evening News, September 23, 1992; NBC Evening News, December 6, 1993; ABC Special, December 6, 1993, VTNA.

20 Ellen McNamara quoted in Mizner, "Reporting an Explosive Truth," 13.
21 Rachel Martin, "Special Series: Scandal in the Church: Five Years On," *Morning Edition*, NPR, January 11–12, 2007, https://www.npr.org.
22 See my various network references above, in which Law's appearance with robes and crosier became a kind of signature of event and locale. For a particularly salient version, see NBC Evening News, February 11, 2002, VTNA.
23 NBC Evening News, Apr 11, 2005, VTNA.
24 Pam Belluck, "Boston Archbishop Will Sell Residence for Abuse Payout," *New York Times*, December 4, 2003.
25 NBC Evening News, September 16, 1990, VTNA.
26 NBC Evening News, June 17, 1993, VTNA.
27 Linda Matchan, "Town Secret," *Boston Globe Magazine*, August 29, 1993.
28 David France, *Our Fathers: The Secret Life of the Catholic Church in an Age of Scandal* (New York: Harmony Books, 2004), 232–35.
29 NBC Evening News, December 7, 1994; CBS Evening News, July 24, 1997; CBS Evening News, July 10, 1998, VTNA.
30 For example, Elizabeth Bruenig, "Everyone Knew about Theodore McCarrick," *New York Times*, Nov. 10, 2020, https://www.nytimes.com.
31 See Christina Mancini and Ryan T. Shields, "Notes on a (Sex Crime) Scandal: The Impact of Media Coverage of Sexual Abuse in the Catholic Church on Public Opinion," *Journal of Criminal Justice* 42 (2014): 221–32, 224 (quotations).
32 Thomas G. Plante and Kathleen L. McChesney, eds., *Sexual Abuse in the Catholic Church: A Decade of Crisis, 2002–2012* (Santa Barbara, CA: Praeger/ABC-CLIO, 2011).
33 Sarah Lawson, "'Spotlight' and Its Revelations," *New Yorker*, December 8, 2015, https://www.newyorker.com.
34 David Weber, "Mom Sues Priest for Alleged Sexual Abuse of Sons," *Boston Herald*, July 11, 1996.
35 Eileen McNamara, "Hardly a Case of Persecution," *Boston Globe*, January 15, 1997.
36 Diego Ribadeniera, "Cardinal Announces Defrocking of Priest Accused of Molestation," *Boston Globe*, June 6, 1998.
37 Mizner, "Reporting an Explosive Truth."
38 Adam Liptak, "Tough Judge at Center of Boston Archdiocese Suits," *New York Times*, December 5, 2002, https://www.nytimes.com.
39 Lawson, "'Spotlight' and Its Revelations."
40 Bella English, "'I Wanted to Run: When He Was an Altar Boy in Salem,' Bernie McDaid Tried to Hide from His Priest's Sexual Advances. But He Couldn't Escape," *Boston Globe*, May 15, 2002, http://archive.boston.com.
41 James Curran, Natalie Fenton, and Des Freedman, *Misunderstanding the Internet*, 2nd ed. (New York and London: Routledge, 2016), 48–84.
42 Nick Allen, "No Better Job: Sacha Pfeiffer on 'Spotlight,'" RogerEbert.com, February 23, 2016, https://www.rogerebert.com.
43 "'Spotlight' on Globe's Coverage of Church Abuse," Dart Center, February 24, 2016, https://dartcenter.org.
44 CNN Evening News, January 18, 2002, VTNA.

45 NBC Nightly News, February 9, 2002, VTNA.
46 Peter Steinfels, "The Media as a Source for the History of the Catholic Sex Abuse Scandal in the United States," *Studies: An Irish Quarterly Review* 105 (2016): 427–40; Timothy Lytton, *Holding Bishops Accountable: How Lawsuits Helped the Catholic Church Confront Clergy Sexual Abuse* (Cambridge, MA: Harvard University Press, 2008), 81–107.
47 NBC Nightly News, January 12, 2002, VTNA.
48 NBC Nightly News, February 9, 2002, VTNA.
49 Raymond Williams, *Television: Technology and Cultural Form* (1974; New York: Routledge, 2003).
50 David Morley, "Domesticating Dislocation in a World of 'New' Technology," in *Electronic Elsewheres: Media, Technology, and the Experience of Social Space*, ed. Chris Berry, Soyoung Kim, and Lynn Spigel (Minneapolis: University of Minnesota Press, 2010), 3–16.
51 Richard Ek, "Media Studies, Geographical Imaginations, and Relational Space," in *Geographies of Communication*, ed. Jesper Flakheimer and Andre Jansson (Lund, Sweden: Nordicom, 2006), 45–66.
52 Fiona Allen, "An Ontology of Everyday Control," in *MediaSpace Place, Scale and Culture in a Media Age*, ed. Nick Couldry and Anna McCarthy (New York: Routledge, 2004), 261.
53 Christine Chinlund, Dick Lehr, and Kevin Cullen, "The Bulger Mystique, Part I: Senate President: A Mix of Family, Southie, Power," *Boston Globe*, September 18, 1988, http://archive.boston.com.
54 "Boston, Massachusetts: Irish-American Brothers," NBC News, January 13, 1995, VTNA; Sara Rimer, "A Tale of 2 Brothers and 2 Divergent Paths," *New York Times*, January 17, 1995, https://www.nytimes.com.
55 CNN Evening News, December 3, 2002, VTNA.
56 See "Whitey Bulger," search term, VTNA.
57 Robert D. McFadden, "Whitey Bulger Is Dead in Prison at 89: Long-Hunted Boston Mob Boss," *New York Times*, October 30, 2018.
58 "Notorious Gangster Whitey Bulger Is Dead," Reuters Now, October 30, 2018, https://www.reuters.com.
59 "Whitey Bulger, Notorious Boston Mob Boss, Killed in West Virginia Prison," WBZ, October 30, 2018, https://www.cbsnews.com; "South Boston Reacts to Death of Whitey Bulger," WBZ, October 30, 2018, https://www.youtube.com; "Death of Notorious Gangster James 'Whitey' Bulger Investigated as Homicide," WCVB Boston, October 30, 2013, https://www.wcvb.com; "Convicted Killer James 'Whitey' Bulger Killed," WGBH, October 30, 2018, https://www.wgbh.org.
60 Myria Georgiou, "Media and the City: Making Sense of Place," *International Journal of Media and Cultural Politics* 6, no. 3 (2010): 345–46.

Section II

1 Keith Hayward, *City Limits: Crime, Consumer Culture and Urban Experience* (Portland, OR: Cavendish, 2004), 7–9.

Chapter Three

1. Nathan Cobb, "Baseball Border War; In Milford, Conn., Geography Brings Sox and Mets Fans; Cheek to Jowl," *Boston Globe*, October 20, 1986.
2. See Benedict Anderson, *Imagined Communities: Reflections on the Origin and Spread of Nationalism* (New York: Verso, 1983). Anderson refers to "political communities" as a component of belonging. I am not sure fandom reaches this level of seriousness but it is certainly worth considering the analogy.
3. Donna L. Halper, "Broadcasting Red Sox Baseball: How the Arrival of Radio Impacted the Team and the Fans," *Baseball Research Journal*, Fall 2017, https://sabr.org; James R. Walker and Pat Hughes, *Crack of the Bat: A History of Baseball on the Radio* (Lincoln: University of Nebraska Press, 2015), 170.
4. See David C. Perry, "Urban Tourism and the Privatizing Discourses of Public Infrastructure," in *The Infrastructure of Play: Building the Tourist City*, ed. Dennis Judd (New York: Routledge, 2015), 36–37.
5. Mark Goodwin, "The City as Commodity: The Contested Spaces of Urban Development," in *Selling Places: The City as Cultural Capital: Past and Present*, ed. Gerry Kearns and Chris Philo (New York: Pergamon Press, 1993), 147.
6. Michael T. Friedman, David L. Andrews, and Michael L. Silk, "Sports and the Façade of Redevelopment in the Postindustrial City," *Sociology of Sport* 21, no. 2 (2004): 122.
7. Mark Gottdiener, *The Production of Urban Space* (Austin: University of Texas Press, 1985), 10–12.
8. Ana Patricia Muñoz et al., "The Color of Wealth in Boston," *Federal Reserve Bank of Boston: A Joint Publication with Duke University and The New School*, May 15, 2015, http://www.bostonfed.org.
9. See Andrew Zimbalist, *The Bottom Line: Observations and Arguments on the Sports Business* (Philadelphia: Temple University Press, 2006), 33–34.
10. Will McDonough, "Tom Yawkey Vows to Move Red Sox without New Stadium," *Boston Globe*, June 21, 1967, https://www.bostonglobe.com.
11. Scott Farmelant and Peter Kadzis, "Fenway's Future: What Stands between the Media Hoopla and Building a New Ballpark?" *Boston Phoenix*, May 7–14, 1998, http://www.bostonphoenix.com.
12. Daniel Rosensweig, *Retro Ballparks: Instant History, Baseball, and the New American City* (Knoxville: University of Tennessee Press, 2005), 37–38.
13. Cornelia Cozmiuc, "City Branding—Just a Compilation of Marketable Assets?" *Economy Transdisciplinarity Cognition* 14, no. 1 (2011): 428–36, 432 (quotation).
14. Benjamin D. Lisle, *Modern Coliseum: Stadiums and American Culture* (Philadelphia: University of Pennsylvania Press, 2017), 7.
15. Michael Ian Borer, *Faithful to Fenway: Believing in Boston, Baseball, and America's Most Beloved Ballpark* (New York: NYU Press, 2008), 146.
16. "Ted Williams: The Greatest Hitter Who Ever Lived," *American Masters*, season 32, episode 3, https://www.pbs.org.
17. John Updike, "Hub Fans Bid Kid Adieu: Ted Williams's Last Game at Fenway Park," *New Yorker*, October 22, 1960.

18. Tim Logan, "Massive Project Would Dramatically Change the Streets around Fenway Park," *Boston Globe*, June 3, 2021.
19. Barry Bluestone and Mary Huff Stevenson, *The Boston Renaissance: Race, Space, and Economic Change in an American Metropolis* (New York: Russell Sage, 2002), 7.
20. Paul Goldberger, *Ballpark: Baseball in the American City* (New York: Knopf, 2019). Goldberger, an architectural critic and historian, successfully places the post–Camden Yards design emphases in context.
21. Bruce Ehrlich and Peter Dreier, "The New Boston Discovers the Old: Tourism and the Struggle for a Livable City," in *The Tourist City*, ed. Dennis R. Judd and Susan S. Fainstein (New Haven, CT: Yale University 1999), 155–78; Costas Spirou, *Urban Tourism and Urban Change: Cities in a Global Economy* (New York: Routledge, 2011).
22. For example, from 1953 to 1958, the Braves moved from Boston to Milwaukee, the Browns from St. Louis to Baltimore, the Athletics from Philadelphia to Kansas City, and the Dodgers and Giants from New York City to Los Angeles and San Francisco, respectively. For an insightful discussion of the emblematic case of the Brooklyn/Los Angeles Dodgers, see Eric Avila, *Popular Culture in the Age of White Flight: Fear and Fantasy in Suburban Los Angeles* (Berkeley: University of California Press, 2006), particularly chap. 5, "Suburbanizing the City Center: The Dodgers Move West," 145–84.
23. McDonough, "Tom Yawkey Vows to Move Red Sox."
24. Travis Korch, "Take Me Out to the 10 Most Expensive Ballparks in America," Bankrate, April 18, 2016, http://www.bankrate.com.
25. Doug Pappas, "Sox Ticket Prices Up 250% in 10 Years," Boston Baseball, 2001, http://roadsidephotos.sabr.org; Korch, "Take Me Out to the 10 Most Expensive Ballparks in America."
26. "State Occupational Employment and Wage Estimates Massachusetts," U.S. Bureau of Labor Statistics, May 2020, http://www.bls.gov; "Occupational Employment and Wage Statistics," U.S. Bureau of Labor Statistics, http://www.bls.gov.
27. Examples of this trend include Minneapolis, Baltimore, Pittsburgh, New York (Queens), Cincinnati, Denver, Detroit, San Francisco, Seattle, and others.
28. "Ford to City: Drop Dead," *New York Daily News*, October 30, 1975.
29. Tom Acitelli, "The Boston Area's Biggest Missed Transit Infrastructure Opportunities, Explained," Boston Curbed, October 30, 2019, https://boston.curbed.com.
30. Nathaniel Baum-Snow and Daniel Hartley, "Gentrification and Changes in the Spatial Structure of Labor Demand," Federal Reserve Bank of Chicago, September 30, 2015, http://marroninstitute.nyu.edu.
31. Thomas B. Edsall, "The Gentrification Effect," *New York Times*, February 25, 2015, http://www.nytimes.com.
32. Suleiman Osman, *The Invention of Brownstone Brooklyn: Gentrification and the Search for Authenticity in Postwar New York* (New York, Oxford University Press, 2011); Loretta Lees, Elvin Wyly, and Tom Slater, *Gentrification* (New York: Routledge, 2008); Samuel Stein, *Capital City: Gentrification and the Real Estate State* (London: Verso, 2019).

33 Lisa Prevost, "Is This Complex Affordable Housing Deal a Promising Model or a Unicorn?" *Next City*, July 3, 2017, https://nextcity.org.
34 Sports and Recreation Business Statistics Analysis, Business and Industry Statistics, https://www.plunkettresearch.com.
35 Scott Lindholm, "Baseball May Be in a Second Golden Age in Terms of Attendance. Is It Real, and Can it Last?" SBNation, February 10, 2014, http://www.beyondtheboxscore.com.
36 "The U.S. Professional Sports Market and Franchise Value Report, 2012," WR Hambrecht Sports Finance Group, September 2013, https://www.wrhambrecht.com.
37 Howard Bryant, *Shut Out: A Story of Race and Baseball in Boston* (New York: Routledge, 2002).
38 Brett M. Palfreyman, "The Boston Draft Riots," *New York Times*, July 16, 2013, http://opinionator.blogs.nytimes.com.
39 After 1976, MLB players were no longer bound to a team for the duration of their careers. In 1975, a federal arbitrator ruled the reserve clause of a standard player's contract invalid. Thus, when a player had completed his contract with a given team, he could enter an open market where teams bid for his services. See Bruce Markusen, "Four Decades Later, Free Agency Still Fuels Baseball," National Baseball Hall of Fame, 2012, https://baseballhall.org.
40 Jacob Bogage, "Yawkey Way Outside Fenway Park Renamed Because of Namesake's Allegedly Racist Past," *Washington Post*, April 26, 2018.
41 Elihu Rubin, *Insuring the City: The Prudential Center and the Postwar Urban Landscape* (New Haven, CT: Yale University Press, 2012).
42 Jonathan Fuerbringer and Marvin E. Milbauer, "Roxbury, Quiet in Past, Finally Breaks into Riot; Why Did Violence Occur?" *Harvard Crimson*, June 15, 1967, http://www.thecrimson.com.
43 Mark Melnick, "Demographic and Socio-Economic Trends in Boston: What We've Learned from the Latest Census Data," Boston Redevelopment Authority, November 29, 2011, http://www.bostonredevelopmentauthority.org; "Boston's Shifting Demographics," BRA Research Vision, 2015, http://www.slideshare.net.
44 Walter Lafeber, *Michael Jordan and the New Global Capitalism* (New York: Norton, 2002), 49.
45 David Harvey, *A Brief History of Neoliberalism* (New York, Oxford University Press, 2007).
46 Michael Haupert, "The Economic History of Major League Baseball," EH.Net Encyclopedia, ed. Robert Whaples, December 3, 2007, https://eh.net; Mike Ozanian, and Juston Teitlebaum, "Red Sox on Forbes Most Valuable Teams List," *Forbes*, March 23, 2023, http://www.forbes.com.
47 Chad Finn, "How NESN Has Changed in 30 Years," *Boston Globe*, May 23, 2014, https://www.bostonglobe.com.
48 Benjamin D. Goss, "Taking the Ballgame Out to the World: An Analysis of the World Baseball Classic as a Global Branding Promotional Strategy for Major League Baseball," *Journal of Applied Sport Management* 1, no. 1 (2009): 75–102.

49 Mike Ozanian and Justin Teitelbaum, "Baseball's Most Valuable Teams 2023," *Forbes*, March 23, 2023, https://www.forbes.com.
50 Greg Ramshaw and Sean Gammon, "More Than Just Nostalgia: Exploring the Heritage/Sport Tourism Nexus," *Journal of Sport Tourism* 10, no. 4 (2005): 229–41.

Chapter Four

1 See, for example, David Roediger, *Colored White: Transcending the Racial Past* (Berkeley: University of California Press, 2002); *Towards the Abolition of Whiteness: Essays on Race, Class and Politics* (London: Verso, 1994); *The Wages of Whiteness: Race and the Making of the American Working Class*, rev. ed. (London: Verso, 1999); and Matthew Frye Jacobson, *Whiteness of a Different Color: European Immigrants and the Alchemy of Race* (Cambridge, MA: Harvard University Press, 1999). See also Gail Dines and Jean M. Humez, eds., *Gender, Race, and Class in Media: A Critical Reader*, 4th ed. (Thousand Oaks, CA: Sage, 2014), for discussions of the intersections of race, class, and media.
2 Joseph R. Fornieri, "Lincoln's America: Tracing the Roots of Lincoln's Democratic Vision," *OAH Magazine of History* 23, no. 1 (January 2009): 11–16. This idea was particularly salient during the New Deal as it provided a basis for visions and policies of inclusion and an alternative reading of a largely exclusionary national historical narrative.
3 "Adam Silver, NBA Teams Express Outrage after George Floyd's Death," NBA.com, June 11, 2020, https://www.nba.com.
4 Douglas Stark, *When Basketball Was Jewish* (Lincoln: University of Nebraska Press, 2017), xi–xii.
5 "A Championship in 1966 Was a Step for Integration," *New York Times*, March 19, 2016, https://www.nytimes.com. The first integrated college team was the Indiana State Team of 1947–48, coached by John Wooden. In 1950, College of the City of New York became the first integrated team to win the national championship. See Arthur Banton, "Running for Integration: CCNY and the Promise of Interracial Cooperation through Basketball" (PhD diss., Purdue University, 2016).
6 Stark, *When Basketball Was Jewish*; Charley Rosen, *The Chosen Game: A Jewish Basketball History* (Lincoln: University of Nebraska Press, 2017); Thomas Aiello, *Hoops: A Cultural History of Basketball in America* (Lanham, MD: Rowman and Littlefield, 2022).
7 "Athletes have always been style icons, but in the past year, fashion's hunger for basketball—both the players and the looks inspired by them—has blown up." Danny Parisi, "What the NBA's Influence on Fashion Tells Us about Men's Shopping Habits," Glossy, September 26, 2019, https://www.glossy.co.
8 . On November 2, 1990, the Phoenix Suns defeated the Utah Jazz in Tokyo, 119–96. This was the first regular season game played outside of North America.
9 Steven J. Jackson and David L. Andrews, "Excavating the (Trans) National Basketball Association: Locating the Global/Local Nexus of America's World and

the World's America," *Australasian Journal of American Studies* 15, no. 1 (July 1996): 57–64, 60 (quotation).
10. David L. Andrews, *Sport Commerce Culture: Essays on Sport in Late Capitalist America* (New York: Peter Lang, 2006), 23.
11. Ian Whittell, "Fans in Europe Tune in for NBA Action," ESPN, May 1, 2007, http://www.espn.com.
12. Lindsay Sarah Krasnoff, "How the NBA Went Global," *Washington Post*, December 26, 2017, https://www.washingtonpost.com; Andrew Sharp, "Coming to America," *Sports Illustrated*, January 18, 2018, https://www.si.com.
13. David L. Andrews, "Sport, Culture, and Late Capitalism," in *Marxism, Cultural Studies, and Sport*, ed. Ben Carrington and Ian McDonald (New York: Routledge, 2009), 225–26.
14. See David Harvey, "Flexible Accumulation through Urbanization: Reflections on 'Post-Modernism' in the American City," *Perspecta* 26 (1990): 251–72.
15. Harvey Araton, "A Not-So-Fond Farewell to a Shrine," *New York Times*, April 22, 1995, https://www.nytimes.com.
16. Game four of the 1988 Stanley Cup series, on May 24, 1988, was played in the fog until it was suspended due to a power failure in the arena. YouTube, https://www.youtube.com.
17. Simon Bronner, *Following Tradition* (Provo: Utah State University Press, 1998), 53–54.
18. Bronner, *Following Tradition*, 54.
19. Michael LaFlash, "The Demolition of Boston Garden: An Examination of Sports Stadia in Historic Preservation" (MA thesis, Cornell University, 2019), 1.
20. The Big Dig project was started in 1992 and not fully completed until 2006. It was among the most expensive public works projects in U.S. history and had the effect of connecting the neighborhoods to the immediate north to the city's downtown and creating a third tunnel to the airport—named after Red Sox icon Ted Williams. It also created acres of new parkland.
21. "The Hub on Causeway Grand Opening," TD Garden, November 6, 2019, https://www.tdgarden.com.
22. Aram Goudsouzian, "Bill Rusell and the Basketball Revolution," *American Studies*, 47, nos. 3–4 (Fall–Winter 2006): 61–85, 69 (quotation).
23. Peter May, "The Passing of a Legend," *Boston Globe*, October 28, 2006, http://archive.boston.com.
24. Michael Wilbon, "Celtics as a White Man's Team? Think Again," NBC News, June 5, 2008, https://www.nbcnews.com.
25. Aram Goudsouzian, *King of the Court: Bill Russell and the Basketball Revolution* (Berkeley: University of California Press, 2010), 152, 150–51.
26. Bill Russell as told to Al Hirshberg, "I Was a 6' 9" Babe in the Woods," *Saturday Evening Post*, January 18, 1958; Gilbert Rogin, "We Are Grown Men Playing a Child's Game," *Sports Illustrated*, November 18, 1963; Fred Katz, "Behind the Laugh and Scowl," *Sport*, March 1966.
27. Goudsouzian, "Bill Russell and the Basketball Revolution," 6–85.
28. Goudsouzian, *King of the Court*, 258.

29 "Celtics Quietly Retire Bill Russell's No. 6," *New York Times*, March 13, 1972, https://www.nytimes.com.
30 Adam J. Criblez, "White Men Playing a Black Man's Game: Basketball's 'Great White Hopes' of the 1970s," *Journal of Sport History* 42, no. 3 (Fall 2015): 371–381, 373 (quotation).
31 Connie Kirchberg, *Hoop Lore: A History of the National Basketball Association* (Jefferson, NC: McFarland Press, 2007), 146.
32 Broadcaster Johnny Most was the longtime voice of the Celtics, from 1953 to 1990, a figure who was very much a part of the team's emergent identity during an era when radio broadcasters were the public projection of the team and idiosyncratic deliveries were allowed. The Volk family had a long connection to the team through Coach Auerbach as a result of the friendship between Jerry Volk and Auerbach. Auerbach used the summer camp owned by Volk as a training camp for the team from 1960 to the 1980s. In 1971, Jerry's son Jan went to work for the team, eventually becoming general manager, from 1984–1997, when he replaced Red Auerbach. Wyc and H. Irving Grousbeck, who I discuss in greater detail later, were two of the principals in the acquisition of the team in 2003. H. Irving Grousbeck was the founder of Continental Cablevision of New England.
33 Harvey Araton, "Auerbach Seen through the Smoke," *New York Times*, November 3, 2006, https://www.nytimes.com. See also Harvey Araton and Flip Bondy, *The Selling of the Green: The Financial Rise and Moral Decline of the Boston Celtics* (New York: HarperCollins, 1992).
34 Roy S. Johnson, "Thomas Explains Comments on Bird," *New York Times*, June 5, 1987, https://www.nytimes.com.
35 J. A. Adande, "The Truth Isn't Always Black and White for the Celtics," ESPN, December 19, 2007, https://www.espn.com.
36 Madeline Fitzgerald, "'No Food, No Drink, No Watermelon': Boston Schoolteacher Claims Her Students Were Racially Profiled at Museum," *Time*, May 24, 2019, https://time.com.
37 Harvey Araton, *Crashing the Borders: How Basketball Won the World and Lost Its Soul at Home* (New York: Free Press, 2005), 53.
38 Bob Sakamoto, "Cocaine—Scourge of the NBA," *Chicago Tribune*, February 16, 1986, https://www.chicagotribune.com. This is just one among many such articles from the era, but this is one of the more informative. See also Sam Goldpaper, "Lloyd and Wiggins of Rockets Arrested for Drug Use," *New York Times*, January 14, 1987, https://www.nytimes.com.
39 Chris Cobbs, "The Punch: Tomjanovich and Washington Both Still Feel the Pain from That Terrible Moment," *Los Angeles Times*, January 28, 1985, https://www.latimes.com.
40 Criblez, "White Men Playing a Black Man's Game," 379.
41 Rachael Withers, "The Reference Point for Dog-Whistle Racism: How 'Willie Horton' Went from Shorthand for Black Depravity to Shorthand for Political Racism," *Vox*, December 1, 2018, https://www.vox.com. See also Thomas Frank, "Bill Clinton's Crime Bill Destroyed Lives, and There's No Point Denying It," *The Guardian*, April 15, 2016, https://www.theguardian.com.

42 Jackson and Andrews, "Excavating the (Trans) National Basketball Association," 58.
43 William Julius Wilson, *The Declining Significance of Race: Blacks and Changing American Institutions* (Chicago: University of Chicago Press, 1978).
44 David L. Andrews and Ron L. Mower, "Spectres of Jordan," *Ethnic and Racial Studies* 35, no. 6 (June 2012): 1059–77, 1061 (quotation).
45 Charles Trevail, "Boston Celtics: The Global Business of Sports, Fans, and Legacy," Outside In with Charles Trevail, August 22, 2017, https://cspace.com.
46 Brian F. Sandford, "NBA Branding Assessment: Boston Celtics," BlueLefant, 2015, https://www.bluelefant.com.
47 Conor Roche, "Wyc Grousbeck: Celtics 'Don't Stand Second to Anybody' When It Comes to Civil Rights," Boston.com, August 31, 2020, https://www.boston.com.
48 Marc J. Spears, "From Russell to KG to Today's Celtics: Being a Black Player in Boston," The Undefeated, February 29, 2020, https://theundefeated.com.
49 Spears, "From Russell to KG to Today's Celtics."
50 Scott Polocek, "Warriors Draymond Green Addresses Celtics Fans' Racist Taunts Ahead of Boston Return," Bleacher Report, January 17, 2023, https://bleacherreport.com.

Section III

1 See Barry Bluestone and Mary Huff Stevenson, *The Boston Renaissance: Race, Space, and Economic Change in an American Metropolis* (New York: Russell Sage, 2002), 1–22, and Elihu Rubin, *Insuring the City: The Prudential Center and the Postwar Urban Landscape* (New Haven, CT: Yale University Press, 2012), 205–20. See also "The Big Dig: Project Background," Mass.gov, https://www.mass.gov.

Chapter Five

1 See Lawrence Webb and Joshua Gleich, eds., *Hollywood on Location: An Industry History* (New Brunswick, NJ: Rutgers University Press, 2019), and R. Barton Palmer, *Shot on Location: Postwar American Cinema and the Exploration of Real Place* (New Brunswick, NJ: Rutgers University Press, 2016). In Massachusetts, as in many other states, local tax programs enhanced location shooting. The program state tax credit for film production has been active since 2006. See Matt Stout, "Supporters of Controversial Mass. Film Tax Credit Aim to Make It Permanent," *Boston Globe*, February 12, 2019, https://www.bostonglobe.com.
2 Scott Bomboy, "The Day the Supreme Court Killed Hollywood's Studio System," Constitution Daily Blog, Constitution Center, May 4, 2023, https://constitutioncenter.org.
3 Lawrence Webb, "The Auteur Renaissance: 1968–1979," in Webb and Gleich, eds., *Hollywood on Location*, 129.
4 For discussions of urban location shooting see, for example, Mark Shiel, *Hollywood Cinema and the Real Los Angeles* (London: Reaktion, 2012). A second

volume that brings his discussion into a more contemporary period is forthcoming from Temple University Press, 2024. See also Joshua Gleich, *Hollywood in San Francisco: Location Shooting and the Aesthetics of Urban Decline* (Austin: University of Texas Press, 2018); Lawrence Webb, *The Cinema of Urban Crisis: Seventies Film and the Reinvention of the City* (Amsterdam: Amsterdam University Press, 2014); and Stanley Corkin, *Starring New York: Filming the Grime and the Glamour of the Long 1970s* (New York: Oxford University Press, 2011).

5 Kevin Lynch, *The Image of the City* (Cambridge, MA: MIT Press, 1959), 1–13.
6 See David Harvey, *A Brief History of Neoliberalism* (New York: Oxford University Press, 2007), for a lucid and compelling discussion of this chronology.
7 Matthew J. O'Brien, "Ethnic Legacy and Immigrant Mobility: The New Irish and Irish America in the 1990s," *Etudes Irlandaises* 28, no. 2 (2003): 119–33; James R. Barrett, *The Irish Way: Becoming American in the Multiethnic City* (New York: Penguin, 2012).
8 Greg Miller, "Maps Reveal How Immigration Transformed Boson's Neighborhoods, *Science*, March 21, 2014, https://www.wired.com.
9 Carmen Rixely Jimenez, "New Bostonians Demographic Report," Mayor's Office of New Bostonians, September 17, 2018, https://www.cityofboston.gov.
10 See Corkin, *Starring New York*, for a discussion of the many films that prominently drew on New York City sites for filming.
11 Barry Bluestone and Mary Huff Stevenson, *The Boston Renaissance: Race, Space, and Economic Change in an American Metropolis* (New York: Russell Sage, 2002), 51–73.
12 Carolyn Adams et al., *Philadelphia: Neighborhoods, Division, and Conflict in a Postindustrial City* (Philadelphia: Temple University Press, 1991).
13 "City Hall Plaza Reopens in Boston," City of Boston, November 10, 2022, https://www.boston.gov.
14 Malcolm X, *The Autobiography of Malcolm X*, as told to Alex Haley (New York: Ballantine Books, 1964), 41.
15 This is available on YouTube, among other places: *Good Will Hunting*, Deleted Scene: St. Patrick's Day Parade, YouTube, https://www.youtube.com.
16 Lawrence Webb, "New Hollywood in the Rust Belt: Urban Decline and Downtown Renaissance in *The King of Marvin Gardens* and *Rocky*," *Cinema Journal* 54, no. 4 (Summer 2015): 100–125.
17 Harvey Weinstein, now a convicted felon for rape and sexual assault, was a former independent film mogul. Weinstein's disgrace occurred after long-suppressed charges of predatory behavior came to light in 2017. For a timeline, see "Harvey Weinstein Timeline: How the Scandal Unfolded," BBC News, May 29, 2020, https://www.bbc.com.
18 Janelle Nanos, "Good Will Hunting: An Oral History," *Boston Magazine*, January 2, 2013, https://www.bostonmagazine.com.
19 Webb, "New Hollywood in the Rust Belt," 125; internal quotation is from Thomas Elsaesser, *The Persistence of Hollywood* (New York: Routledge, 2002), 232.
20 Tim Cresswell, *Place: An Introduction*, 2nd ed. (2004; London: Wiley Blackwell, 2014), 96–97.

21 Cresswell, *Place*, 97. See also Karen Till, "Neotraditional Towns and Urban Villages: The Cultural Production of a Geography of 'Otherness,'" *Environment and Planning* 11 (1993): 717–18.
22 "Whitey Bulger: The Capture of a Legend (Timeline)," *New York Times*, November 14, 2013, https://archive.nytimes.com.
23 Myria Georgiou, *Media and the City: Cosmoplitanism and Difference* (Malden, MA: Polity Press, 2013), 17.
24 "Historical Trends in Boston's Neighborhoods," Boston Planning and Development Agency Research Division, 2017, http://www.bostonplans.org.

Chapter Six

1 Census 2000, Key Neighborhood Characteristics, Comparative Data on Neighborhoods, and Boston U.S. Census 2000 Summary File (SF3) Data, p. 11, http://www.bostonplans.org.
2 Nicolette Rowe, "Centrifugal Boston and Competing Imaginaries in *Mystic River*," *Journal for Cultural Research* 12, no. 1 (January 2008): 81–97, 89 (quotation).
3 Deborah Feyerick and Kristina Sgueglia, "'Whitey' Bulger Says He's Not a Snitch, but FBI File Tells a Different Story," CNN, June 25, 2013, https://www.cnn.com.
4 Bonnie Laufer-Krebs, "Interview: In Deep: *Mystic River*," *Tribute Magazine*, March 2003, https://www.tribute.ca.
5 Adam Epstein, "How the Stranger-Than-Fiction Story of Whitey Bulger Has Been Told on Screen," Quartz, October 30, 2018, https://qz.com.
6 Li Wanlin, "A Cross-Cultural Comparison of Infernal Affairs and *The Departed*," *Style* 52, no. 3 (2018): 321–44, 326 (quotation).
7 North Dorchester neighborhood in Boston, Massachusetts, 02125, 02118, detailed profile, City Data, https://www.city-data.com.
8 Anne Thompson, "The Hollywood Education of Ben Affleck, from 'Chasing Amy, Armageddon' and 'Shakespeare' to His Second Act and 'Argo,'" Indie Wire, February 13, 2013, https://www.indiewire.com.
9 Matthew C. Ehrlich, *Journalism in the Movies* (Champaign-Urbana: University of Illinois Press, 2006); Lou Harry, "110-Plus Journalism Movies, Ranked," *Quill Magazine*, June 3, 2019, https://www.quillmag.com.
10 It is of note that this important thoroughfare is named for a political figure who was John Kennedy's secretary while he was a congressman and senator, and a loyal retainer of his father, Ambassador Joseph Kennedy.
11 See Charles R. Gallagher, *Nazis of Copley Square: The Forgotten History of the Christian Front* (Cambridge, MA: Harvard University Press, 2021), and James Carroll, *Constantine's Sword: The Church and the Jews, A History* (Boston: Houghton-Mifflin, 2001). Both explicate this tendency. Carroll, a priest and Bostonian, does so in more comprehensive historical terms, including examining the World War II and postwar eras, while Gallagher focuses on the regime of populist fascism in Boston during the 1930s and 1940s, particularly among followers of Father Charles Coughlin.

12 Billy Baker, "School Busing Protests Replayed in South Boston: Reenactment for Film Recalls Chaos of Busing Protest," *Boston Globe*, July 1, 2014. See also Richard Brody, "The Blinding Cinematic Whiteness of 'Black Mass,'" *New Yorker*, September 23, 2015, https://www.newyorker.com.
13 Scott Essman, "Scott Cooper Conjures Whitey Bulger in *Black Mass*," Below the Line, October 19, 2015, https://www.btlnews.com.
14 Brody, "Blinding Cinematic Whiteness."

Conclusion

1 Emily Nussbuam, "Good and Bad in 'Orange Is the New Black' and 'Ray Donovan,'" *New Yorker*, July 1, 2013, https://www.newyorker.com; Matt Zoller Seitz, "Seitz on *Ray Donovan*: When Irish Eyes Are Assimilating," *New York Magazine*, June 30, 2013, https://www.vulture.com.
2 Gaylyn Studlar, *This Mad Masquerade: Stardom and Masculinity in the Jazz Age* (New York: Columbia University Press, 1996), 237–38.
3 Yair Galily, Moran Yarchi, and Ilan Tamir, "From Munich to Boston, and from Theater to Social Media: The Evolutionary Landscape of World Sporting Terror," *Studies in Conflict and Terrorism* 38, no. 12 (August 2015): 998–1007.
4 Hayden Bird, "'Today Was Different': When David Ortiz Reminded Boston, 'This Is Our F***** City,'" Boston.com, April 14, 2023, https://www.boston.com.
5 US Census Bureau: QuickFacts, Boston, Massachusetts, https://www.census.gov; Jack Caporal, "Are You Well-Paid? Compare Your Salary to the Average U.S. Income," The Ascent, June 13, 2023, https://www.fool.com; "Key Neighborhood Characteristics: Comparative Data on Neighborhoods and Boston," US Census 2000, Summary File (SF3) Data, https://www.bostonplans.org.

Index

Note: Page references in *italics* denote figures and with "n" endnotes.

ABC, 12, 121
Abdul-Jabbar, Kareem, 151, 152
Abolitionism, 10
Abrams, Dan, 81
Adande, J. A., 150
Affleck, Ben, 163, 173, 175, 176, 183–184, 186, 189, 194, 214–215, 232
Affleck, Casey, 214–215
African Americans, 129, 131; Charles Stuart murder case (*see* Charles Stuart murder case); coaches, 127; and gentrification, 49; harassment in white spaces, 32; migration, 118; players, 115–116, 127, 143, 152; population in Boston, 30; racialized vision of criminality, 45; racially segregated school system, 32; racist policing, 49; and Red Sox, 115–116; students transported to white school, 29; Watts Riot, 118
Agnew, John, 4
Ainge, Danny, 149
'Air Hoodlum,' 151
Ali, Mohammed, 146
Allen, Ray, 156
Allon, Fiona, 84
All the President's Men, 219
Ally McBeal, 175
Altered States, 175
American Basketball League (ABL), 132, 137
American Dream, 113
American Gangster, 187
American League, 109, 116
American Masters series, 107
Americanness, 129, 135, 208

America's Most Wanted, 87
Anderson, Elijah, 31
Andrews, David L., 135, 154, 155
Araton, Harvey, 138, 150, 152
Arbery, Ahmaud, 130
Atlanta Braves, 120–121, 246n22
Auerbach, Red, 139, 143, 144, 147, 149, 250n32
authenticity, 10, 92, 97, 115, 125, 158, 164, 174, 180–181, 185–187, 189; actual, 16; broader crisis in, 11, 15; Irish American, 193; in mass culture, 128; regional accent as measure of, 211; residual notions of, 140; urban, 17, 231; working-class, 57; working-class white, 52

Baby Boom, 133
Bacon, Kevin, 233
Bakhtin, Mikhail M., 6
ballparks, 109–114; *see also* Fenway Park
Bank of Boston, 4
Barkley, Charles, 155
Barry, Rick, 151
basketball, 96, 131–137, 148–153
Basketball Association of America (BAA), 133, 137
Bedford, William, 152
Benjamin, Walter, 61
Bennett, Willie, 43
Berg, Peter, 232, 233
Berry, Jason, 63
Bias, Len, 152
Big Dig project, 14, 26, 112, 114, 141, 249n20
Bill Russell, Legend, 143

255

Bird, Larry, 149–154
Birmingham, Joseph, 74–75
Black criminality,, 42–43, 47, 154
Black Hand, 241n3
Black Mass (film), 2, 14, 17, 59, 164, 218–227, 228
Black Mass (Lehr and O'Neill), 223
black-on-black crime, 49
Blaine, Barbara, 63
Bluestone, Barry, 109
The Boondock Saints, 164, 175
Borden, Lizzie 69
Borenstein, Max, 144
Borer, Michael Ian, 106
Boston: -based sports teams, 15–16; branding, 102–109; before branding, 170–171; busing crisis (*see* busing crisis); Catholics/Catholicism in (*see* Catholicism); in digital age, 78–84; elite educational institutions, 4; and feature films, 16–17; Irish-born residents in, 4–5, 25, 34–39; Johnson on, 1–2; major sports facilities, 101–102; mediated, 183–194; place and space concept, 3–4; population, 3, 30; priest abuse scandal (*see* priest abuse scandal); and race, 114–119; race and ethnicity in, 179–183; *Ray Donovan* and essence of, 228–235; and Red Sox, 114–119; urban *mythos*, 85–87; white spaces, 23, 25–52
Boston Banks and Urban Renewal Group (BBURG), 32
Boston Bruins, 137, 160, 229
Boston Celtics. *See* Celtics
Boston College High School, 87
Boston Garden, 137–138, *138*, 139, 144
Boston Globe, 1, 34, 36, 56, 59–60, 66, 69, 70, 79, 86, 122, 123, 200, 220, 222
Boston Herald, 34, 45, 71, 133
Boston Housing Authority, 139
Boston Legal, 125
Boston Marathon Bombing, 14
Boston noir: and the bonds of tradition, 171–175; novels, 171, 174; re-elaborations of, 164

Boston Properties, 141
Boston Redevelopment Authority, 139
Boston Red Sox. *See* Red Sox
Boston Strangler, 233
Boyle, Kevin, 196
branding: Boston before, 170–171; city, 102–109; digital, 128, 134; place, 15–16, 104, 186; professional sports, 6; team, 102–109; urban, 128–129
Bratton, Bill, 45
The Bridge, 196
Briggs, Walter, 115
The Brinks Job, 17, 163, 167, 169, 173–177, 178–179, 181–182
Brody, Richard, 226
Brokaw, Tom, 69
Bronner, Simon, 140–141
Brooke, Edward, 10
Brown, Jaylen, 160
Brown, Jim, 146, 147
Brown, Walter, 133, 137, 148
Brown vs. Board of Education, 27
Bryant, Howard, 115
Bulger, Bill, 85–87
Bulger, James Whitey, 23, 54, 73, 84–92, 171, 187, 203, 206, 207; background, 58–59, 85; and Catholicism, 55; code of silence, 58; conviction and sentence, 88; death, 90; murder, 59; mythological imprint of story, 89
Bull Durham, 102
busing crisis, 10–12, 15, 22, 26–27, 76; coverage of, 29–30; white resistance, 33

"Cardinal Announces Defrocking of Priest Accused of Molestation," 71
Carlson, Margaret, 48
Carr, Howie, 22
Carroll, James, 253n11
Carroll, Matt, 67
Carter, Gary, 226
Catholic Church, 14, 23, 54–55, 57, 61, 63, 65, 70–71
Catholicism, 14–15, 53, 55, 65, 128, 217, 220, 222; and Boston, 53, 60–62;

and Bulger, 55; priest abuse scandal, 57–58
CBS, 12, 44, 48, 134
CBS News, 70
Celtics (basketball team), 15–16, 95, 127, 137–142, 143, 194, 229, 234, 250n32; and Great White Hope, 149–154; Larry Bird era, 149–154; pride, and race, 127–160
Celtics/Lakers, 144
Chamberlain, Wilt, 143
Charles Stuart murder case, 12–13, 22–23, 26, 42–52, 60, 151, 171
Charlestown, 1, 9–11, 27, 30, 40, 51, 62
Chartoff, Robert, 185
Chasing Amy, 186
Cheers, 125, 175
Cheever, John, 125
Chicago, 2–3, 7, 44, 53, 56, 77, 132, 233
Chicago Tribune, 121
Chiklis, Michael, 144
Chinlund, Christine, 86
chronotopes, 6–7, 21, 30, 39, 61, 84, 105, 129, 183–184, 195, 226–227
city: branding, 102–109; multiethnic, 214–218; neoliberal, 109–114
City on a Hill, 232
A Civil Action, 125, 175
Civil Rights Act in 1964, 132
class mobility, 39–42
clerical criminality, 23
Clifton, Sweetwater, 143
Cobb, Nathan, 99
Cobb, Ty, 115
Coleman, Ken, 199
commercial sports, 95
Common Ground: A Turbulent Decade in the Lives of Three American Families (Lukas), 39–42, 50
Connolly, John J., 58, 88
Cooper, Chick, 143
Cooper, Scott, 223, 226
Copland, 186
cosmopolitan capitalism, 136
Costas, Bob, 107
Costner, Kevin, 106

Coughlin, Father Charles, 253n11
Cousy, Bob, 143
Covid-19 crisis, 114
Cowens, Dave, 145, 148, 151
Coyle, Eddie, 180–181, *181*
Crane, Hart, 196
Criblez, Adam J., 148
Criblez, Alex, 153
crime: black-on-black crime, 49; ethnic, 213; organized, 58, 88, 90, 209, 212, 224; street, 43; urban, 46
criminality: clerical, 23; racialized vision of, 45
crisis of authenticity, 11
Cronkite, Walter, 54
Cullen, Kevin, 86
Cultrera, Joe, 74
Cumberbatch, Benedict, 223
Cunningham, Billy, 151
Cushing, Richard, 74

Daily Mail, 58
Damon, Matt, 163, 183–184, 186, 194, 207, 209, 232, 233
Day, William J., 34
The Declining Significance of Race (Wilson), 155
Delaware North, 141
Deliver Us from Evil, 78
Delmont, Matthew, 30, 33, 239n15
The Departed, 13, 17, 59, 164, 194, 215, 218–219, 233, 234; and the ruptures of time, 207–214
Depp, Johnny, 223
Detroit, 3, 101, 104, 118, 150
Detroit Pistons, 133, 150
DiCaprio, Leonardo, 209
digital age, 78–84
digital branding, 128, 134
digital Celtics, 154–160
digital media, 12, 15; ideals of disclosure, 73; and priest abuse scandal, 74–78
Disney Company, 121
Dolan, Charles, 120
Donahue, Phil, 63, 82
Do the Right Thing, 150

Drew, John, 152
Drugstore Cowboy, 186
Dubuisson, Hervé, 134
Duffy, Sean, 175
Dukakis, Michael, 42
Dumas, Richard, 152

Eastwood, Clint, 125, 196
Edgerton, Joel, 223
Edsall, Thomas B., 113
Eight Mile, 187
Ek, Richard, 83
embedded Calvinism, 128
Encyclopedia Britannica, 58
Epstein, Robert, 157
Erving, Julius, 151
ESPN, 121, 123–124
ethnic: crime, 213; identifiers, 28; whiteness, 27
ethnicity: in Boston, 179–183; Irish 55; white, 104, 128, 226; working-class, 104, 183–184
ethnocentrism, 127

Falk, Peter, 177
feature films, and Boston, 16–17
Fenway Park, 16, 43, 46, 95, 99–100, 102, 105, 107, 140; drawbacks, 103; iconic symbol of a ballpark, 109; new, 104, 111
Fenway Sports Group, 122
Fever Pitch, 125
Field of Dreams, 102, 106, 125, 175
Finney, Jack, 138
Fisk, Carlton, 226
Fitzpatrick, Kevin, 63
Flemmi, Steve "the Rifleman," 88
flexible accumulation, 119
Floyd, George, 130, 159
Flynn, Raymond, 43
Forbes, 122
Ford, John, 13, 168
Forman, Stanley, 38
Formisano, Ronald, 25
Freedom Trail, 110
The French Connection, 175

The Friends of Eddie Coyle, 17, 37, 163, 167, 169–174, 176, 177–179, 181, 184
"Friends of Red," 149
Frontline, 74
The Front Page, 219
functional racism, 48

Gallagher, Charles R., 253n11
Gammon, Sean, 125
Gammons, Peter, 124, 125
Gans, Herbert, 11
Garabedian, Mitchell, 56
Garnett, Kevin, 156, 157, 160
Garrison, William Lloyd, 10
Garrity, W. Arthur, 28, 32, 34, 37, 54
Gauthe, Gilbert, 63
gentrification, 11–12, 25, 30, 52, 56; in 1990s and 2000s, 108–109; of abutting real estate, 40; and African Americans, 49; pressures of, 44; and professional sports, 113
Geoghan, John J., 64, 69, 71–72, 77, 219, 221
Georgiou, Myria, 91, 192
Gervin, George, 151
Giuliani, Rudolph, 45
Glaeser, Edward L., 3
Globe, 68–69, 71–72, 77, 79, 86, 87, 124
Goldberger, Paul, 246n20
Golden State Warriors, 160
Gone Baby Gone, 17, 164, 193, 194, 215–216, 218, 219, 222, 227, 233; and multiethnic city, 214–218
The Good, the Bad, and the Ugly, 205
Goodfellas, 185, 208
Goodman, Ezra, 228
Goodnight Sweet Wife: A Murder in Boston, 44
Good Will Hunting, 17, 104, 125, 163, 167, 172–173, 175, 177, 183–194, 195, 201, 208
Goodwin, Doris Kearns, 125
Goodwin, Mark, 100
Gotham, Rich, 156
Gottdiener, Mark, 101
Gottlieb, Eddie, 133

Goudsouzian, Aram, 144, 146
Gould, Eliott, 228
Great White Hope, 151
Greeley, Andrew, 63
Green, Draymond, 160
Green, Elijah "Pumpsie," 115
Grousbeck, H. Irving, 149, 157, 250n32
Grousbeck, Wyc, 149, 157, 159, 250n32

Halberstam, David, 125
Hand of God, 74
Harlem Globetrotters, 132, 147
Harper, Tommy, 116
Harrington, John, 104, 122
Harvey, David, 52, 119
Havlicek, John, 143, 144–145, 148
Hawthorne, Nathaniel, 211
Hayward, Gordon, 142
Hayward, Keith, 96
Hecht, Jim, 144
Heinsohn, Tom, 143
Henry, John, 104, 122
Henry-Werner-Lucchino group, 107
Hicks, Louise Day, 34–35, 35, 64
Higgins, George V., 171, 174
Hill, Grant, 155
Hispanics: as dominant urban minority, 113; population in Boston, 30
Hodge, Aldis, 233
Hoover, J. Edgar, 168
Horton, Willie, 42, 154
Hotel Madison, 139, 141
The House of the Seven Gables, 211
Howell, Bailey, 143
Hynes, John, 139

immigration: to Boston, 4–5; Irish, 55; Irish-born residents, 4–5; mass, 4, 55
Infernal Affairs, 207
information capital, 119–126
Irish, Ned 133
Irish American: actors, 207; authenticity, 193; brotherhood and brutality, 90; crime network, 171; gangs, 176; political class, 25, 168; population, 10, 137, 159, 188, 196; rogue politicians, 86

Irish-born residents: in Boston, 4–5, 25, 34–39; immigration, 4–5
Irish Dead Rabbits, 241n3
Irish ethnicity, 55
Irish immigration, 55

Jackie Brown, 186
Jackson, Steven J., 135, 154
Janey, Kim, 5
Jean R. Yawkey Trust, 122
John Birch Society, 10
John Hancock Insurance, 9
Johnson, Akilah, 1–2
Johnson, Magic, 151, 152
Jones, KC, 132, 143, 147
Jones, Sam, 143, 144
Jordan, Michael, 119, 155
journalism: coverage of busing crisis, 29–30; ethnic identifiers, 28; *see also* media
Joyce, James, 210

The Keepers, 78
Kennedy, Edward, 33
Kennedy, John F., 13
Kennedy, Joseph P., 197
Kennedy, Ted 10, 36–37
Kiley, Robert, 239n18
King, Martin Luther, Jr., 146
King, Stephen, 125
Kite, Greg, 149
Knight, Phil, 119
Kos, Rudy, 69

Landsmark, Ted 37, 39
The Last Hurrah (film), 168, 175
The Last Hurrah (O'Connor), 13, 168, 175
Law, Bernard, 56, 69, 74
Lead Us Not into Temptation, 63
Lee, Spike, 150, 151
Lefebvre, Henri, 26, 202
The Legend of the Curse of the Bambino (Shaughnessy), 221
Lehane, Dennis, 196, 214, 233
Lehr, Dick, 86, 223–225, 228
Lewis, Reggie, 153–154

Linney, Laura, 203
Lisle, Benjamin D., 105
Live by Night, 175
Lloyd, Earl, 143
Lloyd, Lewis, 152
Louise Day Hicks, 137
Lucchino, Larry, 104, 122
Lukas, J. Anthony, 39–42, 50
Lytton, Timothy, 80

Major League Baseball (MLB), 114, 122–123, 128, 247n39
Malcolm X, 182
Mancini, Christina, 69–70
March on Washington, 146
Martin, Rachel, 64
Martinez, Pedro, 117
Massachusetts Bay Transit Authority (MBTA) tracks, 140
mass culture: authenticity in, 128; tradition in, 128
mass immigration, 4, 55
mass media, 21, 26, 33, 40, 50, 53, 57, 73, 75, 106, 128, 133, 151, 158, 183, 234
Masur, Louis, 37–38
McAdoo, Bob, 151
McCarrick, Theodore, 69
McClean, Charlie, 232
McClendon, John, 144
McCormack, John W., 35
McGoff, Lisa, 50–51
McHale, Kevin, 149
McHugh, Howie, 137, 148
McNamara, Eileen, 64, 71–72
McSorley, Patrick, 56
Mean Streets, 208
Medeiros, Humberto, 74
media: Charles Stuart murder case, 49; coverage of sex scandal, 14–15; digital, 12, 15, 73–78; embedded racism in, 47; local, 12; mass, 21, 26, 33, 40, 50, 53, 57, 73, 75, 106, 128, 133, 151, 158, 183, 234; and priest abuse scandal, 74–78; public, 6; -saturated environment, 4, 6; social, 14, 22, 77, 156; and sports, 119–126

"Media Studies, Geographical Imaginations, and Relational Space" (Ek), 83
mediated Boston, 183–194
Menino, Tom, 5
Miller, Reggie, 155
Milliken v Bradley, 28
Mitchum, Robert, 171, 174
Mizner, David, 59
mobile privatization, 82
"Mom Sues Priest for Alleged Sexual Abuse of Sons," 71
Monahan, William, 207
Money Ball, 125
Monument Ave, 164, 175, 193
Morley, David, 82–83
Most, Johnny, 149, 250n32
Mothers for Adequate Welfare, 118
Mower, Ron L., 155
multiethnic city, 214–218
Murder at Fenway Park (Soos), 125
Murdoch, Rupert, 45
Museum of Fine Arts, 151
Muzzi, Anthony, Jr., 56
My Most Excellent Year: A Novel of Love, Mary Poppins, and Fenway Park (Bush), 125
My Own Private Idaho, 186
Mystery Street, 168
Mystic River, 13, 17, 104, 125, 164, 184, 193, 194, 197, 206, 207, 208–210, 216, 220, 234; and the legacy of place, 196–207

narratives: *Black Mass*, 218–227; *Spotlight*, 218–227; of time and place, 218–227
National Basketball Association (NBA), 114, 131, 134, 142–149
National Basketball League (NBL), 133
National Football League, 114, 131
NBA.com, 158
NBA League Pass, 136, 158
NBATV, 158
NBC News, 12, 56, 68–69, 79–81, 87
NBCSports-Boston, 158
NCAA, 132
Nelson, Avi, 21

neoliberal city, 109–114
neoliberalism, 117, 119, 136, 140
New Balance, 119
New Deal, 248n2
New England Sports Network (NESN), 121–122
New Hollywood: cinema, 187; era/period, 175, 187; filmmakers, 169; moment, 169
New Jersey Nets, 134
Newman, Paul, 174, 175
new old Boston and the old new Boston, 175–179
Newsweek, 35
New York, New York, 185
New York Celtics, 132
New York Daily News, 112
The New Yorker, 70, 73, 107
New York Knicks, 120, 133, 143
New York Rens (or Renaissance), 132
New York Times, 35, 70, 77, 87, 89, 113, 122, 138, 147, 148
Nicholson, Jack, 207
Nightline, 56
Nightly News, 68–69, 79, 87
Nike, 119, 134, 155
Nussbaum, Emily, 228

Oberle, Bill, 79–80
objective space, 30
O'Brien, Hugh, 5
O'Connell, Dick, 116
O'Connor, Edwin, 13, 168
Olmstead, Frederick Law, 46
omerta, 57–58, 81
O'Neil, Gerard, 223–225, 228
On the Waterfront, 176
organized crime, 58, 88, 90, 209, 212, 224
Original Celtics, 132
Ortiz, David, 117, 232
The Out of Towners, 167
Outside In podcast, 156

Pagliucca, Steve, 157
Palladino, Elvira "Pixie," 36
The Paper Chase, 167

Patriots, 16, 104, 193–194, 201
Patriots Day, 232, 233
Penn, Sean, 196
Petrovic, Drazen, 134
Pfeiffer, Sacha, 67, 73, 75–76
Philadelphia Warriors, 133
Phil Donahue Show, 68
Pierce, Charles P., 48, 125, 160
Pierce, Paul, 156
place: branding, 15–16, 104, 186; and events, 84; narratives of, 218–227; and placelessness, 91; urban *mythos*, 85–87
Plain, Jamaica, 36
Plunkett Database, 114
Podhoretz, Jim, 144
Pollard, Sam, 143
Pope John Paul II, 66
Porter, James, 68
Porter, Joseph, 82
The Portrait of the Artist as a Young Man (Joyce), 210
The Post, 219
priest abuse scandal, 14–15, 23, 54, 60, 63–66; Boston dimension, 70–73; Catholicism, 57–58; code of silence, 58; and digital media, 74–78; investigation, 66–70; in Roman Catholic church, 55; and Whitey Bulger saga, 57
The Prince of Fenway Park (Baggott), 125
production of space, 26
professional basketball, 128
professional sports, 95, 102, 157–159, 163; as aspects of information age, 120; as aspects of neoliberal/nonproductive economy, 120; branding, 6; and digital revolution, 120; franchises, 127; and gentrification, 113; and media saturation, 117; and neoliberal city, 109–114; progressive policies/values among, 130; rebirth and blooming of, 112
Prudential Center, 7, 117–118
Prudential Tower, *8*, *9*, 107
public education, 28

race/racism, 50, 127; and Boston, 1, 23, 114–119, 179–183; and Celtics pride, 127–160; functional, 48; inequities, 118–119; and policing, 49; Red Sox (baseball team), 114–119; and segregated school system, 32; white, 118
Raging Bull, 185, 208
Ramirez, Manny, 117
Ramshaw, Greg, 125
Ray Donovan, 2, 13, 17, 59, 125, 229–230, 234
Red Sox, 127, 140, 145, 194
Red Sox (baseball team), 15–16, 95; branding, 102–109; broadcasts, 100; presence enhanced by media, 100; and race, 114–119; racism, 115–116; stadium, 106; valuation, 120; wearing merchandise, 99–102
Red Sox Nation, 99, 119–126
Reebok, 119
Rescue 911, 44, 88
Revere, Paul, 129
Rezendes, Michael, 59, 67
Rice, Jim, 116
Richardson, Michael Ray, 152
Rivers, Doc, 156
Roache, Mickey, 45
ROAR (Restore Our Alienated Rights), 36
Robinson, David, 155
Robinson, Walter, 67
Rocky, 185–186
Rodman, Dennis, 150
Roman Catholic church, 54–55, 65, 72, 91, 183, 220; *see also* Catholic Church
Romney, Mitt, 88
The Rookie, 102
Rose, Gillian, 61
Rosensweig, Daniel, 104
Roush Fenway Racing, 122
Rowe, Nicolette, 198
Roxbury, Boston, 30
Rubin, Elihu, 117
Rupp, Adolph, 147
Russell, Bill, 132, 143, 144, 145–146, 147–148, 151, 152

Ryan, Andrew, 36
Ryan, Bob, 124, 125

Sabonis, Arvydas, 134
Sanders, Tom, 143, 147
Saperstein, Abe, 132
Saturday Evening Post, 146
Saviano, Phil, 56, 81
school integration 54; resistance, in Boston, 9–10
Schreiber, Liev, 220, 228
Schrempf, Deltef, 134
Scorsese, Martin, 185, 207
Scott, Charlie, 148
Seattle Supersonics, 147
segregation: in Massachusetts's urban schools, 27; practice in Boston, 32; spatial, 30, 32
Seitz, Matt Zoller, 228
Sex Abuse in the Church: Code of Silence, 78
sexual abuse: of children by priests, 54, 55; scandal in Catholic church (*see* priest abuse scandal)
Shanley, Paul, 69, 77
Sharman, Bill, 143
Shaughnessy, Dan, 221
Shields, Ryan T., 69–70
Shut Out: A Story of Race and Baseball in Boston (Bryant), 115
Silver, Adam, 130
Simmons, Bill, 125
slum clearance, 7
Small Mercies (Lehane), 233
Smith, Al, 34
Smith, Kevin, 186
Smith, Reggie, 116
social media, 14, 22, 77, 156
Sorvino, Paul, 177
South Boston, 1–2, 10–15, 17, 25, 27, 29–30, 32–34, 36–37, 40, 54–55, 57; Irish-ethnic enclave of 85; "mean streets," of 87
space: crises of, 22; objective, 30; overview, 26; production of, 26; racialized conceptions of, 23; and time, 83; white, 23, 25–52; working-class, 15

spatial segregation, 30, 32
Spears, Marc J., 160
spectator sports, 102, 119, 128, 133, 151, 159
Spenser Confidential, 233
Spin magazine, 151
Sport magazine, 146
sports: marketing, 119; and media, 119–126; professional (*see* professional sports); spectator 102, 119, 128, 133, 151, 159; teams, 96–97
Sports Illustrated, 146
Spotlight, 2, 17, 59, 64, 66, 164, 175, 218–227, 228
Stallone, Sylvester, 185
Starting Over, 175
Steinfels, Peter, 80
St. Elsewhere, 125, 175
Stern, David, 131, 136, 152, 156
Stevenson, Mary Huff, 109
Stivaletta, Arthur, 10
Stockard, Aaron, 214
Storin, Matt, 69
street crime, 43
Stuart, Carol, 22
Stuart, Carole DiMaiti, 42–43
Stuart, Charles, 146, 151, 154, 171
Studlar, Gaylyn, 230
Survivors Network of Those Abused by Priests (SNAP), 63
Sweeney, W., 72–73
Swingers, 186
"symbolic power of cities," 192

Taxi Driver, 208
Taylor, Breonna, 130
team: branding, 102–109; sports, 96–97
Tex Rickard, 138
Thomas, Isiah, 153
The Thomas Crown Affair, 167
Thomas Yawkey Way, 117
Tiant, Luis, 117
time: narratives of, 218–227; ruptures of, 207–214; and space, 83
Times of Acadiana, 63
Tomjanovich, Rudy, 152
The Town, 40, 125, 164, 173, 176, 193, 194

Tracy, Spencer, 13, 168
tradition, 10, 52, 107–108, 115, 129, 158; assumptive, 129; Boston noir and bonds of, 171–175; in mass culture, 128; of *omerta*, 81; and racial inequities, 118–119; right-populist notion of, 62; scholastic, 87
Trouble with the Curve, 102
Turner, Ted, 120

Unicorns, 137
University of San Francisco, 132
Unrepentant: Investigating Abuse in the Canadian Catholic Church, 78
Unsolved Mysteries, 87
Updike, John, 107, 125
urban: authenticity, 17, 231; -based sports franchises, 112; branding, 128–129; crime, 46; *mythos*, 85–86
U.S. Dream Team, 134

Van Sant, Gus, 186, 189
The Verdict, 17, 163, 167, 169–170, 174–176, 178–179, 182–183, 184, 220
Volk, Jan, 149
Volk, Jerry, 149, 250n32

Wahlberg, Mark, 14, 207, 232, 233
"Wake Up America" campaign, 10
Walk East on Beacon, 168
Walker, Antoine, 156
Wallach, Eli, 205
Walton, Bill, 149, 151
Washburn, Chris, 152
Washington, Duane, 152
Washington, Kermit, 152
Washington Capitals, 143
Washington Post, 35, 58
Watts Riot, 118
Webb, Lawrence, 169
Wedman, Scott, 149
Weinstein, Harvey, 252n17
Werner, Tom, 104, 122
West End Redevelopment Project, 7
Westies, 241n3
Westphal, Paul, 148
West Side Story, 176

What Doesn't Kill You, 164
Whirlwinds, 132, 137
White, Jo Jo, 145, 148
White, Kevin, 34, 35
white ethnicity 104, 128, 226
whiteness: of the crowd, 157; ethnic, 14, 26–27, 97; of the fanbase, 234; nostalgic, 140; and racial exclusion, 128; relative, 148; unobstructed, 59; unrelieved, 225; violent, 37; working-class whiteness, 140
white racism, 43, 118
white resentment, 21, 27, 34–39
white Southern revanchism, 226
white spaces, 23, 25–52; Boston's Irish, 34–39; class mobility, 39–42; coverage of busing crisis, 29–30; defined, 31; reproducing assumptions of, 31–34; spatial segregation, 30; white resentment, 34–39; *see also* space
Why Busing Failed: Race, Media, and the National Resistance to School Desegregation (Delmont), 239n15
Wiggins, Mitchell, 152
Williams, Jerry, 21

Williams, Raymond, 82
Williams, Ted, 107, 249n20
Wilson, Earl, 116
Wilson, William Julius, 155
Winkler, Irwin, 185
Winning Time, 144
Winship, Thomas, 123–124
Winstone, Ray, 211
"Winter Hill" gang, 58
Woods, James, 230
working-class: authenticity, 57; ethnicity, 104, 183–184; spaces, 15; white authenticity, 52
"The Work of Art in the Age of Mechanical Reproduction" (Benjamin), 61
World War I, 132
World War II, 131
Worthy, James, 152
Wu, Michelle, 5, 233
Wynegar, Jerome, 37

Yates, Peter, 171
Yawkey, Tom, 103, 111, 115, 127, 234

Zukin, Sharon, 11